W9-BYC-505

Upper School Library
Glenelg Country School
12733 Folly Quarter Road
Ellicott City, MD 21042

The Al Jazeera Effect

ALSO BY PHILIP SEIB

*Headline Diplomacy: How News Coverage Affects
Foreign Policy*
Taken for Granted: The Future of U.S.–British Relations
*Going Live: Getting the News Right in a Real-Time,
Online World*
*The Global Journalist: News and Conscience in a
World of Conflict*
*Beyond the Front Lines: How the News Media
Cover a World Shaped by War*
Media and Conflict in the Twenty-first Century (editor)
*Broadcasts from the Blitz: How Edward R. Murrow Helped Lead
America Into War*
New Media and the New Middle East (editor)

The Al Jazeera Effect

HOW THE NEW GLOBAL MEDIA
ARE RESHAPING WORLD POLITICS

PHILIP SEIB

Potomac Books, Inc.
Washington, D.C.

Copyright © 2008 by Potomac Books, Inc.

Published in the United States by Potomac Books, Inc. All rights
reserved. No part of this book may be reproduced in any manner
whatsoever without written permission from the publisher, except
in the case of brief quotations embodied in critical articles and
reviews.

Library of Congress Cataloging-in-Publication Data
Seib, Philip M., 1949–
   The Al Jazeera effect : how the new global media are reshaping
world politics / Philip Seib.— 1st ed.
      p. cm.
   Includes bibliographical references and index.
   ISBN-13: 978-1-59797-200-0 (alk. paper)
   1. Television broadcasting of news. 2. Online journalism. 3.
Government and the press. 4. Al Jazeera (Television network) I.
Title.
   PN4784.T4S44 2008
   302.23'45—dc22
                                    2008013320

Printed in the United States of America on acid-free paper that
meets the American National Standards Institute Z39-48
Standard.

Potomac Books, Inc.
22841 Quicksilver Drive
Dulles, Virginia 20166

First Edition

10 9 8 7 6 5 4 3 2 1

For Christine

Lo, soul! seest thou not God's purpose from the first?
The earth to be spann'd, connected by net-work,
The people to become brothers and sisters,
The races, neighbors, to marry and be given in marriage,
The oceans to be cross'd, the distant brought near,
The lands to be welded together.

Walt Whitman, *Leaves of Grass*

CONTENTS

PREFACE

The battle for hearts and minds in the Middle East is being fought not only on the streets of Baghdad but also on the newscasts and talk shows of Al Jazeera. China's future is being shaped not solely by Communist Party bureaucrats but also by bloggers working quietly in cybercafes. Al Qaeda's next attacks will not necessarily be directed from Osama bin Laden's cave but from cells around the world connected by the Internet.

In these and many other instances, traditional ways of shaping global politics have been superseded by the influence of new media—satellite television, the Internet, and other high-tech tools. What is involved is more than a refinement of established practices. We are seeing a comprehensive reconnecting of the global village and reshaping of how the world works.

Whenever we ponder the day's news, we need to recognize that beneath the surface of events is a virtual reality that provides a new context for both turmoil and progress. Understanding this is crucial because peaceful change and terrorist attacks share the virtual terrain.

Al Jazeera is a symbol of this new, media-centric world. It affects global politics and culture, particularly by enhancing the Islamic world's clout. As it delivers its programming in Arabic and English (and perhaps soon in additional languages), and as its message meshes with content from Islamic Web sites, blogs, and other online offerings, Al Jazeera helps foster unprecedented cohesion in the worldwide Muslim community.

More than that, Al Jazeera is a paradigm of new media's influence. Ten years ago, there was much talk about "the CNN effect," the theory that news coverage—especially gripping visual storytelling—was influencing foreign policy throughout the world. Today, "the Al Jazeera effect" takes that a significant step farther. Just as "the CNN effect" is not about CNN alone, so too is "the Al Jazeera effect" about much more than the Qatar-based media company. The concept encompasses the use of new media as tools in every aspect of global affairs, ranging from democratization to terrorism and including the concept of "virtual states."

The de facto nation of Kurdistan is a good example of the virtual state. It is not officially recognized by governments and does not appear on commonly used maps, but it exists, knitted together largely by a combination of radio and television stations and an array of Web sites and online communication. Common media reach Kurds who live in Iraq, Turkey, Syria, and elsewhere, sustaining the Kurdish identity and accelerating its political maturation. The phenomenon of the virtual state may encompass entities far larger than Kurdistan, such as individual nations' diasporic populations and the *ummah*, the global Islamic community. If new media bring cohesion to the *ummah*, policymakers throughout the world will have to reckon with a significant new player in international affairs.

The growth of new media has been explosive. In the Middle East, Al Jazeera has plenty of company on the airwaves. From a mere handful of stations a few years ago, more than 450 Arab satellite channels are now on the air and most are privately owned, bringing an end to the dominance of government-run media in the region. In Latin America, Venezuelan president Hugo Chávez is the moving force behind Telesur, a regional channel on the model of Al Jazeera. Chávez says Telesur is a means of "counteracting the media dictatorship of the big international news networks." Similar ventures are being planned for sub-Saharan Africa and elsewhere. In each instance, the new arrivals are wresting influence away from CNN, the BBC, and other Western news organizations on which much of the world has relied for many years.

Many governments dismiss these emerging media, especially Al Jazeera, because they are not "objective" providers of information and therefore presumably have little clout with their audiences.

But to use Western standards of journalistic objectivity to judge the effectiveness of these media misses the point of why they are so influential. They are credible; that's what matters. As Telesur's managing director put it, there is an "urgency to see ourselves through *our own* eyes and to discover *our own* solutions to our problems." Similar sentiments have been expressed by Arab viewers watching Al Jazeera's coverage of the Palestinian *intifada* or anti-Syrian demonstrations in Lebanon.

These new, popular sources of information create challenges for those who govern. In Egypt, opposition groups that are ignored by state-run media are sustained by blogs. The United States, professing concern about winning support for its policies on the "Arab street," finds its public diplomacy efforts overwhelmed by the flood of messages generated by regional and local media. China tries to monitor Internet traffic within its borders, but by late 2007 there were 220 million Internet users in China, more than 47 million blog writers, and in December 2007 66 million search engine queries. The government's watchers cannot keep up.

This kind of thing is happening around the world. In the past, governments could control much of the information flow and therefore keep tight rein on political change. That is no longer the case. Governments can jail some bloggers and knock some satellite stations off the air, but the flood of information, and the intellectual freedom it fosters, is relentless.

Beyond the challenges governments face are larger issues, such as those related to the prospects for a "clash of civilizations" that would cast a shadow on the world for decades to come. The 2006 Danish cartoon controversy, which initially spread on the Internet, seemed to illustrate inescapable conflict between the Islamic world and the West. But the relationship is more complicated than that, and it is affected to some degree by media-carried popular culture. This can be seen when an Indonesian child wears a New York Yankees baseball cap along with his Osama bin Laden T-shirt or when *The Simpsons* is exported to Arab audiences as *Al Shamsoon*, with Homer's behavior becoming far more proper (and much less funny).

New media are also changing the relationship between the public and news providers. In the past, news consumers have passively received whatever news organizations offered, whenever they chose to deliver it. When Ted Turner created CNN in 1980, he let his audience get news when they wanted it. This has been taken to the next level by Web-based news content, which provides a nearly infinite variety of news products available at all times. The Internet also allows more people to become part of the "culture of information," as can be seen by the success of South Korea's OhmyNews, which has featured tens of thousands of bylines and has had tens of millions of daily page views.

"The media" are no longer just the media. They have a larger popular base than ever before and, as a result, have unprecedented impact on international politics. The media can be tools of conflict and instruments of peace; they can make traditional borders irrelevant and unify peoples scattered across the globe. This phenomenon—the Al Jazeera effect—is reshaping the world.

O ⌐ O

As I worked on this book, I received valuable help from many colleagues, including Nadia El-Awady, Mehpare Selcan Kaynak, and Larry Pintak, and research assistance from Stuart Thomas. I also appreciate the support I received from Marquette University and the University of Southern California.

Early versions of some of the material in this book appeared in articles I wrote for *Strategic Insights*, *Transnational Broadcasting Studies Journal*, and *Military Review*, as well as in presentations at conferences organized by the International Studies Association, Arab-U.S. Association for Communication Educators, Eurasian Media Forum, British International Studies Association, Center for the Study of Islam and Democracy, and L'Ecole Nationale d'Administration Publique (Quebec).

Thanks to Don Jacobs and Hilary Claggett at Potomac Books for all their work and to Robbie Anna Hare, the world's most patient and supportive literary agent.

As always, my wife, Christine Wicker, made it possible for me to write by providing much encouragement and love.

1

Beyond the Clash of Civilizations

Blaming the world's most visible conflicts on a clash of civilizations is hard to resist. We eagerly seek and cling to reasons for the things we see, and the simpler and more sweeping the reasons, the better. From simmering tension to full-blown war, Islam and the West seem to have irreconcilable differences that can be ascribed to incompatible cultures. Best to fight it out, get it over with, and move on to the next test. Further clashes loom; China awaits. And beyond China . . . who knows?

For the bellicose, this may be a comfortable worldview, but it is so simplistic that to use it as a basis for policymaking is unforgivably lazy and almost certain to produce tragic results. Adopting this outlook will ensure many years of devastation while armies battle and terrorists strike. To assume the inevitability of a clash of civilizations is to ensure that it will happen.

Armed conflict and lesser disputes may abound, as they have throughout human history, but their causes are not necessarily rooted in civilizational clashes. The troubles between Israelis and Palestinians, for instance, are at heart political—involving territory and rights—not purely civilizational.

People today evaluate such matters and decide on their importance based partly on information delivered at high speed by media that are unobstructed by conventional borders. Satellite television, the Internet, and other new media accelerate the global public's reaction to news and shrink the time governments have for responding to that news.

Ideally, new media might knit together people and nations,

1

creating a harmonious global village. CNN founder Ted Turner said, "My main concern is to be a benefit to the world, to build up a global communications system that helps humanity come together." But, as George Packer noted, "in some ways, global satellite TV and Internet access have actually made the world a less understanding, less tolerant place. What the media provide is superficial familiarity—images without context, indignation without remedy."

The global village, wrote Packer, is "not the utopian community promised by the boosters of globalization but a parochial place of manifold suspicions, rumors, resentments, and half-truths. If the world seems to be growing more, rather than less, nasty these days, it might have something to do with the images all of us now carry around in our heads."[1] Along similar lines, Thomas Friedman observed, "Maybe the Internet, fiber optics, and satellites really are, together, like a high-tech Tower of Babel. It's as though God suddenly gave us all the tools to communicate and none of the tools to understand."[2] For Americans, how the United States is depicted and understood matters. When perception is linked to the virtual contiguity that is a facet of globalization, new capabilities and threats come into play. Those who are intent on doing harm find previously distant targets now within range, as the September 2001 attacks on the United States demonstrated. The 9/11 Commission stated that America was a subject "for admiration, envy, and blame. This created a kind of cultural asymmetry. To us, Afghanistan seemed very far away. To members of al Qaeda, America seemed very close. In a sense, they were more globalized than we were."[3]

Al Qaeda exemplifies the new, globalized menace. It is a stateless state, a virtual entity that has enhanced its power by being able to organize and maneuver within cyberspace in ways that profoundly affect traditional, earthbound political processes. In 2005, for example, announcements on some Islamic Internet forums asked for pledges of loyalty to al Qaeda's leaders "so that Osama bin Laden will have an army in Afghanistan, an army in Iraq, and a massive army in the waiting list on the Internet. This is the Internet that Allah operates in the service of jihad and of the mujahideen."[4]

Al Qaeda and other terrorist organizations have made good use of new media, taking advantage of satellite television news channels' hunger for content and using it to disseminate propaganda, display hostages, and otherwise gain exposure. On a grander scale, they count on the media to help spread terror. Thousands were killed on 9/11, but millions were terrified by the images the media delivered to them. And still others who saw those media reports regarded them as evidence that the mighty can be humbled and that supporting al Qaeda would be worthwhile. While the uncomprehending mass audience partakes of the stew of journalism heavily seasoned with entertainment that is served up by mainstream news organizations, terrorist groups use those same media, particularly the Internet, to proselytize, recruit, train, and dispatch orders to their followers.

Governments—especially those that protect free speech—have been at a loss as to how to deal with the use of mass communication for such evil purposes. The European Commission recommended in 2005 that news organizations draft a code of conduct to ensure that they did not inadvertently serve as propagandists for terrorists. Journalists, stated the commission, "face the difficult responsibility of reconciling their duty to inform the public with the need not to facilitate the aims of terrorists." Further, the commission urged the news media to beware of reinforcing prejudices by casually reinforcing stereotypes such as "Islamic terrorists."[5] But, as Osama bin Laden and others of his ilk realize, guidelines will not override the allure of delivering threatening images to a credulous public, and concerns about stereotyping will have little effect when news judgments are grounded in condescension toward the audience.

New technological capabilities should be accompanied by a new sense of responsibility. Media technologies have effect and the people who use them have responsibilities; they are not mere bystanders while conflict and change occur. More specifically, any appraisal of the many elements of international relations should include careful evaluation of media roles. This is not a new concern, but the increasing speed, pervasiveness, and influence of media-borne information require revised evaluations of these phenomena.

An example of how media can shake up the world is the Danish cartoon controversy of 2006. This case illustrates what can happen when premodern sensibilities are mixed with modern politics and postmodern technologies.

It started with jokes. A comedian told Flemming Rose, editor of the Danish newspaper *Jyllands-Posten*, that he wouldn't dare crack jokes about the Quran, although he'd have no reluctance about making fun of the Bible. Then Rose read that a Danish author of a children's book about religion could not find illustrators willing to draw a likeness of the Prophet Muhammad. So, in September 2005 Rose decided to ask twenty-five Danish newspaper cartoonists to draw Muhammad as each saw him. A dozen responded, and *Jyllands-Posten* published the work.

Leaders of Denmark's Muslim community—about one hundred thousand of a population of five million—protested to the newspaper and the Danish minister of culture but received no response from either. They gathered seventeen thousand signatures on a petition, which they submitted to Danish Prime Minister Anders Fogh Rasmussen, and met with ambassadors from eleven Muslim countries, who then sought a meeting with the prime minister, all to no avail.

Leaders of the protest then traveled to the Middle East with the *Jyllands-Posten* cartoons, similar illustrations from another Danish newspaper, and several obscene drawings of Muhammad that had been sent anonymously to some Danish Muslims. The group held a news conference in Egypt that was heavily covered by Arab media and then traveled to Lebanon and Syria to meet with clerics.

By this time, there had been some news stories about the cartoons, and word of the controversy was spreading privately through e-mail, text messaging, and Web sites. Individuals began sending e-mails to lists of acquaintances, urging a boycott of Danish goods. Recipients of the messages sent them to their friends and the audience grew exponentially. The process was similar to the chain letters of a previous generation, except much faster and with instantaneous global reach.

With the boycott and other protests growing, Prime Minister Rasmussen said he would not have published the drawings, but he would not apologize for the newspaper's act of free speech. Rose himself said that the cartoons "were not intended to be offensive." These partial apologies spurred other Western news organizations, such as the German newspaper *Die Welt*, to run some of the cartoons to demonstrate their commitment to press freedom. *Die Welt* editor Roger Koppel said that a newspaper publishing the drawings in a Muslim country might be punished but that was not the case in Germany, where the news media's free speech is protected.

Of course, "published in . . . " means little in the era of globalized communication. If the drawings are published anywhere, they can be assumed to have been virtually published everywhere. Within days, protests about the cartoons occurred in Indonesia, Malaysia, the Palestinian territories, and Iraq. They were quickly followed by protests in Syria during which the Danish and Norwegian embassies were burned. The Syrian demonstrators were galvanized by text messages such as, "Join us in defending our prophet and what is sacred." In Lebanon, protestors set fire to the building housing the Danish embassy, and the next day demonstrations in Afghanistan targeted a U.S. air base. This was followed by protests in Pakistan. In all, about two dozen people died.[6]

One communications expert said the cartoon case illustrated how the Internet can serve as a "rage enabler," delivering quick and persistent jabs that keep people mindful of the dispute. The Internet becomes a venue for anger and its content may make the angry even angrier.[7] Aside from the principal online efforts to organize the boycott and demonstrations, the chatter of bloggers, Web site proprietors, and other cybercitizens contributed to what some perceived as a stirring chorus and what others considered a disturbing cacophony. Once someone has access to the Web, one enters an egalitarian space. Everyone can talk, and sometimes everyone does. No longer must someone be able to afford a printing press to "publish" or be dependent on a news organization to reach an audience.

Governments that want to keep unrest localized are certain to be overwhelmed by the flood of information through public and private new media channels. Even if news coverage can be curtailed, word will get out by cell phone and Internet. Information—not all of it accurate—will spread, and there is no way to stop it all. When anger remains at flash point for prolonged periods, something will probably set it off. Information can provide the spark.

To cite a region that attracts much attention, the continuing high level of anger in the Arab world has been ascribed by some to a feeling among Arabs that they have been passed by while much of the rest of the world has advanced in many ways. This feeling has developed over centuries and becomes manifest when looking at enviable aspects of Western—and now Asian—society and when fellow Muslims, such as the Palestinians, appear to be victimized by Western governments' anti-Muslim/Arab policies. As Bernard Lewis wrote, the prevailing question among many in the Middle East and larger Islamic world is, "What went wrong?" Lewis added, "Whatever the form and manner of the question and of the answers that it evokes, there is no mistaking the growing anguish, the mounting urgency, and of late the seething anger with which both question and answers are expressed."[8]

The Danish cartoon controversy has been pointed to as clear evidence of that anger leading to a clash of civilizations—in this episode, Scandinavian free speech versus Muslim intolerance; bad manners countered by deadly rioting.

But the same media that facilitate hostility ensure that in some ways Islam and the non-Islamic can connect. People pick and choose among cultural and political offerings, some of which are shared. Turn on a computer in Cairo and read the *New York Times.* While browsing the Web in Omaha, take a look at *Al-Ahram.* Or consider the young Indonesian boy wearing a New York Yankees cap and an Osama bin Laden t-shirt.[9] Here, America and anti-America merge neatly and, given the globalized flow of information and goods, predictably.

Sometimes, however, media-based attempts to bring East and West together prove awkward, as in the effort to send *The Simpsons* to the Arab world as *Al Shamsoon.* The original animation was used, but the programs were dubbed by Arabic speakers reading scripts written to meet the standards of the audience. Homer Simpson became Omar Shamsoon, and Bart became Badr. Homer's beer turned into a soft drink, his hot dogs became Egyptian beef sausages, and his donuts were transformed into Arab cookies known as *kahk*. Despite these alterations, with 60 percent of the Arab world under age twenty and 40 percent under age fifteen, an avid *Simpsons/Shamsoon* audience would seem guaranteed. The problem, according to some American *Simpsons* fans who speak Arabic and saw the Arabized version, was that it simply wasn't funny. Making Homer suitable for Muslim audiences removes the raunchiness that Americans find amusing and perfectly proper (or at least perfectly tolerable).[10] The twain wouldn't meet.

The notoriety of the Danish cartoons and the presumed popularity of Homer Simpson are functions of the globalized stream of information that new communications technologies make possible. In less than two decades, people have come to see the world much differently. Using 1991 as a starting point, the Gulf War that year was in many ways the last gasp of Western communications hegemony. CNN's slogan at the time was, "The world is watching CNN." That was true because most of the world didn't have much choice. Beyond CNN and other American and European information providers was a near vacuum in terms of global media. The dominant news, entertainment, and other information products may have had global reach but not global outlook. Political and cultural dominance could be perpetuated by such a limited system; other voices were not heard.

Shortly after the Gulf War, two factors began to rattle the status quo: the growing number of satellite television channels based outside the West, such as Al Jazeera, and the Internet's expanding role. On one level, more satellite television channels gave news consumers a choice between "us" and "the other"—the option to turn away from outsiders and instead gravitate to information providers that might be more parochial but also more deserving of trust. Once they began to build an audience, the satellite news channels affected politics. Reports about an event such as the 2000 intifada could reach Arab populations without being filtered through Western lenses or government censors. As Israelis soon realized, political feelings in the countries around them were becoming even more highly charged.

When this proliferation of television is supplemented by the Internet's vast capabilities, the political universe expands greatly.

Once people gain access to the Internet they can tap into almost unlimited information sources, from established news organizations to newborn blogs, and they can communicate with each other. The Internet's interactive nature as a medium for debate and mobilization holds great power, although its galvanizing effect is still more speculative than proven.

By the time the world was shaken by the events of September 11, 2001, globalized communication was becoming more diverse and important, not just as a provider of information to the public but also as an integral part of globalization more broadly. Thomas Friedman wrote that globalization is "the overarching international system shaping the domestic politics and foreign relations of virtually every country, and we need to understand it as such." More specifically, according to Friedman, globalization involves "the inexorable integration of markets, transportation systems, and communication systems to a degree never witnessed before. . . . In the broadest sense we have gone from an international system built around division and walls to a system increasingly built around integration and webs."[11]

Jean Chalaby noted that as part of this, "the globalization of communication plays a determining role in the deterritorialization of capitalism and economic liberalism, and is central to the globalizing process at large. Many fields of activities are currently integrating on a world scale and progressively turning into global systems. Global communication adds to the flow of information, networks of communication, and systems of exchange that intensify the interconnectedness of these fields and facilitate their worldwide integration."[12]

Most appraisals of globalization are suffused with the glow of optimism, which is unrealistic given the obstacles that globalization is certain to encounter. Conflict can disrupt constructive aspects of globalization, and it should be remembered that globalization has its negative elements—such as the ease with which terrorists can travel across the world to a target or the speed with which an epidemic can transform itself from local to global.

But globalization also fosters openness, albeit to varying degrees. Given this, globalization and a clash of civilizations might seem mutually exclusive, and it may be that globalization's potential rewards will dampen the ardor for such a clash. Perhaps the most significant conflicts in the near future will be *intra*civilizational, struggles between progressives and reactionaries within individual civilizations.

Even that sounds grim, and while such struggles proceed either global progress will markedly diminish or the battling part of the world will be left behind while the rest advances. Whichever scenario prevails, media roles will be significant. Media, playing on fears and exacerbating tension, can have incendiary effect. History is replete with examples of politicians who have mastered this malicious skill, Adolf Hitler and the *genocidaires* of Rwanda among them. Meanwhile, the media can also discourage internal conflict by fostering transparency and giving those who might be caught up in disorder a chance to see a preferable world outside their own borders and experience.

The heightened pervasiveness and influence of information can be seen in how people in Islamic countries, particularly in the Middle East, have refocused their views of the world and themselves. Jon Alterman observed, "For most in the Arab world, technological change means that they are exposed to a broader variety of views than has ever been true before. As literacy and bandwidth both expand dramatically, publics are exposed to a broad, often unregulated, spectrum of views that range from secular to religious, from nationalist to global, and from material to spiritual. Under the new paradigm, information is demand-driven rather than supply-driven, and the universe of available views is far broader than ever before."[13]

The greater variety of viewpoints available to a large public has expanded the range of discourse and fostered new levels of public debate. Evaluating the new array of Arab media, Marc Lynch notes, "Rather than imposing a single, overwhelming consensus, the new satellite television stations, along with newspapers, Internet sites, and many other sites of public communication, challenged Arabs to argue, to disagree, and to question the status quo."[14] These new media also make the public's news environment more intense. They see more of what is going on in the world from different perspectives, partly because their governments are unable to control most of what comes flowing onto television and computer screens.

The new technologies have been accompanied by a new journalism, graphic and contentious, that can raise the public's temperature and become a significant factor in the competition to influence public opinion. As Gilles Kepel observes, "With the occupation of Iraq, the war for Muslim minds entered the global jungle of the Internet. Photographs of Iraqi prisoners being tortured or sexually humiliated by their American guards circulated freely, along with videos of hostages being mistreated by their terrorist captors. . . . Through its coverage on the Internet, the Iraq War erased the geographical boundaries of *Dar al-Islam* (the domain of Islam) and *Dar al-Harb* (the domain of war) that had structured Muslim geopolitics for fourteen centuries."[15]

This process involves more than stirring Arab anger directly against the United States. It also affects the way Arab Muslims see themselves, an image that may be unflattering. Writing about Saudi reactions to news coverage of conflict in the region, John Bradley notes, "The images of Israeli soldiers abusing and murdering Palestinians . . . only further enrage Saudi youth aware of their own safety, indulgence, indolence, and impotence. The Palestinians, by contrast, are poor, oppressed, and brave—and manly."[16]

Yet another dimension of media-based change in the Middle East is the coverage of Israel by Arab news organizations. Yossi Alpher reported that during the removal of Jewish settlers from Gaza in 2005, reporters for Al Jazeera and Al Arabiya "stuck their microphones in the faces of anguished settlers and weeping soldiers, and even occasionally expressed empathy for their plight. They even interviewed the Israeli military's chief of staff." Alpher noted, "the phenomenon of Arab media bringing a relatively straightforward portrayal of Israel into living rooms in Riyadh, Baghdad, and Beirut is food for thought." Just a few years earlier, this kind of coverage would not have been available. Western news organizations, even if they had shown it, would not have been credible, and the stodgy government-run Arab channels would never have dared to portray Israelis in any way except as propagandistic caricatures.

Alpher, a former Mossad official and academic, and Ghassan

Khatib, vice president of Birzeit University and former minister of planning and labor in the Palestinian Authority, are coeditors of bitterlemons.org, an online magazine that offers Israeli and Palestinian viewpoints on issues of mutual concern. By mid-2007, it had more than fourteen thousand e-mail subscribers and was read online by more than one hundred thousand people each week. Opinion pieces from bitterlemons are reprinted by other media, including Arab news organizations that carry articles by Israeli writers. As Alpher said, this is "not a revolution, but nevertheless a change."[17]

Another change can be seen in attitudes about the role of Islam in political life. In a survey conducted in May 2005, the Pew Global Attitudes Project found that in five of six Muslim countries surveyed, respondents saw a growing role for Islam in politics. This opinion had solid majority support in Indonesia and Morocco and slightly less in Pakistan, Turkey, and Lebanon. Only in Jordan was there a substantial plurality who saw a lesser role for Islam.[18] While Islam's global political clout evolves, considerable jockeying for leadership is evident, as in the political competition between Saudi Arabia and Iran. The two Islamic powers use well-funded public diplomacy in this contest, as each finances schools, mosques, and other popular projects in Muslim countries.

When evaluating the future of Islam, it is important not to overlook its far-flung presence that extends well beyond the Arab world. For example, with about 21 million Muslims, China has an Islamic population almost as large as that of Saudi Arabia. Protests occurred among Chinese Muslims when the Iraq War began in 2003 and during the Danish cartoon controversy of 2006, but the government moved quickly to suppress the dissent, instructing imams not to incite the Muslim population. The director of an Islamic school in Linxia said, "We have to cooperate with our government. They asked us to be calm. They said they would speak on our behalf and express our unhappiness." Even while it was cooperating with the government and remaining calm, that same school acquired two computers so it could get news directly from the Middle East.[19]

As they grow larger and more visible, Muslim communities

outside the Middle East will contribute to a redefinition of global Islam. Olivier Roy noted, "Globalization is a good opportunity to dissociate Islam from any given culture and to provide a model that could work beyond any culture." Already, Islam is beginning to reach out and look to the future. Roy reported, "Muslim preachers are increasingly relying on Western languages for their sermons for two simple reasons: they want to address the new generation, and they want to reach a multi-ethnic congregation."[20] Imams and others in the Islamic hierarchy have incentive to expand their ambitions this way because they know they can reach these new audiences through satellite television and the Internet. High-tech proselytizing is within their grasp.

While Islam is reshaping its perspective on itself and the rest of the world, the world is taking a new look at Islam. This occurs in various ways, most of which have political ramifications. Lebanese journalist Diana Mukkaled wrote in 2005 that Muslim leaders who used inflammatory rhetoric when speaking to Arabic media but who were more circumspect when speaking English on international networks were increasingly surprised to find that English speakers had read translations of their earlier comments. Mukkaled noted, "The world is closely watching. There are Western institutions that specialize in translating material that is used by all forms of Arab media" and so extremist comments cause "Muslim and Arab immigrants and their children in the West to pay the price for such words."[21]

Much of what the rest of the world sees in the Islamic world, particularly the Arab states, is viewed through a filter of myth and stereotyping. In his online news story about American television coverage of the 2006 Israel-Hezbollah War, Al Jazeera's Habib Battah said that an MSNBC analysis featured "field reporters and pundits, many blatantly supportive of Israel's fight against 'terror acts' and the 'worldwide Islamic threat'—still no mention of the widespread devastation and human loss in Lebanon."[22] As an example of depiction through journalistic rhetoric, Battah's story was just one more volley in an ongoing battle. Accusations abound about pro- or anti-Arab or pro- or anti-Israel slants in news reporting.

On a larger scale, the growing Islamic presence in traditionally non-Muslim countries has led to recognition, as Olivier Roy noted, that "Islam had become a permanent feature of their societies, and this prompted a reassessment of European national identities."[23] Although estimates of Muslim populations in non-Muslim countries are usually imprecise, it is reasonable to put the size at about 3 percent in Britain, 4 percent in Germany, 8 percent in France, and 10 percent in Russia. These relatively small but often rapidly growing populations have created new and broader awareness of Islam. When a mosque opens down the street in what had been a predominantly Christian neighborhood, it attracts attention.

Mutual reassessment proceeds, as Muslims warily look beyond their homelands, traditional or adopted, and the rest of the world appraises the Islamic world, deciding if it is friend or foe. A survey by the Pew Global Attitudes Project that was released in summer 2006 reported that "for the most part, Muslim publics feel more embittered toward the West and its people than vice versa. Muslim opinions about the West and its people have worsened over the past year and by overwhelming margins Muslims blame Westerners for the strained relationship between the two sides. But there are some positive indicators as well, including the fact that in most Muslim countries surveyed there has been a decline in support for terrorism." In the West, said the Pew report, "Solid majorities of the general publics in Germany and Spain say that there is a natural conflict between being a devout Muslim and living in a modern society. But most Muslims in both of those countries disagree. And in France, the scene of recent riots in heavily Muslim areas, large percentages of both the general public and the Muslim minority population feel there is no conflict in being a devout Muslim and living in a modern society."

The survey also found

> both hopeful and troubling signs with respect to Muslim support for terrorism and the viability of democracy in Muslim countries. In Jordan, Pakistan and Indonesia, there have been substantial declines in the percentages saying suicide bombings and other forms of violence against civilian targets can be justified to defend Islam against its enemies. The shift has been especially dramatic in Jordan, likely in response

to the devastating terrorist attack in Amman in 2005. Twenty-nine percent of Jordanians view suicide attacks as often or sometimes justified, down from 57 percent in May 2005.

The belief that terrorism is justifiable in the defense of Islam, while less extensive than in previous surveys, still has a sizable number of adherents. Among Nigeria's Muslim population, for instance, nearly half (46 percent) feel that suicide bombings can be justified often or sometimes in the defense of Islam. Even among Europe's Muslim minorities, roughly one-in-seven in France, Spain, and Great Britain feel that suicide bombings against civilian targets can at least sometimes be justified to defend Islam against its enemies. Anti-Jewish sentiment remains overwhelming in predominantly Muslim countries.

The survey found some cause for optimism as Muslims and non-Muslims appraised the chances for democracy to work in Muslim countries. "Pluralities or majorities in every Muslim country surveyed say that democracy is not just for the West and can work in their countries. But Western publics are divided—majorities in Germany and Spain say democracy is a Western way of doing things that would not work in most Muslim countries. Most of the French and British, and about half of Americans, say democracy can work in Muslim countries." Among other findings in the survey are these: "Concerns over Islamic extremism are widely shared in Western publics and Muslim publics alike. But an exception is China, where 59 percent express little or no concern over Islamic extremism." Also, "Muslims differ over whether there is a struggle in their country between Islamic fundamentalists and groups wanting to modernize society. But solid majorities of those who perceive such a struggle side with the modernizers."[24]

The Pew survey and others clearly indicate that attitudes among Muslims and non-Muslims remain highly changeable. All are using the increased flows of information provided by new communications technologies and news organizations. The most visible of these suppliers is Al Jazeera, which is both a prototype for the new breed of news organizations appearing around the world and a player in global politics.

To understand Al Jazeera's influence, it is necessary to look at the channel not from the perspective of Western policymakers who consider it to be a malignant nuisance, but rather from the standpoint of its Arab audience, which sees it as a magnifier of shared frustrations and aspirations and as a truth-teller. Relatively free from the control of governments (except its own Qatari government), near or far, Al Jazeera is trusted as a chronicler of Arab and Muslim interests. In the opinion of many of its viewers, if its news coverage stirs passions, fine; if those passions swirl out of control, so be it. In the surge of journalistic-political freedom that Al Jazeera's freewheeling style exemplifies, restraint is often merely an afterthought.

As Gilles Kepel observed, during the intifada that began in 2000 "Al Jazeera relayed the daily news of a war in which 'martyrdom operations' were acts of heroism. Funerals of fallen heroes were broadcast on Arab satellite television, and viewers mourned for victims of the Israeli army's attacks. In many cases, Arab and Muslim sentiment spilled over unreservedly into anti-Jewish hatred. Muslims perceived themselves as the collective target of a humiliation campaign inflicted by Israel, in collusion with the United States and its Western allies."[25]

Al Jazeera's sometimes incendiary effect dismays some governments within and beyond the Middle East, but its style and the reactions it elicits from its viewers tell much about the popular politics of the region. Marc Lynch noted that when Saddam Hussein's regime was collapsing in 2003, Al Jazeera's talk shows "were broadcast live and uncensored, offering an unmatchable window into Arab public political argumentation."[26] These programs let viewers in the Middle East and elsewhere participate, even if just vicariously, in the dramatic events of the moment and certainly fostered thoughts about what might happen if other regimes were to fall.

The Qatar-based station has played a historic role in transforming media not only in the Middle East but also globally, proving that the hegemony of the predominantly Western media establishment can be successfully challenged. Beyond Al Jazeera's own success in this regard, the channel serves as a model within the Arab world and beyond, an example of news organizations with regional and global reach that are certain to proliferate during the next decade.

The effects of Al Jazeera, its principal competitor Al Arabiya, and other Arab news organizations could be seen during the 2006 Israel-Hezbollah War. As the *Washington Post* noted, the Arab world tuned in every night "to a bloodier, more painful, and more devastating conflict than the rest of the world sees." The coverage stimulated large numbers of calls to Al Jazeera's talk shows, and one producer said of the callers, "Usually what they want to do is criticize Arab leaders" for not more forcefully supporting Hezbollah.[27]

While the Arab channels' news products became more sophisticated, so too did their use of technology. By October 2006, a majority of the channels broadcasting on Arabsat and Nilesat satellite systems had a corresponding Web site or portal tied to the channel. As the Arab media market expands, indigenous news providers have been joined by other voices. In March 2006 the state-owned Spanish news agency EFE began an Arabic service, with funding provided by the Spanish foreign ministry. Based in Cairo, the EFE project is targeting viewers in countries closest to Spain: Morocco, Tunisia, and Mauritania. Javier Martín, director of EFE's Arabic venture, said, "We want to be a piece of the big puzzle and try to offer a bridge between civilizations." In Denmark, in the aftermath of the 2006 cartoon controversy, plans have been developed to begin television and radio broadcasts in Arabic with the stated goal of advancing democracy. Deutsche Welle and a new French all-news channel also want to reach the Arabic-speaking audience, as does the BBC, which is expanding its longtime presence in the region.[28]

Most of the news organizations entering the Arab market are mixing their broadcast products with online presence for two purposes: to broaden initial name recognition of the television offerings (which will, at least for the immediate future, make more money than the Web sites will) and to cultivate the younger, educated online audience that will grow rapidly as Internet access increases throughout the region. Meanwhile, the level of competition on the Web is expanding far faster than on the broadcast airwaves, as even the financially strapped expatriate has the wherewithal to start up a Web site to deliver news, gossip, or diatribes. The Web pulls together the Arab homeland and centers of the Arab diaspora such as Paris and Detroit.

Such sites challenge conventional broadcast and Web providers and stir up trouble or provide a useful outlet for political frustrations—probably a bit of both. The Ya Mohammed site, launched by Muslim students at universities around the world in response to the Danish cartoon dispute, was designed, said one of its managers, to be part of the "Internet Jihad to fight against the front of blasphemy" and as a "protest against the insults of the Western media." A less contentious site is al-Hakawati, started by an Arab-American living in New Jersey, to "provide a virtual library of Arab culture, to make learning and knowledge about the Arab world available to all, to promote Arab culture, and to promote understanding of Arab culture."[29] All kinds of Arab political and cultural sites abound, and their audiences range from minuscule to vast, their impact from negligible to significant influence on public opinion.

Whatever medium is being appraised, questions remain about whether financial support for so many projects can be found, given the segmented Arab audience and the still-developing economies in many of the Arab states. As has been seen in Iraq, among other places, media start-ups are numerous, but successes are far fewer. Nevertheless, these ventures will increase the amount and diversity of discourse within the Middle East, which will inevitably alter the region's politics and, more broadly, its collective intellectual and political life.

Greater availability of information leads, at least theoretically, to expanded knowledge. Even if that is the case, effects of knowledge are difficult to predict. Mark Allen wrote that in the Arab world today, "knowledge is in spate; a plurality of views undercuts certainties and their emotional securities, but a systematic technique for dealing with contradiction and dissent is lacking. Pluralism is not available."[30]

Allen correctly implied that pluralism will not simply appear; it will require nurturing through systemic change. New media, with satellite television in the vanguard, might help stimulate such change, and not just in the Arab world. Although it might lack the Internet's technological pizzazz, satellite television has been the driving force of intellectual globalization. While in much of the world only a tiny percentage of the population has Internet access, television is much more readily available (although it is not available everywhere). That will change, as the coffee shop with the television in the corner gives way to the Internet café and the home Internet connection supplements the satellite dish. But for now, Al Jazeera, the BBC, CNN, and their brethren are providing a river of information that can nourish people throughout the world.

When the world is more connected, globalization's optimists contend, conflict will be less likely; civilizations knowing more about each other and in consistent contact will be less likely to clash. Details about how this new global arrangement will work remain open to speculation, but one thing is certain: the role of the United States will change markedly.

For the foreseeable future, America will remain unavoidable, if not indispensable. No country will be able to stand up to U.S. military power in a conventional battlefield war, although the Iraq experience shows how alternate forms of combat reduce the American advantage. The U.S. economy will evolve adequately to maintain a position of preeminence, if not dominance. Life on the summit will, however, be precarious in some respects. Wars might not be fought with armies facing each other but rather in twisting, crowded urban alleys. An armory will no longer consist of thousands of missiles but rather of a few suitcases loaded with nuclear trash or anthrax spores. Attacks may occur not on beachheads but in cyberspace. The roster of major economic players will keep expanding—today, China and India, tomorrow Brazil and Kazakhstan. Similarly, the focal points of international tension will change.

As is discussed in later chapters, the Al Jazeera effect is being felt in places distant from the Middle East. Virtually every aspect of the new global order will be shaped by the unprecedented expansion of information and communications technologies. They are linking the world, with effects that deserve careful attention.

2
Channels and More Channels

They are everywhere. Not just an occasional seedling popping up on an otherwise barren plain but rather a whole forest—young and perhaps vulnerable but maturing and expanding with a speed and vigor that makes certain the survival of at least the fittest among them.

They are broadcasting stations funded by royal families and blogs based in tiny apartments. They are sophisticated Web sites and casual e-mail networks. They feature carefully crafted documentaries and cell phone video shot on the run. Some of their proprietors take bows on the world stage, while others live in fear of being raided by the police. Some have built global audiences, and some reach just a handful of like-minded friends.

This diversity makes these media fascinating and influential. No precise definition encompasses all the manifestations of new information and communication technologies, but already some paradigms have emerged. One of the most prominent of these is Al Jazeera.

Al Jazeera and Company

Egyptian journalist Fahmy Howeidy wrote, "Before the emergence of Al Jazeera, I only watched entertainment programs or football matches on Arab TV channels, only stopping at the latter during times of relaxation, laziness, or boredom. I researched important events or ideas through chasing news bulletins, reports, and discussion programs broadcast on Western television channels, particularly British and American ones. I never thought that

I would find 'food' of that nature on any Arab channel."[1]

That intellectual "food" is an important ingredient in Al Jazeera's appeal. The channel has proved to a skeptical audience that Arab media can be useful and that it is no longer necessary to rely on Western news organizations for information about important events. Through a mix of innovative programming, credible journalism, and persistent marketing, Al Jazeera has established itself as the go-to information resource in much of the Middle East. Walk into cafés from Morocco to Kuwait and you'll see that the television in the corner is tuned to Al Jazeera. A 2004–2005 survey of television viewers in Cairo found that 46 percent of households watched satellite television, and of these 88 percent watched Al Jazeera.[2]

Affection for the channel is by no means universal, even among Arabs. Some dislike the fractiousness of the talk shows, some see a religious slant in the news coverage, and others simply don't care for rock-the-boat journalism. The channel's presumed political leanings make some viewers wary. Al Jazeera's director general Wadah Khanfar said, "We have been accused from the beginning that we were created by international agencies like the Mossad, the CIA, and that the Americans are behind us, that this regime or that regime is behind us, that Osama bin Laden is behind us. This kind of nonsense is for us a sign that what we are doing is right. . . . We do not carry slogans or propaganda, not at all. We are just ordinary people with a love for journalism."[3]

But there is more to Al Jazeera than journalism. It may not be a stalking horse for the United States, Israel, Islam, or even Qatar's ruling family, but it is the latest in a line of media ventures that have sought to use mass media to help establish a pan-Arab identity. In 1953 Cairo Radio first broadcast a program called *The Voice of the Arabs*, which soon had a station of its own broadcasting eighteen hours a day. Its message was Gamal Abdel Nasser's Arabism—a revolutionary mix of socialism and anticolonialism that targeted conservative Arab governments.[4] The Egyptian leader was among the first in the Middle East to understand how broadcasting could affect regional politics. Marc Lynch noted that the Voice of the Arabs radio service "was an instrument of a powerful state, used purely for strategic reasons and aimed primarily at mobilizing pressure from below on rival regimes. Radio broadcasting transformed the potential for Arab political action by bringing Arabist political speech (if not rational discourse) directly to the increasingly mobilized masses. This allowed pan-Arab movements to fundamentally challenge the legitimacy of relatively new Arab states."[5]

Al Jazeera is a descendant of Voice of the Arabs in that it supplies cohesion to the notion of "Arabness." Faisal Al Kasim, host of Al Jazeera's talk show *The Opposite Direction*, observed,

> If anything, satellite talk shows have brought the Arab masses together and given them a pan-Arab identity. In other words, to a certain extent they have played a nationalist role by narrowing and sometimes bridging divides. In fact, one might argue that popular talk shows on Al Jazeera and other channels have succeeded where Gamal Abdel Nasser failed. Debate programs and live talks on satellite broadcasting are watched avidly by millions of Arabs and are contributing a great deal to the formation of pan-Arab public opinion over many issues. Arab viewers can now share each other's problems, issues, and concerns.[6]

The early pan-Arabism associated with Nasser has evolved, changing as the political chemistry and the media landscape of the Middle East have changed. At one level, wrote Thomas Friedman in 2002, these changes could be seen in the "explosion of Arab satellite TV and Internet, which are taking the horrific images from the Intifada and beaming them directly to the new Arab-Muslim generation. If 100 million Arab-Muslims are brought up with these images, Israel won't survive." Another facet of this issue, wrote Friedman, was that for decades Arab leaders had "used the Palestinian cause to buttress their own legitimacy or to deflect attention from their own failures. But in the old days, they could regulate how their own people saw the conflict through their state-controlled media. No more. This is the cyber-intifada in the age of globalization. Thanks to independent Arab satellite TV beaming images from Palestine to Arab youths twenty-four hours a day, and thanks to the Internet, which allows those youths to tell each other exactly how they feel about those images, the Arab regimes are losing their grip on public opinion."[7]

A half-century earlier Nasser had used his Voice of the Arabs broadcasts to shake up rival regimes, but by the time of the second intifada there was far less direct political control of media messages. The images, however, had the same kind of destabilizing effect that Nasser had aimed for, as Arabs became frustrated by what they perceived as the failure of their governments to help the Palestinians.

In 2002 Al Jazeera was an important player in this process, but the dominance the channel had enjoyed during its first years was diminishing, primarily because of the emergence of competitors such as Al Arabiya, Abu Dhabi Television, the Lebanese Broadcasting Corporation, and others. Laws, beginning with a 1994 Lebanese statute that revoked the state's broadcasting monopoly, facilitated private ownership of broadcast stations.[8] Costs of satellite hardware dropped substantially, allowing more players into the game.

Growth has occurred despite an economic environment that cannot support a Western-style broadcasting model. In the Arab world in 2005, advertising revenue totaled US$1.5 billion for television, radio, print, and other media, while annual operating costs for these media were about US$16 billion.[9] This lopsided balance sheet, coupled with lack of direct foreign investment in the region, has meant that funding for media infrastructure must come largely from elites such as the region's royal families and other investors who may be more interested in having a political platform than in providing honest information to the public.[10]

In parts of the region, Al Jazeera's strongest competition comes from Al Arabiya. The twenty-four-hour news channel is part of the Middle East Broadcasting Center (MBC) group, which is largely Saudi-owned and based in Dubai. MBC began broadcasting in 1991, and its entertainment and news programs reach more than 150 million Arabic speakers worldwide, with its MBC 1 "family entertainment channel" claiming more viewers than any other channel in the Middle East.

Al Arabiya was created in 2003 in response, says MBC, to "the perceived need from the Arabic audience for a truly relevant, balanced, and responsible source of news."[11] Read that as meaning the region's political establishment, particularly the Saudis, desired a channel more restrained in its politics and programming than Al Jazeera. Sheikh Walid al-Ibrahim, brother-in-law of Saudi Arabia's late King Fahd and owner of MBC, said that he hoped to position Al Arabiya as a moderate CNN compared to Al Jazeera's more extreme Fox News approach. Al Arabiya's billboards claim, "With us, you are closer to the truth."[12]

Al Arabiya may have positioned itself in the spot its owner wants, but it has struggled to match Al Jazeera's popularity. A survey conducted in spring 2004 found that Al Arabiya trailed Al Jazeera by a considerable margin in percentage of the audience throughout the Middle East, although a respectable 39 percent of satellite news viewers said they tuned in to Al Arabiya at some point every day.[13] Like Al Jazeera, Al Arabiya mixes its newscasts with an array of talk shows such as *From Iraq* (which, the channel says, has a large Iraqi audience, as evidenced by "the large quantities of pirated CDs and video sold the day after" the program airs); *Across the Ocean*, from Washington; *Last Edition* and *Fourth Estate*, which respectively examine Arab and Western media; and *Poll-on-Air*, which asks the audience to vote on a question and takes live phone and e-mail responses about a topic.

The journalists who lead Al Arabiya recognize the power that the satellite news channels possess. General manager Abdul Rahman al-Rashed said that Al Jazeera and Al Arabiya "are more dangerous than nuclear bombs, and they radiate on a large scale." Their news, he added, could push viewers "to go into a war, or it could make the people believe in peace and change their lives." He also said, "The region is being filled with inaccuracies and partial truths. I think people will always make good judgments if they have the right information and the whole information. What we lack now is the truth and information. After that, we'll have a sane society. Right now it is an insane society because of the way information is being delivered to individuals."[14]

Before joining Al Arabiya, al-Rashed, a Saudi educated in the United States, had been editor of *Asharq Alawsat*, a well-known Arab-language newspaper published in London. He wrote a widely quoted column for the paper in 2004 after Chechen terrorists seized a school in North Ossetia and more than three hundred people, many of them children, died. "It is a certain fact," he wrote, "that not all Muslims are terrorists, but it is equally certain, and exceptionally painful, that almost all terrorists are Muslims." Referring to suicide bombings, he wrote, "What a pathetic record. What an abominable achievement. Does this tell us anything about ourselves, our societies, and our culture?" In the column, al-Rashed also criticized influential Muslim cleric Sheik Yusuf al-Qaradawi for endorsing the murder of American civilians working in Iraq. Al-Qaradawi regularly broadcasts on Al Jazeera.[15]

Al Arabiya's executive editor, Nabil Khatib, is a Palestinian who has covered the Israeli-Palestinian conflict. Like al-Rashed, Khatib has little tolerance for those who encourage violence, particularly if they are in the news business. "Sensationalism," he said in 2004, "incites people to hatred. I have smelled the blood of hatred, and I cannot understand how someone in an air-conditioned newsroom feels that he has the right to manipulate people's emotions, to rile people up or to generalize about a group, when he sees the repercussions."[16]

Those comments by al-Rashed and Khatib show how Al Arabiya is trying to define a new mainstream for Arab news—neither blandly mirroring a government line nor being as provocative as Al Jazeera. Khatib also said he wants to bring the news agenda closer to the public's daily concerns. "For 50 years," he said, "all Arabs have heard about is Israelis, Palestinians, Americans, Arab summits, and so on, and nothing about real answers to the real questions of why he is poor, frustrated, and unhappy with the level of health care and education for his kids. These are the concerns of any human being and any Arab. But if you ask someone what he is concerned about most, he will tell you Jerusalem or Iraq, because you keep telling him this."[17]

News executives worldwide share the task of deciding what the audience needs and wants. But nowhere else in the world at this time do a handful of television channels have so much influence on the content and tenor of political discourse. It is easy to use the CNN-Fox analogy for Al Arabiya and Al Jazeera, but CNN and Fox moved easily into the stable continuum of American news media. The Arab news channels, in contrast, emerged into a vacuum; in their part of the world they were pioneers in establishing a freewheeling journalism for a mass audience. They have changed journalism, and perhaps more important, they have changed the public's expectations about the availability of information.

Although many of the Arab satellite channels principally offer entertainment programming, numerous Arab channels—terrestrial as well as satellite—also provide some news. Each can maintain a solid, if not huge, audience by providing localized content. People will always be interested in what their own government is doing and how their own close-to-home issues are being addressed, topics that the regional and global channels cannot fully cover (much as local television news in the United States often inspires greater audience loyalty than do the national networks). Audience measurement for these channels is far less intensive than the ratings system that dominates the U.S. television industry, but surveys are gradually increasing in number and sophistication. A 2005 study conducted in Jordan, Lebanon, Morocco, Saudi Arabia, and the United Arab Emirates found that 45 percent of respondents watched Al Jazeera, 12 percent watched MBC and the Lebanese Broadcasting Corporation (LBC) respectively, 9 percent Al Arabiya, Abu Dhabi 6 percent, Hezbollah's Al Manar 4 percent, and the U.S. government's Al Hurra 1 percent. When viewers preferred national rather than regional stations, Al Jazeera and Al Arabiya were most often the audience's second choice.[18]

Lebanese, Palestinian, and Other Players

The recent history of Lebanese television illustrates how technology and politics combine to shape what the audience receives. The LBC went on the air in 1985, in the midst of a civil war. The company's headquarters was periodically shelled, and at one point in 1992 the channel had a single day to move all its people and equipment out of its offices before government troops took over the building. They loaded their gear into fifty trucks, quickly set up a makeshift studio, and got their evening newscast on the air. After the fighting ended (for a while), LBC launched its free satellite channel in 1996, providing Arabic entertainment programs aimed primarily at fifteen to twenty-four year olds. It followed this with three additional channels to reach the global Arab population: LBC Europe, LBC America, and LBC Australia. In 2006, recognizing variations in the interests of Arabs living in the Middle East and North Africa, LBC began LBC Maghreb, which promised localized content with "Lebanese flair."[19]

LBC's evolution illustrates how the Middle East's television industry is maturing. Sophisticated market segmentation is driving expansion, while on the technical side newsrooms such as those of Al Jazeera and Al Arabiya are state-of-the-art, unsurpassed by any elsewhere in the world. Despite such progress, politics remains inescapable, inexorably affecting the media's product and their larger role.

Lebanon provides examples of this dynamic. Late 2006 saw yet another surge of instability in Lebanon as the militant Shiites of Hezbollah stepped up their challenge to the national government, organizing massive demonstrations in Beirut to demand the resignation of Prime Minister Fouad Siniora. Like other political groups, Hezbollah has its own television station, Al Manar, which heavily covered the protests, even replacing some regular programs with a talk show originating in the midst of the protestors. Defending the government was Future TV, owned by the Sunni family of Rafik Hariri, who had been assassinated in February 2005. Hariri's death evoked outrage against Syria, the alleged sponsor of the murder and an ally of Hezbollah. Future TV's coverage of the Beirut demonstrations depicted them as part of an effort by Syria to seize control of Lebanon. Meanwhile, Al Manar portrayed Syria as Lebanon's ally against a "U.S.-Israeli project" to dominate the country.[20]

Al Manar, which is discussed in chapter 7, is a significant example of nonstate political media, a phenomenon that is certain to expand as political organizations try to elevate themselves to the kind of de facto legitimacy that having their own media outlets purportedly provides. In addition to its impact within Lebanon, Al Manar is seen by some as having considerable influence among Muslim minority communities around the world. In late 2004 French officials ordered the cable provider Eutelsat to stop carrying Al Manar because of the channel's overtly anti-

Semitic content, which was allegedly fostering increased radicalization and isolation among French Muslims.[21]

Taken together, the television offerings from Lebanon illustrate how a small country (population about five million) can establish a regional, and to a lesser degree global, presence through mass media. Television's ability to stir *domestic* political passions is also seen in the effects of Al Manar, Future TV, and others.

Within this microcosm is the fusion of media and politics that continues to develop throughout the region. Agendas vary, from Al Jazeera's globalized audience-building to Al Manar's targeted provocation. And new channels keep appearing.

Dissatisfied with information from Israeli news organizations, Palestinians in 1994 launched the Voice of Palestine radio station and in 1996 began television programming as the Palestinian Broadcasting Corporation (PBC).

With about eighty television and radio stations offering varying content in the West Bank and Gaza and with growing access to satellite channels such as Al Jazeera, Palestinians can increasingly tap into diverse information sources from around the world. At the heart of the Palestinians' own media is the politics of the conflict with Israel. When the second intifada began in 2000, Palestinian media urged their viewers and listeners to join the battle. Nabil Shaath, who served as foreign minister in Yasser Arafat's government, said, "During the Intifada, television and radio became a tool for generating resistance and generating steadfastness facing very difficult times." The PBC dropped its regular programming and broadcast minute-by-minute coverage of the fighting. When images were broadcast of twelve-year-old Mohammed el-Dura dying in his father's arms after being caught in the gunfire of a street battle, Palestinian television carried messages to young people telling them to "Drop your toys and pick up rocks." In one such spot, an actor playing the slain boy in "child heaven" said to young viewers, "I wave to you not to say goodbye but to say, 'Follow me.'" Not until mid-2004 did the Palestinian media begin to return to non-conflict-related programs.[22]

In 2003 Hamas launched the Voice of Al Aqsa, which soon became one of the most popular radio stations in Gaza. In early 2006, on the eve of the Palestinian elections that it won, Hamas expanded its broadcasting with Al Aqsa TV. Emulating Hezbollah's Al Manar, Hamas used the channel to bolster its claim to legitimacy as a political party and to proselytize in ways that some would consider insidious.

As part of the channel's programming for young viewers, "Uncle Hazim," portrayed by host Hazim Sharawi, introduced children to characters in animal suits, but even though parts of the show had the look of a typical children's program, much of its content was decidedly political. This was Hamas, after all, and so, Uncle Hazim said, "I will show them our rights through history: 'This is Nablus, this is Gaza, this is Al Aqsa mosque, which is with the Israelis and should be in our hands.'" Although he promised to avoid graphic scenes of violence, Sharawi said he intended to teach children about the disputed status of Jerusalem, the demands of Palestinians to be allowed to return to land taken by Israel in 1948, and other such issues. He said, "I cannot turn the children's lives into a beautiful garden while outside it's the contrary."[23]

In a similar vein, among the characters on the children's show *Pioneers of Tomorrow* was Farfour, who resembled Mickey Mouse. During one program Farfour told children about "placing the cornerstone for the ruling of the world by an Islamic leadership." In 2007 the Farfour character achieved "martyrdom" at the hands of an Israeli soldier and was replaced on the show by Nahoul the Bee, who said to the child host of the program that he wanted "to continue in the path of Farfour" and to "take revenge upon the enemies of Allah." During an episode of the show later in 2007, Nahoul told the audience, "We must arise in order to take revenge upon the criminal Jews, the occupying Zionists. We must liberate Al Aqsa."[24] This is the often overlooked side of expanded television offerings—programming that was not previously available is now feeding an impressionable audience of children political material disguised as entertainment.

Political content was also part of yet another new venture that was announced in 2006 by Prince Al-Waleed ibn Talal, a member of the Saudi royal family and CEO of the international investment group Kingdom Holding Company. Al-Waleed created Al Resalah television, saying that the satellite channel's content would project "our Arab heritage through a modern medium" and would counteract misconceptions about Islam in other societies. Using Arabic-language entertainment programming with moral content, the channel was designed, according to its proponents, to lead Muslim youth away from extremism. The channel's general manager, Tarek Al-Suwaidan, said the programming would represent "pure and moderate Islam." The prince said that he planned to eventually add an English-language version for Western audiences.[25]

The channel has a pan-Islamic rather than just pan-Arab orientation. In 2006 its Web site posted a long open letter, in Arabic and English, to Pope Benedict XVI concerning his speech in Regensburg, Germany, in which he allegedly mischaracterized Islam. The letter was written to "point out some errors in the way you mentioned Islam" and was temperate enough to be in the spirit of Prince Al-Waleed's commitment to moderation and tolerance. But another example of Al Resalah's content was less moderate. In an interview on the channel, an Islamic cleric said that "the West's conflict with Islam and the Muslims is eternal, a preordained destiny that cannot be avoided until Judgment Day."[26] Considering Kingdom Holding Company's massive investments in Western businesses—Citigroup, Time Warner, Motorola, and many others—the cleric's message might not have been appreciated by the channel's owner. But it can sometimes be difficult to determine whether political or financial agendas take precedence, and even media that purport to be "moderate" merit scrutiny concerning how they affect their audience.

The American Presence

Politics is pervasive, and media organizations that say they will deliver ideologically neutral news and wholesome entertainment are unlikely to be truly apolitical. This is an issue not only for Arab channels but also for Arabic-language channels broadcasting from outside the region. The U.S. government-funded television channel Al Hurra was created, according to President George W. Bush, to be part of an attempt to "cut through the barriers of hateful propaganda" generated by Arabic television stations and provide "reliable news and information across the

region."[27] When it began broadcasting in February 2004 with a
$62 million budget for its first year, Al Hurra received mixed re-
views. (In late 2003 Congress added $40 million to the Al Hurra
budget for a sister station broadcasting solely to Iraq.) Critics referred to it as "Fox News in Arabic" and noted its pro-U.S. political
leanings.

Al Hurra notably lagged behind the Arab networks in the
prominence and quantity of coverage of Palestinian issues. This
was one factor that led Hussein Amin of the American University
in Cairo to observe of Al Hurra's staff, "Their credibility is open
to question right now. If they take the position of the U.S. and
color everything with its policies, then people will reject the message and it will not achieve success in any form."[28] Nabil Dajani,
a professor at the American University of Beirut asked, "Can they
expect the Arabs to watch them if they don't show Palestinians
being killed and don't portray Israelis as oppressors?"[29] Harsher
criticism came from a Saudi jurist, Sheikh Ibrahim Al-Khudairi,
who said that Al Hurra was "waging a war against Islam and Ameri-
canizing the world. . . . The objective of the channel is to facilitate
American hegemony over the world in the religious, political, and
social fields."[30]

Offering a mix of news, cooking shows, entertainment and
other such fare, Al Hurra made little initial impact in terms of
winning an audience. Surveys conducted in mid-2004 found Al
Hurra trailing Al Jazeera and Al Arabiya. Among 3,300 respondents to a poll in Egypt, Saudi Arabia, Morocco, Jordan, Lebanon,
and the United Arab Emirates, no one said Al Hurra was his or
her first choice for news and only 4 percent picked it as second
choice.[31] Another survey of viewers in Saudi Arabia found that 82
percent of households watched Al Jazeera, 75 percent watched Al
Arabiya, 16 percent watched Al Hurra, and 12 percent watched
CNN. Only 17 percent of respondents said they considered Al
Hurra to be very trustworthy or trustworthy, while 20 percent
viewed it as untrustworthy. (The remainder expressed no opinion about its trustworthiness.)[32] Other figures, derived from A. C.
Nielsen surveys and cited by Al Hurra, reflect more interest in the
broadcasts and much higher credibility ratings.[33]

Shibley Telhami observed that part of the problem for Al

Hurra is that its apparent detached objectivity does not match the mood of its intended viewers. "Its aim," said Telhami, "is to be precisely dispassionate while facing a passionate audience."[34] As seen in its reluctance to air graphic images or to use language perceived as critical of U.S. policy, Al Hurra has sometimes tied itself in knots while trying to offer objective journalism and at the same time trying to advance the U.S. political agenda in the Arab world. Although Al Hurra's staff includes journalists who pride themselves on their objectivity, their ultimate boss—as their audience well knows—is the U.S. government and that inevitably affects the station's credibility. Fundamentally, it is government-run journalism, a genre that always involves constraints. Anne Marie Baylouny observed in late 2005 that Al Hurra had become "largely irrelevant, serving mainly to clearly identify a news point of view as 'American' and thus facilitate rejection of its content due to this taint." She added the channel had proved counterproductive in terms of advancing U.S. interests.[35]

Despite Al Hurra's shaky performance in the competition for the Arab audience, the BBC's World Service, which is funded by the British Foreign Office, announced in 2005 that it was prepared to invest about US$35 million a year to operate an Arabic-language channel. (The funding was available partly because the World Service ended its broadcasts in ten other languages, many of which—such as those in Bulgarian and Czech—were judged to be vestiges of the Cold War and no longer politically necessary.) Arabic radio was the BBC's first foreign language venture, beginning in 1938, and the BBC brand has built credibility in the region over the years through its radio and online products. The BBC estimated in 2005 that its Arabic radio broadcasts had an audience of about 12 million listeners a week and its online news in Arabic received 17 million page impressions each month. BBC officials said their survey research in 2003 and 2005 found a substantial number of respondents indicating that they would be likely to watch a BBC television channel.[36] The channel began broadcasting in March 2008, and BBC officials said they hope to attract 20 million viewers per week by 2010.

Because of its longtime presence in the region and its image of not being overtly political, the BBC may have an advantage over Al Hurra. But Al Arabiya spokesman Jihad Ballout noted that the media environment had become more crowded and "there are now better sources about our region." That leads to some important questions about the future of news media in the Middle East: At what point does the market become saturated? Will the Arab audience, now with so many homegrown news products available, enter a period of information chauvinism and ignore outside sources such as the BBC and Al Hurra?

The population of the Arab world is about 300 million. That is roughly the same as that of the United States, where the television news market has been segmented in ways that have undercut the dominance of the traditional "big three" leaders. The argument can be made—at least on financial, if not journalistic, grounds—that the finite audience/revenue pie can be sliced only so many times before the pieces become too small to support all the channels. Similarly in the Middle East today, if the regional television leaders are Al Jazeera and Al Arabiya, how much room is there for competitors who want more than just small niche audiences?[37]

Answers to these questions will affect the financial prospects for media ventures and also will determine the amount of influence news providers—particularly "outsiders"—will have. Merely speaking Arabic does not confer credibility. If a station is funded by a foreign government, its protestations about journalistic independence will convince relatively few audience members that what is being broadcast is news rather than propaganda. The relationship between media ownership and news product integrity is a global issue, whether it involves the Emir of Qatar and Al Jazeera or the U.S. government and Al Hurra or, for that matter, the Disney Company and ABC News. In the Middle East, where trust is a limited commodity, the issue is particularly significant for any news organization trying to enter or expand in the market.

Telesur

Outside the Middle East, a facet of the Al Jazeera effect can be seen in the development of regional satellite television in areas where indigenous news media have long been overshadowed by big media organizations based elsewhere. An example of this is Telesur.

Politics led to the creation of Telesur, which is shorthand for La Nueva Televisión del Sur (New Television of the South). In Latin America, as in the Middle East, there was growing resentment about the infringement on intellectual and political autonomy represented by the dominance of outside media. The view of the world through others' eyes is not always trustworthy, and before outside perspectives become useful, there must be an indigenous frame of reference.

This was the view of Venezuela's president Hugo Chávez, who, along with Cuba's Fidel Castro, developed the idea of a regional television channel. Telesur, said Chávez, would be aimed at "counteracting the media dictatorship of the big international news networks." Similar to the rhetoric of the founders of the Arab channels, Telesur journalists speak of the "anti-hegemonic" nature of their effort, and the channel's director general, Aram Aharonian, noted the "urgency to see ourselves through our own eyes and to discover our own solutions to our problems."[38]

While promoting the channel, Chávez asked, "Why do we have to be told everything we know about ourselves by a network from the North, like CNN?" Aharonian said, "Today we know much more about Chechnya than what's happening on the corner, in Colombia or in Central America, because all the information that the North generates comes into focus about the subjects that interest the North."[39]

Initial funding for the channel, which went on the air in 2005 from its base in Caracas, came from Venezuela and other Latin American countries. As of late 2006, the Venezuelan government owned 51 percent of Telesur, while Argentina owned 20 percent, Cuba owned 14 percent, and Uruguay and Bolivia together owned 15 percent. Despite the initial reliance on these governments' money, Aharonian said that the channel would not be state-controlled. This would be more likely if he could secure support from private corporate sponsors, which he said would come soon. Aharonian also promised that Telesur would not adopt the format of some other state-funded channels, which devote inordinate amounts of airtime to government officials' speeches and other activities. He predicted, "No one would watch it," if Telesur were to become a propaganda tool.[40]

That is not to say that Telesur will remove itself from politics. For one thing, Chávez has his own media-related agenda. He remained resentful after opposition media aided a briefly successful coup against his presidency in 2002. He has hosted his own television program, *Alo, Presidente* (Hello, President), on which he takes questions from a studio audience and callers. Also, the journalists running the channel have clearly defined their own political goals. Aharonian said, "We will focus on doing the opposite of commercial television. We will search out the protagonist role of social movements, people, communities, and towns." He cited Fidel Castro's call for creating "a CNN of the people," and said, "Television cannot be left in the hands of the enemy. The Venezuelan government has given great importance to community and alternative radio, but has left mass media to the enemy. Today it is apparent that mass communication is important, since alternative media only reach 5 or 7 percent of the general audience. . . . The people are no longer passive in the face of what is said on television. They watch and try to read between the lines, to discover what is hidden, what is not said."[41]

Given this political context, Telesur's managers embarked on developing a new model for content. In addition to having their own correspondents in Latin America and the United States, they planned to contract with independent media in the region for regular news reporting and also longer pieces and documentaries. To stimulate production of this material, Telesur promised to support a Factory of Latin American Content and to broadcast material developed there on the channel itself or help find other venues for it.

Beyond such operational matters, Telesur's leadership echoed Chávez's calls for political integration within Latin America. Writing for the *Rebelión* Web site in summer 2005, Aharonian, a veteran Uruguayan journalist, argued that Telesur was "aimed at realizing the Bolivarian ideal. To see each other is to know each other. . . . If the goal is integration, Telesur is the means." Aharonian added, "The media image that is portrayed in the region is not representative of its reality, because at present there is no medium that is willing and has the resources to build bridges between the peoples and nations of Latin America. . . . It will be the audio-visual alternative that will help to foster a Latin American identity." He also wrote that Telesur and other such channels could be tools "in the battle of ideas against the hegemonic globalization process." He concluded, "We will not stop until we have democratized the spectrum of television in our region."[42]

Aharonian made some interesting points about Telesur's political outlook, which is shared to some extent by Al Jazeera and others. The idea that globalization strengthens traditional hegemonic practices does not attract much attention in the most-developed nations, partly because globalization means a continuation of their dominance. If you're a member of the club, hegemony is quite nice. But states that are outside this circle look for ways to assert their own interests. Regional bonding, with communication technology as the glue, has appeal. And so Arab states, Latin America, and others who lack economic and military clout can use media to assert collective identity. But how "collected" people want to be is open to question. In Latin America, Bolivarian integration is not universally applauded, as Chávez found out when he tried to meddle in the politics of neighboring countries. Similarly, in the Middle East, Al Jazeera has found that pan-Arabism wins approval as an abstraction, but many Arabs cling to their national identities.

Assuming that the news media are able to enjoy at least a semblance of journalistic freedom, broader reform should benefit. This, however, is where the Telesur model runs into problems. Although Aharonian claimed that Telesur would democratize Latin American television, the shift of media from private to state hands seems an unlikely path toward greater media democracy. Granted, state influence on media content—sometimes overt, sometimes subtle—will always be with us. Al Jazeera, for instance, does not probe into the affairs of the Qatari royal family. In the United States, government pressure can, at least temporarily, keep news organizations on a leash. Those Latin American journalists who do not admire Chávez's political philosophy or tactics are unlikely to adopt Aharonian's rosy view.

Nonetheless, Telesur has some interesting characteristics. In keeping with its professed populist approach, rather than following the slick Western model for newscasts it included among its on-air talent a Colombian Indian journalist wearing the white robes of her Arhuaco tribe. A program offering movies was called *Nojolivud*, Spanish phonetic spelling of "No Hollywood." Recognizing that it must compete for viewers with CNN en Español, Univision, Televisión Española, and other channels, Telesur has aggressively worked to distinguish itself. In early 2006 Telesur signed an agreement with Al Jazeera to share content and technical expertise. Later that year, Telesur acquired additional studio and office space in Caracas as it planned its expansion into Spanish-speaking markets in Europe and northwestern Africa, as well as into additional Latin American markets.[43]

Assuming that Telesur can maintain a stream of governmental and private revenue, it may assume an important role among Latin American media. Chávez's ambition is to see Latin America less dominated by its neighbors in *el Norte* and more unified as a political entity. This works well with Telesur's capabilities. Reactions to Telesur from outside the region are likely to be muted in comparison to those directed at Al Jazeera, but if Latin America should ever become involved in turmoil that is perceived as a threat to broader international stability (or if Chávez assumes the role of the new Castro), Telesur could become more of a political target.

Others in the Game

Politics is in some way involved with almost every development in new media, as can be seen in the reasons behind the creation of satellite channels with extended international reach. French journalist Ulysse Gosset, who helped develop France's entry into this field, France 24, said, "Today news channels are part of the global battle in the world. It's as important as traditional diplomacy and economic strength." He added, "If we have a real desire to communicate around the world, we need to do it with the right medium, and that's English."[44]

Just about everywhere in the world, there are people—particularly among the political and economic elite—who speak

English and are part of the far-flung audience for the American and British broadcasting giants. For governments that want to participate in the global conversation about important issues, English-language media are essential. France 24, born in 2006, is an example of this.

France 24, referred to by some as "CNN a la Francaise," was constructed as a joint venture between TF1, France's largest independent network, and state-run France Télévisions. News bulletins are presented in French and English from adjoining newsrooms. Arabic broadcasts were added in 2007. The channel's Web site also offers news in French, English, and Arabic. Its annual startup budget was about US$100 million, and its staff at the channel's launch included 180 journalists representing twenty-eight nationalities and with an average age of thirty-three.[45]

Alain de Pouzilhac, the French channel's CEO, argued that CNN's coverage of the Iraq War was not objective but reflected an American view that the invading forces were trying to "bring freedom" to Iraq. He said, "This channel will not be anti-American. But this channel has to discover international news with French eyes, like CNN discovers international news with American eyes." The eyes that see the news before it is reported make a difference, he contended: "Objectivity doesn't exist in the world. Honesty exists. Impartiality exists. But objectivity doesn't exist." France 24 will devote more airtime to French positions than other channels do. Mark Owen, an anchor who moved from Britain's ITV to the French channel, said that during the 2006 Israel-Hezbollah War the BBC paid little attention to French president Jacques Chirac's calls for a halt to Israeli attacks within Lebanon, while instead highlighting British prime minister Tony Blair's support of the U.S. position of letting Israel proceed.[46]

France 24 was designed to help spread what it defines as French political values: paying more attention to the less well-covered parts of the world, encouraging debate, and emphasizing cultural as well as economic development. De Pouzilhac said, "It's the opposite of what the U.S. does. The vision from Washington tries to show that the world is unified, whereas we will try to demonstrate the opposite: that the world has a lot of diversity. Diversity of culture, diversity of religion, and diversity of opinion."[47]

Chirac's spokesman Jerome Bonnafont said that Chirac's interest in creating France 24 developed during the aftermath of the 9/11 attacks. The president believed that France and other nations had to step forward to correct misunderstandings among cultures and had to do so with their individual voices, rather than succumbing to "the trend toward uniformity" created by globalization. Chirac was determined that French views would be heard. Bonnafont said, "If you don't try to be present in the world in a dynamic way, then the world will ignore you. You have to show that you are somebody."[48] (In early 2008, Chirac's successor, Nicolas Sarkozy said he wanted to shut down the English and Arabic channels, arguing, "With taxpayers' money, I am not prepared to broadcast a channel that does not speak French." France 24 strongly objected, and as of this writing, the issue was still pending.)

In times past, "showing that you are somebody" often meant flexing your military muscle, so relying on television rather than armies can be considered progress. The significance of that change is clear when considering Russia's effort to use the airwaves rather than its traditional means to assert itself. English-language channel Russia Today was created in 2005 to reshape Russia's image. According to Svetlana Mironyuk, the general director of the news agency Novosti, "Unfortunately, at the level of the mass consciousness in the West, Russia is associated with three words: 'communism,' 'snow,' and 'poverty.' We would like to present a more complete picture of life in our country."[49]

Critics immediately branded the channel as a tool of the government. Political commentator Boris Kagarlitsky said, "Russia Today is very much a continuation of the old Soviet propaganda services. They want good news and they want a positive vision of Russia." But Mironyuk said this was not the case: "It is almost impossible to impose your own point of view among other opinions because the information space is too huge. There are literally scores of alternatives. But the idea is to provide an international audience with an understanding of what is going on in Russia from Russia's point of view."[50]

The truth lies somewhere between the critics and the defenders. There was more behind the creation of Russia Today than the motive of counteracting obsolete images of the frigid Soviet Union. President Vladimir Putin was reportedly angry about the consistently negative tone of international coverage of Russian policies, such as allegations about human rights abuses by Russian forces during the fighting in Chechnya, a conflict that Putin considered to be part of the global war on terror.[51] Mironyuk was correct, however, when she pointed out that heavy-handed propaganda will be quickly and frequently challenged today. Because the information marketplace is crowded with everything from large news organizations to individual bloggers, Soviet-style information management cannot work, at least not for long. Like Jacques Chirac, Putin recognizes the new levels of competition for world opinion. Like France 24, Russia Today provides news with a spin that favors the interests of its proprietors. The product is professionally slick and features a subtle but distinctly Putinesque view of the world. Many news consumers presumably recognize how the game is played and judge the information they receive accordingly.

Such alertness is important because the English-language news arena is becoming even more crowded. CNN was created in 1980, BBC World arrived in 1991, Deutsche Welle began its television broadcasts in English in 1992, and the list goes on, with further additions in the works. A pan-African channel is being contemplated that would broadcast in English and French. One of the planners, Salim Amin, echoed his colleagues at other channels when he described the rationale for the channel: "We don't have a network or media that enables us to talk to each other and to send the message out to the rest of the world. All we see on the international networks about Africa is very negative: famine, war, disease, death, HIV. There are positive things happening here that never get highlighted."[52]

For this African project and other prospective channels, finances are difficult, particularly if the journalists involved want to maintain their independence. Today's major satellite channels have not copied the CNN start-up model of a privately funded corporation. Most rely heavily on government subsidies, which sometimes are accompanied by a full government partnership in the channel's operation. For all the prestige and influence that these channels may have, the market is too crowded for profits to be likely. The best-known channel, Al Jazeera, has always required large amounts of money from Qatar's emir. BBC World, the BBC's commercially funded international venue, claims a weekly audience of 65 million viewers and reported in 2006 that its advertising revenues had grown 20 percent every year since 2001. Nevertheless, channel executives conceded that it would not break even until 2010.[53]

Despite the financial challenges, English-language broadcasting will continue to grow. Deutsche Welle is a good example of a channel that has established a foothold in the market. Its television broadcasts are primarily in English and German, with Spanish and Arabic programs, as well, and—as of 2002—some Dari and Pashto programming that is provided for broadcast by RTA, Afghanistan's television service. The channel's managing director, Cristoph Lanz, said, "There are more viewers watching it in the English language than German. And that doesn't have to do with a small amount of Germans watching. It just has to do with the fact that the world is six billion people and there are just 80 million Germans and there are maybe 150 million German speakers. If you have a mission statement to reach out to the world, then you have to reach across the language gap."[54]

Deutsche Welle is funded by the German government, and its statutory mandate is "to make Germany understood as a European-grown cultural nation and democratic constitutional state founded on the rule of law." The company has noted that its broadcasts are designed partly to enhance "Germany's external media image" and their "most important target groups are international opinion leaders with an interest in Germany and Europe." The Deutsche Welle mission statement cites as one of its roles to "use our credibility to promote Germany's reputation worldwide." The television channel's daily audience is estimated at 28 million people.[55]

Since its first German-language radio broadcasts in 1953, Deutsche Welle has developed as a model for broadcasting enterprises that are created primarily to serve governments' political purposes. The other principal model, which is free from formal government connections, is CNN's global arm, CNN International.

It is private and for-profit, and it plays a significant de facto political role in the world. Born in 1985 as CNN Europe, CNN International competed primarily with BBC World News during the 1990s and over the years has seen its reach extend into more than two hundred countries. An aging star, the entire CNN enterprise has lost some of its luster; in the United States, it often trails the acerbic and conservative Fox News Channel in the ratings contest, and internationally it is overshadowed by younger, zippier channels such as Al Jazeera.

But CNN is still very much in the game, particularly as a result of the partnerships it has formed with indigenous broadcasters around the world. One example is CNN-IBN (India Broadcast News), a twenty-four-hour English-language news channel created in 2005 to link CNN to one of India's leading broadcast companies, the TV18 Group. CNN provides international coverage, while IBN concentrates on national and local reports. CNN International's managing director, Chris Cramer, cited this partnership as one of "CNN's efforts to move closer to its audience," and the new channel's editor in chief, Rajdeep Sardesai, said the appeal of working with CNN was partly the demand for more international news "in a fast-globalizing India."[56]

Those dual rationales say much about the state of the international news business. CNN has recognized that because of the credibility and general appeal of local and regional news organizations, it must change its image from that of an outsider (and a Western one, at that) to that of a local colleague. Regardless of the quality of its journalism and its worldwide presence, CNN itself is still seen as an American entity, which limits its appeal. This is one aspect of the Al Jazeera effect at work. While broadcasting is becoming more transnational in its reach, it is also increasingly seen as a tool of home countries' or home regions' interests.

In the CNN-IBN case, Sardesai's point underscores Indians' desire to become more fully integrated with the global community. The route to that goal runs partly through the United States and certainly requires reliance on English, which shows no signs of being replaced as the dominant language of the world's business. Taken together, these factors make forging this kind of partnership a logical strategy for all parties.

Al Jazeera itself recognized that if it were to expand its world-wide influence, it could not do so wholly in Arabic. And so, after several years of preparation, it launched Al Jazeera English, the first English-language news channel to be headquartered in the Middle East. With its principal broadcast centers in Doha, Washington, London, and Kuala Lumpur, the channel faced the task of proving itself to be more than a curiosity or a junior version of the BBC or CNN.

During its first months, Al Jazeera English seemed to be well on its way to defining its place in the market. The breadth of its coverage, particularly its emphasis on reporting from the South to the North, distinguished it from many of its competitors. Thorough coverage from the Middle East and from Africa provided a perspective that other major satellite channels had not offered their audiences.

Initially, Al Jazeera English was available to 80 million cable and satellite households. It was, however, accessible by only a small number of viewers in the United States (mainly those accessing it through several online providers) primarily because of political reasons. Al Jazeera had been thoroughly demonized by the U.S. government—called "the Osama bin Laden channel" and such—and so the principal cable and satellite services declined to carry it. Although these companies said they would not add Al Jazeera English for lack of space, they were clearly worried about negative reactions from politicians and the public.

That was a backhanded compliment to Al Jazeera's significance. The Arabic channel was seen as a force that could galvanize public sentiment in the Middle East in ways that were contrary to American political interests. Another way of looking at it was that Western news organizations were doing a poor job of reporting the complex realities of events in that part of the world and so Al Jazeera was filling a vacuum. Whatever the diagnosis, Al Jazeera will continue to be judged according to political as well as journalistic criteria. Gaining access to a larger global market will depend on audience demand. If Al Jazeera English does a better job of covering major stories, particularly in the Middle East, than other channels do, and if its competitors find themselves saying,

"As Al Jazeera English reported today . . . ," news consumers will eventually demand access. When the cable and satellite giants are convinced they can make money by offering Al Jazeera English, they will set aside their political concerns and new markets will open for the channel.

Meanwhile, Al Jazeera and other international channels have circumvented some political and technical obstructions and have reached a growing audience by delivering their television product via the Internet. Providers such as JumpTV, which is based in the United States, sell access to single channels or packages of channels from around the world. By early 2008, JumpTV was carrying more than 300 channels from eighty countries, including thirty-seven Arabic-language channels (including Al Jazeera), an Israeli twenty-four-hour soccer channel, and Al Jazeera English. The Arabic package offered programming ranging from *American Idol*-type shows to gavel-to-gavel coverage of Saddam Hussein's trial. By primarily targeting expatriates, JumpTV had signed up thirty-five thousand subscribers for its international channels by late 2007 and hoped to increase that many times over by capitalizing on increased consumer broadband access and a growing thirst for diverse views of the world. As convergence pushes Internet-based content ahead of conventional television offerings, services such as JumpTV may be well positioned to become the new versions of the traditional networks.[57]

Link TV, another U.S.-based provider, delivers its product through the Internet and by satellite. A nonprofit organization, Link offers an eclectic array of news, documentaries, and entertainment programs such as *Accordion Tribe*, *The Afghan Ladies Driving School*, and *La Guerra*, a Mexican animated antiwar video. Its best known programming is *Mosaic*, which presents English translations of news stories from Arabic-language channels.

Yet another example of the expanding content that is available is Bridges TV, also based in the United States, which bills itself as "a lifestyle and cultural network with family-friendly programming" in English for Muslims living in the United States. Available by satellite or Internet, Bridges was created to serve American-born children of Muslim immigrants by presenting programs with "a focus on Muslim life in North America." The Bridges

Web site states, "The programming on the foreign channels is about life back home, not North America." The channel's principal audience, it says, is the "unserved market of eight million American Muslims," a group that is growing much more rapidly and is better educated and wealthier than the overall U.S. population.[58] (Other estimates place the size of the U.S. Muslim population at closer to three million.)

As this array of television/Internet programming has been expanding, discussions have been under way among some Middle Eastern government officials, media professionals, and investors concerning the need to become more involved in Western media. Citing Islamophobia generally and some people's assumption that Islam and terrorism are one and the same, Ekmeleddin Ihsanoglu, secretary general of the Organization of the Islamic Conference, told a 2006 meeting of information ministers, "Muslim investors must invest in the large media institutions of the world, which generally make considerable profits, so that they have the ability to affect their policies via their administrative boards." He added, "This would benefit us in terms of correcting the image of Islam worldwide." Additional suggestions included providing more English-language versions of Arabic media and improving the credibility of the media in Muslim countries so news outlets would not be considered to be merely government mouthpieces.[59]

Part of this prescribed process has been under way since the 1990s, as Kingdom Holding Company based in Saudi Arabia, has invested heavily in Western media organizations. Kingdom Holding has a large stake in News Corporation, Rupert Murdoch's global media company, as well as substantial investments in Time Warner and Disney.[60] How much clout Prince Al-Waleed ibn Talal has acquired is debatable, although some media critics trace back to his influence such things as a disclaimer about anti-Muslim sentiment that was aired with the dramatic series 24 on the Fox network (part of News Corporation), which had a story line involving Muslim terrorists. But in terms of the news coverage from News Corporation–owned broadcast or print properties, Prince Al-Waleed's investment appears to have had no significant effect.

Even more uncertain is the possibility that Muslim countries' news media will become more credible—and therefore more influential—around the world. When in competition with outside news sources, such as Western satellite channels, local and regional news providers may be trusted more simply because they are "ours." But even then, the audience remains skeptical because in many Islamic countries, news organizations have always been controlled by the government and their product reflects that.

Those characteristics are not universal; some excellent news organizations—particularly print—thrive despite political and religious pressure. Overall, however, there are limits; criticism of politicians or clerics can lead to harsh reprisals or subtler reprimands. In a system such as this, despite the audience's wanting to rely on homegrown news, credibility remains elusive. Nevertheless, the expanded array of news providers alters political dynamics throughout the world. Policymakers are, however slowly, recognizing this.

○ ⌨ ○

Satellite television channels continue to proliferate and their impact on politics and society generally continues to grow. As the satellites these channels use whirl through space, the Al Jazeera effect is also receiving a boost from the tools of cyberspace.

3
The Internet Surge

As robust as the expansion of satellite television has been, it is nothing when compared to the growth of Internet-based media. This growth, however, has been uneven, with part of the world reaping its benefits while another part lags behind. This is the "digital divide," which may be defined as the situation in which some people—usually because of socioeconomic reasons—are unable to access information and communication technologies (ICT) with sufficient regularity or ease or are unable to access them at all.[1]

Disparities in technological capabilities have been studied for many years, particularly in terms of their impact on economic progress. In 1984 the Commission for Worldwide Telecommunication Development cited the lack of telephone infrastructure in developing countries as a barrier to economic growth. Although emphasis has shifted from telephone to computer issues, differences between developed and less-developed nations have remained striking. In 2002 the Telecommunications Union reported, "The 400,000 citizens of Luxembourg between them share more international bandwidth than Africa's 760 million citizens."[2] Such statistics could be cited time and again, particularly through the first years of the new century. Now, however, the divide is narrowing, but as that occurs the value of aspects of ICT-related development is being debated.

Nevertheless, the potential for Internet-based political change remains enormous. On the positive side, the Al Jazeera effect can help governments become more transparent and more responsive. Even mundane matters such as paying a parking ticket can be made less onerous when online services are available. More grandly, the Internet and other new communication mechanisms can be splendid tools of democratization, adding new dimensions to freedom of expression and political action. Negatives exist, too, as the Internet can move information—regardless of its accuracy—so quickly that the distance between discussion and riot has narrowed considerably. And the Internet has also proved to be invaluable to terrorist organizations.

Setting Priorities

Former UN Secretary General Kofi Annan noted in his Millennium Report, "New technology offers an unprecedented chance for developing countries to 'leapfrog' earlier stages of development. Everything must be done to maximize their peoples' access to new information networks." Meanwhile, Microsoft chairman Bill Gates has argued that the emphasis on ICT is a distraction from more pressing issues. Gates asked, "Do people have a clear view of what it means to live on $1 a day? About 99 percent of the benefits of having a personal computer come when you've provided reasonable health and literacy to the person who's going to sit down and use it." The Bill and Melinda Gates Foundation has devoted most of its resources not to ICT-related grants but to improving basic health care and education.[3]

Those who believe that priority should be given to fighting malaria, AIDS, and other diseases and who favor improving basic sanitation facilities ahead of expanding Internet access make a compelling case. The two paths need not be mutually exclusive, however, and the problems that Gates and others have cited might be somewhat alleviated through ICT use. In India, the nonprofit "knowledge centers" that have been established in some villages use solar power and wireless technology to provide residents with information about government welfare programs, health advice, market prices for crops, and other useful material. Students at local schools can practice computer skills and search for jobs online. The knowledge centers also provide people living in small villages with a sense of being connected to a larger community.[4]

By no means have such efforts eliminated the digital divide.

Even in the villages with knowledge centers, the Internet access is mostly used by the relatively well off, while the poorest residents remain uninvolved. Some of the Internet-based tools are of limited use: satellite mapping of the movements of large schools of fish was created to benefit fishermen in the Indian villages, but only the wealthiest fishermen had the navigation equipment and large enough boats to make use of the information. Also, the great majority of the material on the Web is in English, although that is gradually changing.[5]

So the Internet should be seen as a factor in incremental progress, not a panacea that will immediately restructure social and economic order. There is no denying, however, that changes are taking place, even if their long-term effects are uncertain. In Macedonia, a Wi-Fi network spanning a thousand square miles and reaching thirty cities is in the works. In Irbid, Jordan, a street about a half-mile long had, as of 2002, the world's largest concentration of cybercafes. Wimax, a successor to Wi-Fi, may allow broadband to reach rural areas that were previously considered outside Internet range.[6]

As these changes occur, technology keeps evolving. A practical as well as symbolic example of this progress is One Laptop per Child, a project born at the Massachusetts Institute of Technology and dedicated to creating an inexpensive laptop computer, millions of which could be distributed to schoolchildren around the world. Initially touted as the "$100 laptop," the cost may actually be closer to US$150, but it remains a remarkable achievement. As originally proposed, the machine will be Linux-based with a dual-mode display—both a full-color DVD mode and a black and white display that is readable even in bright sunlight. The laptop will have a 500MHz processor and 128MB of DRAM, with 500MB of Flash memory. It will not have a hard disk, but it will have four USB ports. The laptops will have wireless broadband that, among other things, allows them to work as a mesh network; each laptop will be able to talk to its nearest neighbors, creating an ad hoc local area network. According to MIT, the laptops will be able to do most everything except store huge amounts of data, and they will be powered by batteries that can be charged by turning a crank. With the prospect of broadened

Internet connectivity, these computers promise to put their users in touch with the larger world. As MIT's Seymour Papert observed, "There is no other way that has been suggested of giving people a radical change in their access to knowledge except through digital media."[7]

Mass production of these laptops began in late 2007. The need for this tool has increased because of the recent upsurge in the number of children attending school in developing countries. Sub-Saharan Africa saw 22 million more students enroll between 1999 and 2004, an 18 percent increase in the enrollment rate. This rush has far outstripped the countries' resources, and so textbooks and other supplies are scarce.[8] This region would be fertile ground for One Laptop per Child, partly because the project would give each student something that she or he could use in the classroom and take home.

Response to the project has been mixed. In 2006 Libya signed up for 1.2 million of the laptops, one for every schoolage child in the country. Schools in Nigeria have the computers, and Uruguay and Rwanda are among the other nations participating. Brazil embraced the idea not only to help its children, but also to seize an opportunity to build some of the laptops and further its aspirations to become a major electronics producer. Other countries, such as Chile and India, declined—at least initially—to participate, citing a large financial outlay that could prevent spending on other needs.[9] Another reason for resistance to the One Laptop program, as well as to computer proliferation generally, is fear of precisely what the project's advocates have promised: introducing the outside world to the laptops' users. Some Middle Eastern governments cite concerns that the Internet might foster dissemination of Western political thought and culture. Political and religious leaders are therefore wary about giving so many young people access to "unacceptable" information.[10]

Still another concern in some quarters about heavily investing in laptops is the expectation that the laptop will soon be bypassed as a personal information tool. Its likely successor: the cell phone—not just the cell phone for telephone calls but the cell phone with many of the capabilities of a desktop computer. Inexpensive, portable, and popular, the cell phone might become the means for significantly narrowing the digital divide by providing widespread access to the Internet. The growth of cell phone use has been fast and pervasive. In Russia, for example, there were one million cell phone users in 2000; by the end of 2005, there were 120 million, with three million more signing up each month. Worldwide, according to the International Telecommunications Union, the number of cell phone subscribers passed the three billion mark in 2007 (roughly triple the number of Internet users).[11]

Villagers in Bangladesh have gotten their first Internet access exclusively through cell phones. With a population of 150 million, Bangladesh has just one million landline telephones but as of late 2006 had 16 million cell phone subscribers and two million new users each month. The rate of growth there has been stunning. In January 2006 only 370,000 Bangladeshis had access to the Internet; by the end of the year the number was in the millions and climbing.[12]

The range of tasks cell phones can perform, including delivery of increasingly sophisticated Internet access that can provide television-quality video, keeps expanding. This affects the way people receive information: they can now get it fast and on the run. This may in turn affect how they react to it. The emotional ambience of watching news at home on a television set or computer monitor is different from that of hearing news by way of a cell phone in the midst of a crowd of strangers on a bus or a street corner. And if others in that crowd are receiving the same information, a chain reaction among the recipients could occur. News providers should recognize this and consider it when delivering potentially inflammatory news reports.

During the Iraq War, the expanded number of news providers and their varied approaches to covering events affected the volatility of news. In 2004 Arab media reports about alleged abuse of prisoners by U.S. forces ran the gamut from cautious to incendiary. In its coverage of the Abu Ghraib controversy, the Saudi English-language newspaper *Arab News* did not publish some of the most disturbing photographs from the prison. The editor, Khaled Al-Maeena, said, "They're distasteful. I don't want to inflame passions. I don't want to see the whole American nation condemned for what only a handful of people did, just as we don't want to have the application of collective guilt on all Saudis because 16 of the 19 [9/11] hijackers came from here." Meanwhile, the Egyptian newspaper *Al-Wafd* ran photos that purported to show U.S. soldiers abusing Iraqi women. The images had circulated widely on the Internet, but the U.S. embassy in Cairo said they were staged photos taken from pornographic Web sites.[13]

In 2005 coverage of another abuse-related scandal led to at least fifteen deaths and more than one hundred injuries in riots sparked by the news report. *Newsweek* magazine carried a story based on the unconfirmed statement of a single anonymous source that American interrogators at the Guantanamo Bay detention center had flushed a copy of the Quran down a toilet to torment Muslim prisoners. Several days later, at a news conference in Islamabad, Pakistani politician (and former cricket star) Imran Khan waved a copy of the magazine and accused the United States of "desecrating the book on which our entire faith is based." Radio carried Khan's remarks and those of angry Islamic clerics. Cell phone and e-mail messages further spread the word, local newspapers picked up the story, and protests erupted in the Muslim world. *Newsweek* then backed away from its story, citing problems with its source.[14]

The deadly storm resulted from sloppy journalism made worse by speed. The original story said "sources tell *Newsweek*" though there was only one source, not several. It also said that the Quran desecration episode was "expected" to be included in a Pentagon report. As *Washington Post* ombudsman Michael Getler pointed out, "That's like saying somebody is 'expected' to be indicted or found guilty, and journalists simply don't do that."[15] Once a story like that is out, it will quickly spread across the world and will have different effects depending on the audience it reaches.

What takes this beyond most journalistic foul-ups is the violent reaction to the report. People died. Later evidence suggested that the *Newsweek* story was true, and as Hendrik Hertzberg pointed out, the real issue was torture and abuse, not journalistic practice.[16] Nevertheless, when information travels so far and so fast, news organizations should feel obligated to raise their standards and anticipate their product's possible impact.

As the news media's ranks grow even larger, issues of journalistic competence and integrity become even more important. People will be barraged by information from countless sources, and although most news consumers will have a few favorite providers, they will also be in range of news-flingers of uncertain provenance. Rumors and errors will be plentiful, and dealing with this is a shared duty. Just as news organizations must perform at a high standard, so too must the public take responsibility for being knowledgeable enough to sift through information and judge what is reliable.

This is part of a shifting news media landscape in which change is more sweeping than it has ever been in the past. Newspapers were able to weather the rise of radio and television, but they are being put to new tests by the newest media. This is not a matter of technology per se; the audience for old media is not departing solely because it is infatuated with the bells and whistles of new gizmos. Rather, the issue involves the relationship between the news provider and news consumer.

The New Partnership

In 2005 Rupert Murdoch declared, "I believe too many of us editors and reporters are out of touch with our readers." He said that his own News Corporation had to become smarter in its use of the Internet and make its products "places for conversation" in which the public could "engage our reporters and editors in extended discussions." Murdoch cited the differences between "digital immigrants"—older people who balance old and new media—and "digital natives" who rely on Web portals such as Yahoo and Google and regularly get information from blogs. This younger audience sees information gathering as a participatory process, as exemplified by wikis, which allow readers to edit and contribute content.[17]

When a big story breaks, such as the 2003 invasion of Iraq, certain patterns of media use come into play, as was found by American University's Center for Social Media:[18]

○   There is interaction between traditional media and

newer informal media: for example, bloggers quoting
CNN and the *New York Times* tracking blogs.

○ Despite this interplay, much ad hoc/informal media
content reflects distrust of mainstream news media.

○ Informal media rely on users trusting the individual
voice—the e-mail they receive rather than the network
television newscast.

Much of mainstream journalism is patronizing in the way it
deals with the public. News organizations have set the content
agenda and delivery schedule. Blogs and other vehicles for participatory journalism have challenged and changed that and by
doing so have engaged in a contest for the loyalties of the next
generation of news consumers.

The Russian experience with blogging illustrates how blogs
can serve as a venue for independent journalism that is impractical in Russia's traditional media. With the Russian government
keeping tight rein on mainstream media freedom, the
blogosphere allows its denizens anonymity and worldwide reach.
In the tradition of Soviet dissidents who relied on samizdat—the
clandestine distribution of printed, antigovernment material—
bloggers debate government policies and sometimes advertise
protests.[19]

Russia's Garry Kasparov, the former world chess champion
who became a leading critic of the Putin government, wrote, "The
Web is quickly becoming the last refuge of dissent in my country." Kasparov was cofounder of an opposition coalition, the Other
Russia, which relies on its Web site to disseminate video of its
rallies—including security forces attacking participants—and to
publicize what it calls "the Putin regime's disdain for dissent and
the law." Opposition efforts also use blogs, and Kasparov noted
that the popular blog Russian Live Journal has 2.2 million weekly
readers, a million of whom reside outside Russia. This substantial external audience helps disseminate the Russian opposition's
message to news media around the world.[20]

Beyond basic blogging, one of the most important models
for citizen journalism is OhmyNews, based in South Korea.
OhmyNews has taken blogging to a level more closely related to

conventional journalism in the sense that it has "reporters" (60,000 by late 2007) and editors who impose quality control that makes the product more credible. But it is still a populist venture. Jean K. Min, OhmyNews's head of international business relations and corporate communications, observed, "Contrary to initial thinking, the Internet is not just another channel for news to travel along. Instead it's a space that everyone can use, and that means that journalism is going to stop being a lecture given by a few 'special' people, and start being a conversation."[21]

OhmyNews is a model for other news services, such as U.S.-based iTalkNews. Elizabeth Lee, cofounder of iTalkNews, said that these online ventures are changing the nature of news because "traditionally it's been a percolation from the top down. We want to see news that comes from the people, upwards. I don't see citizen journalism replacing traditional news, but instead we'll have a reciprocal flow." The iTalkNews Web site declared that the project was born in response to "the need for an interactive community where people can read breaking news, discuss it, and post their own articles." The site notes, "The difference between blogging and citizen journalism is that the latter tries to preserve the accountability and factual accuracy that was present in your grandparents' journalism and not always present in everyday blogs."[22]

Global Voices is another Web-based news service that goes beyond standard blogging. Its cofounder, Ethan Zuckerman, said that Global Voices is a "network of bloggers, activists, and citizen media people" responding to the "herd mentality" of most news organizations that cover the hottest story of the moment to the exclusion of other important matters. Zuckerman added, "Keep in mind we are not a news site. We are a citizen media site. A great deal of what we are covering is observation and opinion." The site provides a forum for "bridge bloggers," who write about their country or region for an international audience. The organization's blogger-editors select and provide links to the most interesting blogs from various regions of the world. Global Voices uses a number of technologies, including blogs, wikis, podcasts, and online chats, to call attention to stories that might not be noticed by traditional media organizations. It then offers its product to those news organizations as a source of story ideas.

The Global Voices philosophy is similar to that of some of the emerging satellite television channels and news-oriented Web sites: "Because North American and Western European voices and perspectives dominate both the international news media and the global Internet, Global Voices focuses on the rest of the world. We aim to bring previously unheard voices into the mainstream media."[23]

Sometimes those previously unheard voices can emerge and resonate with striking suddenness. During the moments following the London bombings on July 7, 2005, the BBC began receiving images from people at the scenes of the attacks. Within an hour, the number of still and video images, primarily from cell phones, had risen to fifty and several days after the attacks they topped a thousand. The BBC displayed these images in an online gallery. Other Web sites also featured such images, and overall this do-it-yourself journalism was more comprehensive than what the mainstream media could offer. The Internet also was used as a giant message board for those searching for missing people, seeking comfort, or wanting to discuss the event.

This represents an important shift in mainstream news organizations' approach to gathering information. Traditionally, early news reports about an event such as the 7/7 bombings might have included no images because no professional news photographers were on scene. Now, the public is counted on to provide images. News organizations vet submissions to weed out phony material, but generally news gathering in such circumstances now involves an open, trusting partnership with the public.

Despite the availability of online venues, people still turn primarily to traditional news sites. On 7/7, news Web sites received 6 percent of all online traffic, up 50 percent from the previous day, with BBC News's site accounting for 29 percent of all the page views of news sites. The *Guardian* reported 1.3 million visitors and 8 million page views that day, with 500,000 of the visitors coming from the United States. Madrid, scene of train bombings in March 2004, accounted for more visitors than any city other than London itself.[24]

The public's use of new media as a means to supply as well as retrieve information about the 7/7 attacks illustrated the change in the relationship between news consumers and news providers. Such events, as well as the maturing of blogs, indicate that convergence will not necessarily mean the replacement of old media by newer ones, but rather it will be a process of cooperative expansion, with the public becoming active participants in a new kind of journalism, rather than being passive recipients of information.

"Citizen journalism" as seen in the coverage of 7/7 will become more common, both as a facet of the conventional news process and as independent journalism disseminated through the Internet. Dissemination of the cell phone video footage of Saddam Hussein's execution in 2006 illustrated that the Web provides a forum unfettered by traditional journalistic criteria concerning graphic images. Soon after the hanging, the video became available on a Web site and later on the Associated Press's video service. It spread virally across the Internet and attracted 13 million hits just on YouTube, Google Video, and Break.com.[25]

Anyone with Internet access who wanted to see it could, and this raises questions for television news divisions and other conventional news providers: Should news organizations provide video that they normally would withhold, or at least edit, just because it is on the Web? Are these news organizations superfluous because the public can get the product on their own? Answers to such questions can partly be found in the fundamental journalistic role of providing historical and political context for what is being seen. Presumably, at least some of the people looking at the Saddam Hussein video wondered, "What does this mean?" That is a query journalists can help answer.

Beyond News

New media are also being employed for a range of quasi-journalistic purposes. Within a week of the December 2004 tsunami, Web sites such as the Phuket Disaster Message Board were available with lists of names, descriptions of the damage, photos of missing people, and links for people needing help of various kinds. The thirteen thousand postings on the Phuket

Disaster Message Board were visited by more than three million people. Some found hope; others had fears confirmed. Some of the postings described victims: "Boy, blue t-shirt with a full print of Spiderman on front."

The Internet also proved to be a fast and efficient mechanism for raising relief funds. The charity organization Oxfam announced a goal of US$5 million for tsunami relief and reached that total just a day later. By the following week, Oxfam had raised US$15 million from 73,000 donations, most of which were made online. In the United States after Hurricane Katrina in 2005, Americans donated $738 million within ten days, half of which came online. It should be noted that the Internet was also a tool for disaster-related fraud, as Internet users had to deal with e-mail solicitations from fake charities.[26]

The Live 8 concerts of 2005 illustrated how the Internet can enhance the impact of charitable fundraising. Organized by U2 singer Bono and others to combat poverty in Africa, concerts performed around the world were carried online and organizers claimed that over time they were seen by three billion people. By late 2005 the organization had donated about US$6 million. More significant than the money, said the Live 8 organizers, was the political pressure on the Group of Eight, a forum for the world's eight wealthiest nations, to provide aid and debt relief to Africa. On one day, more than 26 million people around the world sent text messages in support of the Live 8 campaign. (The previous daily record was the nearly six million messages sent by *American Idol* voters.) The theory was that politicians would take note of the massive audience Live 8 reached and shape policy toward Africa accordingly.[27]

Promises were made, but beyond the donations, the real impact of Live 8, as with other rallies and protests, remains speculative. Tuning in to an online concert and sending money and a text message are not evidence of continuing political commitment. It is a start, maybe, but little more. Those who wield real political power understand this.

The speed, as well as the reach, of the new media can be enormously helpful in the aftermath of an event such as the 2004 tsunami, but speed and online access can also exacerbate a volatile situation. During riots in France in 2005, blogs, Web sites, and cell phone messaging were used by antigovernment protestors to galvanize their supporters. One blog urged its readers to "Go to the nearest police station and burn it," while other online messages called for arson attacks to take place at specific times. Many of the blogs were posted on Skyblog, operated for the nationwide radio station Skyrock, which claims to have the largest audience of French thirteen to twenty-four year olds. With violent incidents occurring in more than two hundred towns and with about two thousand cars being burned, the French government began monitoring blogs to anticipate protestors' movements. But at the time, Skyblog hosted three million blogs, with twenty thousand new ones added each day, and the demonstrators also used cell phones for calls and text messages. The government quickly found itself overmatched.[28]

New media do not cause disorder, but they can help perpetuate and spread it, whether the case at hand involves urban rioting, larger-scale conflict, or terrorism. In Africa, the Internet has been used for political debate and, as a leader of the Côte d'Ivoire rebel group New Forces put it, as "a war weapon." New Forces used its Web site and television station to help launch a mutiny that led to the government's fall. Aboude Coulibaly, director of New Forces, wrote, "In these matters of revolution, we have to be wired to win." In Congo, Mai Mai insurgents believe water protects them from bullets, but they also have a Web site to promote their cause.[29]

The Indonesian paramilitary group Laskar Jihad (Holy War Warriors), wrote Robert Hefner,

> relied heavily on new communications technologies that became broadly available across Indonesia in the 1990s. This began with the fax machine and new software programs for desktop publishing in the early 1990s, but quickly came to include the Internet, which was introduced into large Indonesian cities in late 1997 and early 1998. No mass organization in Indonesia has relied more heavily on these technologies to coordinate its operations. . . . The combination of abstract, electronic communication with face-to-face

mobilization extended the Laskar Jihad's appeals well beyond what would have been possible using web-based or face-to-face communication alone.

Hefner noted that by 2000, laskarjihad.org was carrying daily news reports about the fighting and alleged Christian atrocities in Maluku and also featured stories and links to Web sites of jihadists in Chechnya, Kashmir, and Afghanistan. The organization used the Internet to send these daily reports to its twenty-four branch offices around the country, where the reports—already in desktop-publishing format—could be downloaded and then printed for distribution to the people who did not have Internet access.[30]

The Internet is also used to proselytize to a transnational audience. This example is from the Saudi online journal *Voice of Jihad*: "My Muslim and Mujahid brothers, don't you see the Muslims being killed in Afghanistan and Iraq?! Don't you see, on the televisions screens, the bereaved women crying out for the Muslims' help?! Don't you see the torn body parts of children, and their skulls and brains scattered . . . ?" Faisal Devji wrote that this quotation demonstrates how the case is made that "the media's representation of martyrdom creates a global community whose witnessing imposes certain responsibilities upon its members."[31] The pervasiveness of such messages gives them added weight. When their audience receives them constantly, they are likely to intrude into political consciousness and nudge their recipients toward action.

Online information moves quickly and widely, which may be a good thing—unless the information is false. Thomas Friedman wrote that an Indonesian working for the U.S. embassy in Jakarta told him, "Internet users are only 5 percent of the population—but these 5 percent spread rumors to everyone else. They say, 'He got it from the Internet.' They think it's the Bible." Friedman added,

At its best, the Internet can educate more people faster than any media tool we've ever had. At its worst, it can make people dumber than any media tool we've ever had. The lie that four thousand Jews were warned not to go into the World Trade Center on September 11 was spread entirely over the Internet and is now thoroughly believed in the Muslim world. Because the Internet has the aura of 'technology' surrounding it, the uneducated believe information from it even more. They don't realize that the Internet, at its ugliest, is just an open sewer: an electronic conduit for untreated, unfiltered information.[32]

Examples such as the one Friedman offered illustrate the multifaceted nature of "information." Trust should be awarded carefully; skepticism is invaluable. Not everything on the Web is true, just as not everything in the *New York Times* is true. But information in the *Times* is subject to a reporting and editing process that increases the likelihood that it will be accurate. Most Web-distributed information does not undergo such testing. That distinction is important, and the influence of the Internet will remain unpredictable while standards evolve and the public around the world decides how much to trust its content.

In addition to the Internet, older companion technologies are being put to greater use around the world. Sometimes their arrival represents a dramatic leap forward, as has been the case in Afghanistan. When the Taliban fell in 2002, there were just twenty thousand telephone lines in the country of 30 million people, and there was no way to call abroad. By early 2006 there were 1.3 million mobile phone users in the country taking advantage of service that extended even into rural areas. In April 2006 a conference in Kabul focused on constructing a fiber-optic voice-and-data system that would connect Afghanistan to the rest of the world. An indication of the magnitude of this change could be seen in how some invitations to this conference were sent: on a Morse telegraph system.[33]

Text messaging through mobile phones is particularly popular in areas with weak Internet infrastructure or restrictions on Internet use. In Saudi Arabia, 60 percent of cell phone users send text messages, and one aspect of that is SMS—Short Message Service—which allows people to send messages that will be displayed as crawls on television screens. *Star Academy*, an Arab reality show that featured aspiring pop music stars living under one roof, did much to popularize SMS. Viewers could vote for their favorites on the show and also carry on conversations that ran across the bottom of the screen, making television an interactive medium. SMS became so popular that some television channels abandoned their regular programming and devoted the entire screen to streams of messages, turning television into a chat room. The next step is MMS—Multimedia Messaging Service—which features sending and receiving personal videos.[34]

Making and sharing videos is another of the transformative changes in communication. On Web sites such as YouTube, visitors see videos ranging from quirky to newsworthy. As of late 2006, YouTube received 20 million visitors a month, watching 100 million videos each day, with 65,000 new videos posted every day. By early 2008, more than 150,000 new videos were being uploaded every day. People with cameras are everywhere, capturing politicians' gaffes, graphic scenes from war zones, and much else that was once the preserve of professional journalists but is now "covered" by anyone with a cell phone that can record video.

Just as the "CNN effect" purportedly influenced governments' policy priorities by showing the public disturbing news reports—refugees under fire and the like—YouTube's content might have similar impact. Some of the online videos are picked up by major news organizations and others are disseminated by bloggers or on Web sites. The speed and reach of this process continue to increase, further lessening news consumers' dependence on mainstream news organizations and providing countless new sources of information.

Some of the videos are undoubtedly phony, but given the volume of material there is certainly much truth to be found. Governments have reacted with dismay to this unsupervised flow of images. American officials ordered U.S. soldiers in Iraq not to post videos until they had been vetted, which of course runs counter to the whole point of this new medium. The Iranian government reduced Internet connection speeds to limit access to video streaming. More obstructions are certain to be created.[35]

YouTube and similar enterprises already have so many video providers and video watchers that government-imposed obstructions will amount to little more than bumps in the road. To take the Iraq war as an example, despite the best efforts of the American government—and for that matter the mainstream news media—to sanitize depictions of the war, YouTube and related sites ensured that harsh reality was available to those who wanted to see it. Videos from U.S. service personnel, Iraqi insurgents, and others could supplement—and, for some viewers, replace—the fare of traditional television news. Over time, perhaps there will be a measurable "YouTube effect" as this online material influences viewers' political attitudes.

The world of new media is fascinating. It is dynamic and growing, and it offers much more than a collection of high-tech curiosities. New media are also contributing to changes in how the world works, altering the shape of the traditional political structures on which the international system is based. This is one facet of the Al Jazeera effect, and it will lead to still more changes in global affairs.

4

The Rise of the Virtual State

The traditional state is a physical presence—territory defined by borders, a place on the map of the world. We should be able to spin a globe and point out any country: "Here is France; here is Nigeria; here is Chile." Political geography, in this sense, is mastered by children when they first contemplate the larger world, seeing it as a jigsaw puzzle in which they learn to fit the pieces in their proper places.

Borders may expand, shrink, or otherwise change, as when the United States purchased the Louisiana Territory or when colonial powers carved up their acquisitions. Conflict is often related to disputes about borders, and wars have produced new borders and sometimes new countries. Such events are promptly reflected on maps, although sometimes the precise lines are disputed. Regardless of how boundaries may be altered, states retain physical dimensions.

At least, that's the conventional way of looking at geopolitics. But just as the concept of sovereignty has changed over time, so too have assumptions about statehood. As Benedict Anderson noted, a nation is "an imagined political community" that features "a deep horizontal comradeship"—a fraternity that has made it possible, "over the past two centuries, for so many millions of people not so much to kill as to willingly die for such limited imaginings."[1]

Can an imagined community exist within imagined borders? If so, it must still have something to hold it together, to create identity, and to maintain the cohesion of the "horizontal comradeship."

New communications media can contribute to this, providing common intellectual ground for the community and enabling it to sustain itself without regard to conventional boundaries.

All this matters because a virtual state can provide influence and dispense hope to those who may have neither within regular political structures. Particularly in parts of the world where states and borders are vestiges of faded empires, reality may give birth to new states that lack diplomatic and cartographic recognition but nevertheless possess significant political dynamism. Enhanced by communication technologies, a political presence may develop on several levels. The Internet, as Merlyna Lim observed, "can strengthen national identity while also fostering a de-territorialized identity" and in some cases may help establish "a new de-territorialized pattern of hierarchy."[2]

Hezbollah has existed for years in Lebanon as a state within a state, evolving from its first incarnation as a militia to become a political organization that has held seats in the Lebanese cabinet and sponsored social programs ranging from health care to soccer teams. Encouraged by Syria and Iran, Hezbollah apparently considered itself substantial enough to begin a war with Israel, and it has been a mentor for groups such as Hamas. But Hezbollah never went so far as to define itself as a singular national entity, focusing instead on acquiring power within Lebanon. It has a more or less conventional political identity as a substate.

Looking beyond Hezbollah, no all-purpose blueprint exists for building a virtual state. Although political will and leadership are required, a steady flow of information is also essential. At its heart, the virtual state is a marriage of politics and communication.

The Virtual Sovereignty of Kurdistan

Kurds sometimes say that they constitute the largest nation in the world without a state of their own. They number close to 25 million and most live in the area where Iraq, Turkey, and Syria converge, although their diaspora has taken them to countries throughout the world.[3]

"Kurdistan" remains something of a mirage. Kurds will be happy to provide a map of Kurdistan to anyone expressing interest, and the United States and others have implicitly recognized the freestanding Kurdish area of northern Iraq since the aftermath of the 1991 Gulf War and particularly since the fall of Saddam Hussein's regime in 2003. But in that tense region, the established nations and various political factors mitigate against the birth of another "real" state.

The Kurds' ongoing political identity crisis is rooted in decisions made by the victors of World War I. Winston Churchill wanted to create a Kurdistan that would, he hoped, be a "friendly state providing a barrier against Turks and Russians." But by the time of the 1921 Cairo Conference at which the region was carved up, Churchill had been persuaded that having a Kurdish state was neither necessary nor wise.[4] As was often to be the case, other matters took precedence over the Kurds' status.

So, the Kurds have endured continuing subjugation, primarily at the hands of Iraqis, Turks, and Syrians, although they have never relinquished the Kurdistan idea. Retaining cohesion has not been easy. For one thing, there is not a common Kurdish language. As Christiane Bird noted, "Kermanji speakers cannot understand Sorani speakers, and vice versa," although wars and other political upheaval have increased the intermingling of speakers of these and other Kurdish dialects.[5] Political divisions among the Kurds have also diminished their political clout. Uneasy unity prevailed during the post-Saddam reconstruction, when the Kurdish north established itself as the safest and most prosperous part of the new Iraq. But Kurdish political life remains intensely factionalized, with the two principal groups duplicating administrative and security roles. There have even been two cell phone companies—one for each faction—which means users have had to switch memory cards when crossing from one group's turf to the other's.[6]

All this seems to add up to a diffuse and ineffectual "nation" that cannot hold itself together. Nevertheless, despite political discord, a unifying tool has emerged during the past decade—a new generation of Kurdish media. Satellite television and more recently the Internet have given Kurdistan the substantive identity that for so long had been elusive, but even these steps toward virtual cohesion have encountered political obstacles.

In 1995 the first Kurdish satellite television channel, MED-TV, went on the air. (MED is derived from Medes, the Kurds' Indo-European ancestors, whose country was, interestingly in this context, known as Media.) The channel was the project of Kurdish expatriates who were granted a license in the United Kingdom by the Independent Television Commission (ITC) and set about establishing "sovereignty in the sky." Programming focused on reinforcing the Kurdish identity, offering adults newscasts with a Kurdish interpretation of events and providing children classes in the Kurdish language. The Kurdish flag and national anthem were part of the broadcasts.[7]

The channel immediately captured attention within "Kurdistan." It broadcast up to eighteen hours each day in several Kurdish dialects as well as in Turkish, Assyrian, Arabic, and English. Kurds in Europe and the Middle East could watch it, and satellite dishes began popping up in remote Kurdish villages, especially in Turkey. According to a group of jailed Kurdish members of the Turkish parliament, "Thanks to MED-TV the Kurdish language was coming alive, something which threatened those who wanted to suffocate it. MED-TV epitomized the hope of the Kurdish people for recognition; it was a magnet which drew the Kurds together." Turkish officials took a much different view; one said, "MED-TV threatens the security of this nation more than the guerrilla attacks of the PKK [Kurdish Workers Party]."[8]

Within Turkey, satellite dish vendors and users were intimidated and occasionally electricity was cut off from Kurdish villages during MED-TV's prime-time hours. In 1999 Turkey presented British regulators with transcripts of MED-TV interviews in which Kurds urged action against the Turkish government. The UK's ITC then revoked the channel's license and it went off the air. Although the ITC cited "legal grounds" for its action, MED-TV supporters charged that the British decision was the result of Turkish pressure.[9]

MED-TV was promptly replaced by Medya TV, which was licensed in France and, like its predecessor, emphasized Kurdish language and culture. Also like MED-TV, Medya was short-lived, presumably because of Turkish protests. In February 2004 a French court ruled that because of the appearances of PKK spokespersons on the channel, Medya posed "risks to public order" and so was not entitled to its license.[10]

Within a few days of Medya's demise, the Kurds had yet another new channel on the air—Roj (sun) TV. This time the channel's home was established in Denmark, which immediately received complaints from Turkish officials about Roj's alleged ties to the PKK. In response, fifty-four mayors from southeastern Turkey's Kurdish region sent a letter to the Danish government asking that the station be allowed to remain on the air. Roj has claimed that it keeps its distance from the PKK, although it has run PKK-provided footage showing guerrillas in action against the Turkish military. As of spring 2008, Denmark's Media Secretariat had rejected the Turkish complaints and allowed Roj to continue operating.

Turkey, as part of its effort to be admitted to the European Union, dropped its ban on Kurdish-language broadcasting but retained rules limiting such broadcasts to four hours a week and barring children's programs and discussions of "political" subjects. The Turkish approach cannot prevail forever; the media-enhanced Kurdish identity will become stronger. With a growing number of homes in Turkey, as elsewhere, sporting satellite dishes, and with more satellites available to broadcasters at lower cost, Roj and other Kurdish stations will be able reach expanding audiences of Kurds in Turkey and wherever else in the world they may be. They can also watch several Kurdish channels streamed on the Internet.

A good example of such viewers is a Kurdish woman who lives in Turkey but does not speak Turkish and is a faithful fan of Roj. She told a reporter, "Roj TV reflects the emotions of the Kurds, our opinions. It's a mirror of the Kurds."[11] She is now connected to the larger Kurdish community, a community that is steadily becoming a more defined cultural and political entity partly because of the connections fostered by satellite television. She is part of Kurdistan.

Ties among Kurds are further enhanced by Internet offerings such as KurdistanWeb.org, which provides this as its raison d'etre:

The Internet has opened the unprecedented opportunity for

the Kurds in various corners of the earth to discuss among themselves and provide to others information on their culture, politics and human heritage. It has also laid for open discussion these hitherto forbidden topics to millions of Kurds living in such restrictive societies as Turkey. It has likewise reinvigorated the voice of smaller Kurdish communities as the Guraní, Kalhurí, Pehlí, Hewramí, Kirmashaní and their rich, millennial literature. . . . In inculcating such knowledge, we at KurWeb believe our service will facilitate Kurdish attainment of equal rights and liberties with other great nations of the world. The Kurds' legitimate and peaceful aspirations are not any different from the same basic rights enjoyed by the non-Kurdish callers of KurWeb pages, that include life, liberty and equality.[12]

Another site, KurdishMedia.com, promotes itself as a "one-stop-shop information provider on Kurds and Kurdistan," and cites among its goals to "introduce Kurds as a civilized nation in the international arena" and to portray Kurdistan as "an isle of peace at the heart of the Middle East."[13] This site provides links to about seven hundred other Kurd-related Web sites, such as Kurdland.com, which offers Kurdish news, music, and even ringtones, and Kurd Net, which features links to a Kurdish dating service as well as news and other sites. Collectively, these hundreds of Web sites constitute a thriving virtual community. In conjunction with the growing political and economic maturity of the Kurdish region of Iraq, the Kurdish Internet presence brings increased visibility and an air of legitimacy to Kurds' aspirations to be widely recognized as a nation.

There is a state here, despite its being absent from conventional maps and lacking the official legitimacy of diplomatic recognition. This state should be taken seriously because the Kurds' virtual nationalism is more than a manifestation of communications gadgetry. Their political purposefulness has long existed but it has been given new vitality because of the reach of the Kurdish presence on satellite television and the Web (in addition to expanded use of print and radio). Kurdish communities in countries such as Syria and Turkey and individuals who are part of the global Kurdish diaspora have in common their ability to reinforce their shared culture and politics through Roj and other television channels and through Web sites.

The Internet is especially important because its interactivity encourages Kurds not just to receive information but also to stay in touch with each other. As Internet access becomes more widely available, such personal involvement with the virtual state will become even more important, increasing the sense of belonging to the greater Kurdish community. Communication that fosters conversation and other involvement nurtures the "horizontal comradeship" that Anderson described.

Kurdistan as virtual state is significant as a paradigm because it illustrates a path that might be taken by others among the "un-mapped," primarily in the less-developed world, who aspire to better establish their identity. Policymakers should take note of this because it may encourage separatism and affect the stability of traditional states that include elements wanting to break away from the geopolitical status quo. It can also affect regional stability as new players assert themselves and change the balance of political and economic power.

Even without going so far as to formally secede and pro-claim itself the independent Republic of Kurdistan, the Kurdish virtual state continues to become more of a player in the region as its oil reserves and relative peacefulness contribute to economic growth. Turkey watches this warily, gauging its effect on the res-tive Kurdish community within its borders. (Kurds constitute about 20 percent of Turkey's total population.) Turkish troops have crossed into Kurdish Iraq in pursuit of militants, and vari-ous scenarios could further exacerbate tensions between Iraqi Kurds and Turkish authorities. Such incidents create diplomatic difficulties for the United States and others among Turkey's NATO allies.

Syria, with its own Kurdish population (less than 10 percent of the country's total) and a penchant for troublemaking, could be an unwelcome addition to any Kurd-related dispute. If ten-sions rise about such matters, the communications media that contribute to Kurdistan's virtual existence could also contribute to heating or cooling the politics of the moment. Anyone seeking to prevent or resolve conflict should recognize the significance of these media.

Having satellite television and an Internet presence will not in itself open the door to statehood, virtual or otherwise. There must also be strong political leadership and widespread resolve among constituent groups if the tools of cohesion are to be effectively used. But even with such caveats, the Kurdish example shows how the maps and politics of the world can change. No longer will the configuration of the globe depend so much on the machinations of postwar conferences or other big-power decisions that split or assemble peoples and nations with little regard for the realities on the ground or the wishes of those affected. New media can enhance national identity. The era of the virtual state is under way.

The Middle East and Global Islam

Before addressing virtual dynamics within the global Muslim community, it may be helpful to examine the structure of that community. How broad is it? How do leadership and influence flow—how far and from where to where? Do distant issues stir interest and passion, or do local concerns trump larger matters? Is globalization strengthening or diluting the power of Islam throughout the world?

Such questions elicit varied answers. First, concerning the breadth of Muslim expansion, Olivier Roy defines "global Muslims" as "either Muslims who settled permanently in non-Muslim countries (mainly in the West), or Muslims who try to distance themselves from a given Muslim culture and to stress their belonging to a universal *ummah*, whether in a purely quietist way or through political action." He observes, "The blurring of the borders between Islam and the West is not just a consequence of immigration. It is linked with a more general phenomenon: deterritorialization. Islam is less and less ascribed to a specific territory and civilizational area. . . . Through the increase in migratory and population flows, more and more Muslims are living in societies that are not Muslim." He adds that globalization "is de-ethnicizing Islam. . . . The endeavor to build a community whose sole criterion is religious faith presupposes the negation of any specific culture and ethnicity."[14]

That is a critical issue. Regardless of the power of religious faith, is it strong enough to override other facets of individual cultures and ethnicities? Whether that is possible or necessary has yet to be determined, but the residual power of state/cultural identity should not be underrated. In a secular context, this has been an issue for the European Union, as it has been seen that the notion of transnational "community" can proceed only so far before constituencies assert their individual interests. Some may argue that the religious principles of Islam have greater appeal and substance than do EU politics, and so have greater unifying potential, but true globalization of *anything* does not come easily.

The Quran (49:10) says, "The believers are a band of brothers." This principle is at the heart of the idea of the *ummah*, although it has been interpreted in different ways concerning matters such as inclusiveness. Anthony Shadid defined the *ummah* in historical context as "the notion of an Islamic community created when Mohammed's followers began to look beyond their clan and tribal affiliations in Arabia to see themselves foremost as Muslims." Today, some Islamic scholars and political figures, such as Ali Bulac and Abul-Ela Maadi, have asserted that the *ummah* should be a broad-based, modern alternative to Western-style secular civil society, but should still be democratic. Some activists insist, reported Shadid, that "community action is both a religious obligation and a successful political program. By nature, that action has been a democratizing force, drawing its legitimacy and vitality from the community rather than imposing itself from above."[15] Fundamentalists may, however, look askance at democratic structure as impeding true Islamic cohesion.

Population shifts complicate consideration of the *ummah*'s unity. Within the Islamic world, even in some of the Arab states of the Middle East, ethnic movement reflects a broadening of Islam's base. Faisal Devji argued, "In general the importance of non-Arab Muslims and of non-Arab Islam to the Middle East has been underestimated. . . . The presence of large non-Arab working populations in the Arabian Peninsula, as well as the dominance of non-Arab Muslims in the formulation and dissemination of Islamic

ideas globally, especially in languages like English, renders non-
sensical any notion that the Arab Middle East is the original
homeland of radical Islam."

He notes that in Dubai, for instance, "One is as likely to
encounter Urdu or Swahili in public places as one is of encountering Arabic," and he adds, "The new world of social and other
relations that is represented by Dubai is the same one from which
the jihad is constituted. And maybe this explains why the jihad
reconstitutes the Middle East or Arab world by narratives other
than those of the nation or region as distinct demographic and
geographical entities characterized by collective political or economic cultures."[16]

Determining whether the impetus for jihad can be ascribed
to one group or another is just one facet of understanding the
globalized mingling of Muslim constituencies. Anyone who has
spent time in Kuwait, Qatar, or any of the other Gulf states and,
to a lesser extent, elsewhere in the Middle East will have encountered many of the non-Arab Muslims of whom Devji speaks. They
are mostly South Asians, many of whom do not speak much, if
any, Arabic. These people are the foundation of the region's service industries, many of them doing the work that the native Arab
population does not want to do. The ease with which people
travel from country to country to find jobs is an element of globalization, and this has ramifications beyond reconfiguring the
work force. Although they are often regarded as second-class residents (and usually barred from full citizenship), they are changing
the face of the Middle East just as immigrants have done elsewhere in the world.

Information, like people, flows with ease, and that also affects Islam's political character. Satellite television and the Internet
have brought the conflict between Palestinians and Israelis to a
global audience. As the ranks of information providers have grown
to include more with Islamic and pro-Palestinian viewpoints, news
of this conflict has had greater effect on Muslim audiences.
Stephen P. Cohen noted, "This Israeli-Palestinian war is not just
a local ethnic conflict that we can ignore. It resonates with too
many millions of people, connected by too many satellite TVs,
with too many dangerous weapons."[17]

An example of this reach and resonance: in spring 2002 a Zogby poll found that 65 percent of Indonesians rated Palestine as "the most important" or "a very important" issue, and the 2003 Pew Global Attitudes Survey reported that in Indonesia 68 percent of poll respondents named Yasser Arafat as the world figure in whom they had most confidence.[18] Ayman al-Zawahiri, al Qaeda's second in command, wrote in his book *Knights Under the Banner of the Prophet*, "The fact that must be acknowledged is that the issue of Palestine is the cause that has been firing up the feelings of the Muslim nation from Morocco to Indonesia for the past 50 years. In addition, it is a rallying point for all the Arabs, be they believers or non-believers, good or evil."[19]

Communications media can make the remote seem proximate, particularly when news is presented in a steady stream, often in real time, and is delivered by so many providers. In this way the Palestinian becomes the Indonesian's neighbor, and within the global village a neighbor's plight attracts much interest. That is not to say, however, that a single political outlook will take hold throughout the Muslim world or that priorities will be uniform.

Even when there is agreement about an issue's importance, different values may dictate different courses of action. Quintan Wiktorowicz described how the Salafi movement, so potent in Saudi Arabia, could encounter fragmentation when it sought to spread its influence elsewhere in the world. In Chechnya, he wrote, "where Sufi practices predominate, the Salafi ideology of the Arab mujahidin directly contradicted local understandings of Islam and fomented tensions between Chechens and their Arab allies. . . . Dialogue between the Chechen religious leaders and the Salafi fighters was unsuccessful, leading to factional clashes and internal conflict."[20] Within the Middle East, tensions exist among Arab states and can be exacerbated when satellite television channels and other media are seen as vehicles for proselytizing. Naomi Sakr noted that during the early 1990s, "Egyptian commentators were warning against Saudi efforts to use the satellite media to stamp their own 'tribal Saudi version of Islamic values' on Egypt's socio-political life."[21]

In Indonesia, the clash between global and local could be seen when Islamist ideas arrived from the Middle East as part of

some Indonesian Muslims' efforts to develop stronger ties between Islam, politics, and culture. Anthony Bubalo and Greg Fealy
wrote,

> Some Indonesian students who traveled to the Middle East
> came back influenced by the ideas of the Muslim Brother-
> hood. More malign influences would also be imported by
> Indonesians who went to Afghanistan in the 1980s and 90s
> to fight in the *jihad* against the Soviets and forged links with
> the future leaders and activists of Al Qaeda. But Islamist and,
> in particular, neo-fundamentalist ideas have also been im-
> ported from the Middle East. Most notably, missionary
> activities by official and non-official organizations from
> Saudi Arabia played a critical role in the emergence of a
> Salafist current within the Indonesian Muslim community.
> The impact of these ideas has varied. Elements of Muslim
> Brotherhood thinking helped the Islamist Prosperous and
> Welfare Party (PKS) play a positive role in Indonesian poli-
> tics, though darker aspects of the PKS, notably the
> anti-Semitic views and anti-western conspiracy theories of
> some of its members, have also been influenced by thinking
> from the Middle East. Many of the Indonesian groups sup-
> ported by Saudi Arabia limit their activism to the promotion
> of Islamic piety—albeit of a fairly puritanical form—though
> some have participated in violent sectarian conflict. More
> insidious has been the influence of Al Qaeda and other
> Middle Eastern sources on doctrine and operational tech-
> niques of the Indonesian terrorist group Jemaah Islamiyah.[22]

Such missionary efforts based in the Middle East and directed at Muslims elsewhere in the world are not new, but they
are substantially enhanced through pervasive global media.
Among Muslims, as with almost everyone else in the world, the
messages delivered by these media affect everyday life and long-
term personal and societal aspirations.

Information changes how people look at other people and
ideas. It alters expectations and can foster intellectual and spiritual growth. That, in turn, can lead to profound political change,

positive and negative. Islam may be on the cusp of such a transformation, with ramifications affecting the rest of the world.

The Virtual *Ummah*

On a grander scale than virtual Kurdistan, consider the virtual state in the context of globalized Islam. Conventional wisdom
has long had it that despite increased knowledge about issues
affecting fellow Muslims around the world, the *ummah* as a cohesive entity is, and will remain, an illusion.

Presumably, the Muslim in Amman and the Muslim in
Djakarta and the Muslim in Dakar and the Muslim in Toronto
have little to say to each other because their languages, national
cultures, and politics differ greatly, and those differences outweigh
any linkage provided by their common religious beliefs. Writing
from Indonesia in the aftermath of the 2006 Danish cartoon controversy, Karim Raslan observed, "Yes, we are part of the extended
family of believers, the *ummah*. We cannot help but feel some
sense of solidarity with our co-religionists in Damascus, Tehran,
or Cairo. But the explosiveness of the Arab street doesn't trans-
late, somehow, to the tropics. Many of us have a growing suspicion
that we are culturally different from our Arabic- and Urdu-speak-
ing brethren, perhaps more tolerant and less emotional."[23] That
may be, but there is at least increased awareness of religious and
political matters that affect the distant brethren. The salience of
these issues depends on the level of kinship felt among the scattered coreligionists, but the flow of information can stimulate
interest and at least tentative comradeship. From that point closer
ties might develop.

As Dale Eickelman and Jon Anderson noted, "Muslims, of
course, act not just as Muslims but according to class interests, out
of a sense of nationalism, on behalf of tribal or family networks,
and from all the diverse motives that characterize human endeavor. Increasingly, however, large numbers of Muslims explain
their goals in terms of the normative language of Islam."[24] Plenty
of differences exist among Muslims, but the pieces of global Islam might be drawn together in unprecedented ways by media
that enhance the sharing of Islam as a dominant, unifying factor.

In political terms, the bottom line is this: If satellite television and the Internet were to provide an environment conducive to Islamic discourse and serve as a platform on which to build a new level of cohesion within the *ummah* and its 1.3 billion members, global geopolitical balances could be altered significantly.

Western policymakers would be wise to consider how even a partially unified *ummah* would make for a very different world. In the United States, for instance, when the public and political leaders consider Islam they tend to slip into a simplistic mind-set in which "Muslim" and "Arab" are synonymous, and so they do not look beyond the Middle East and North Africa. These 280 million Arabs in a relatively well defined region may seem a manageable entity for which a one-size-fits-all policy approach is feasible. Of course, even for the Arab world alone, such an approach is dangerously naïve, as differences between the Arab in Tangier and the Arab in Doha may be substantial. Beyond that, the continuing misery of Iraq illustrates the devastating effects of the antipathy so easily roused between Sunni and Shia.

The principal flaw in this myopic worldview is its failure to appreciate that the Islamic community comprises much more than the Middle East. Global Islam is the Arab population more than quadrupled and spread across the world. If this massive group were to develop a meaningful level of unity, its potential power would be enormous, and crafting policy related to the community of Islam would become a far more challenging task.

That possibility is not as farfetched as it once seemed, primarily because of the reach and speed of new mass media. The surge of anger in reaction to the 2005 *Newsweek* story about desecration of the Quran at the U.S. detention facility in Guantanamo Bay, Cuba, and the swift spread of the 2006 Danish cartoon controversy illustrated how a story told on television and computer screens could quickly resonate in the farthest reaches of the Muslim world.

Prospects for media-based cohesion are enhanced by the nature of the Internet and satellite television. Members of dispersed groups, wherever they are, can collect information from sources ranging from Al Jazeera to individual bloggers. In addition to people in predominantly Muslim countries, deracinated Muslim communities in Europe and elsewhere may be particularly eager to connect to media offerings that engender a sense of belonging and provide electronic ties to home and religion.

How this affects assimilation of Muslims who live in largely non-Muslim environments is not yet known. It could provide a reassuring comfort zone that makes their new home amid a different culture seem less threatening because of links to the larger Islamic world maintained through media. Or, those virtual connections might make that former homeland seem close enough at hand to make integration into the new community appear less necessary or desirable.

One reason there is so much uncertainty about Islamic connections is that attitudes about Muslim identity vary from country to country, even in predominantly Muslim nations. A survey by the Pew Global Attitudes Project published in 2005 asked, "Do you consider yourself a national citizen first or a Muslim first?" These were the answers from Muslim respondents in six countries:

○ Pakistan: national citizen 7 percent; Muslim 79 percent.
○ Morocco: national citizen 7 percent; Muslim 70 percent.
○ Jordan: national citizen 23 percent; Muslim 63 percent.
○ Turkey: national citizen 29 percent; Muslim 43 percent.
○ Indonesia: national citizen 35 percent; Muslim 39 percent.
○ Lebanon: national citizen 30 percent; Muslim 30 percent.[25]

These results, affected by the individual countries' political and cultural characteristics, illustrate that the strength of Muslim identity is far from uniform. The variations also indicate that shifts might occur within a given country depending on the politics of the moment or particular events, perhaps including how news is covered and information provided through the Internet or other sources. The results from Lebanon, for instance, presumably reflected the nationalist tremors that were shaking that country around the time the polling was done. Blogs and Web sites, as well as traditional media, helped fuel the surge in nationalist political activism there, as was evident after the assassination in 2005 of Rafik Hariri.

Given the varied social dynamics throughout the Muslim world, change is more likely than a sustained status quo. Building media bridges that will further Islamic cohesion may be one facet of such change and may be welcomed particularly by those Muslims who believe that they are increasingly menaced by the non-Islamic world.

Pulling the *ummah* closer together is not a new idea. In the twentieth century, groundwork was laid by men such as Hassan Al-Banna, a founder of the Muslim Brotherhood. Beginning in the 1920s, Al-Banna championed "the Islamization of society." His movement, according to Reza Aslan, "represented the first modern attempt to present Islam as an all-encompassing religious, political, social, economic, and cultural system. Islam, in Al-Banna's view, represented a universal ideology superior to all other systems of social organization the world had known."[26] Another Egyptian Islamist, Sayyid Qutb, endorsed "a unified *ummah* in the novel sense of a transterritorial ideocracy."[27] Now, more than four decades after Qutb's death, "transterritorial" has an expanded meaning as the concept is reshaped by technologies that make conventional boundaries less relevant. Olivier Roy has observed that the *ummah* "no longer has anything to do with a territorial entity. It has to be thought of in abstract or imaginary terms."[28]

Roy's point is grounded in the realities of new media and access to information. While satellite television is transterritorial, the Internet may be considered *supra*territorial because boundaries within and among states are not merely inconsequential, they need not, in the cyberworld, be acknowledged at all. An example of how this theory takes shape in practice can be seen in the success of Islam Online (www.islamonline.net), which provides news, general information about Islam, "Living *Shari'ah*" featuring "live *fatwas*," and much more, all available in Arabic and English. (The Arabic and English sites have different staff members, content, and audiences, and one rarely translates material from the other.) The site lists among its goals: "To strengthen the ties of unity and affiliation between the members of the Islamic community and support informational and cultural exchange. To expand awareness of important events in the Arab, Islamic and larger worlds. To build confidence and a spirit of hope among Muslims."[29]

Absent new media, such connection within the *ummah* would simply not happen. In early 2006 Islam Online was attracting an average of about 13 million page views and 1.5 million unique visitors per month, and its management wants to expand this audience by offering content in additional languages, such as French and Turkish. It employs about three hundred staff members, most working in Cairo, and uses material from approximately fifteen hundred correspondents, Islamic scholars, and other contributors, many of whom are not Muslims. For the English-language version, which attracts 25 percent of the page views, about half the audience is in the United States. Part of Islam Online's agenda involves working offline with international organizations. Staff members of the site's Health and Science section, for instance, cooperate with the World Federation of Science Journalists to improve skills of science journalists around the world.

For Islam Online and other such media organizations, translated material is an essential part of reaching a truly global audience. Al Jazeera made its name through its Arabic newscasts and then attracted much attention when it announced its plans for Al Jazeera English. There was considerable public discussion, especially in the non-Islamic world, about how this channel's content and political tone might differ from that of the Arabic channel and how it would be received by Western audiences and governments. Because of the hostility toward Al Jazeera from some quarters—notably the U.S. government—the potential expansion of Al Jazeera's influence was viewed with concern, despite the new channel, as it was unveiled, looking more like CNN or the BBC than its Arabic sibling.

While this was debated and the launch of Al Jazeera English was delayed because of technical problems (and, some insiders say, tensions between the Arab channel's journalists and their mostly non-Arab AJE colleagues), the parent organization's management quietly announced that it hoped to also begin Al Jazeera Urdu. With editorial content and translation supervised by the

Al Jazeera bureau in Pakistan, this channel would consist primarily of the Arabic channel's contents dubbed into Urdu for a potential audience estimated at 110 million, which is roughly triple the size of the Arabic channel's viewership. Al Jazeera also plans to deliver its product in additional languages, such as Turkish. This expansion probably will not happen, however, until Al Jazeera English shows it can make a profit and the overall Al Jazeera organization finds firmer financial footing.

Nevertheless, for policymakers the potential political repercussions of these prospective ventures are worth considering. If one buys into the argument (debatable though it may be) that Al Jazeera's Arabic coverage features an anti-American slant that rouses "the Arab street" against U.S. and other Western interests, delivering that coverage to an additional huge Muslim audience could significantly affect the wider contest for global public opinion. And if it reinforces an "us-against-them" mentality among its viewers, it may escalate the adversarial nature of their relationship with the non-Islamic West—something else that U.S. policy planners must weigh. Common sense would dictate a reappraisal of Western governments' relationships with Al Jazeera, with greater emphasis on cooperation and less on feuding. There is, however, little evidence that common sense will prevail.

Regardless of what the West does, effects of such globalized media influence may be enhanced by the disillusionment some Muslims feel toward secular citizenship in their own states. As Olivier Roy asked, "What is a true Muslim land, in a time when many radical Muslims consider that all the regimes ruling Muslim countries are illegitimate?"[30] For Muslims who feel greater loyalty to Islam itself than to any particular homeland, the *ummah* as superstate may be the "true Muslim land," tangible or not.

In a virtual community, wrote Jon Anderson, the Internet serves as "a new public space, which enables a new class of interpreters, who are facilitated by this medium to address and thereby to reframe Islam's authority and expression for those like themselves and others who come there." The virtual space, said Anderson, "does not facilitate the spokesperson-activists of established institutions, but draws instead on a broader range of new interpreters or newly visible interpreters of Islam."[31]

Among these is Yusuf al-Qaradawi, who, through his presence on Al Jazeera and Islam Online, has established himself as one of the Islamic world's best-known public figures. Born in 1926, al-Qaradawi studied theology at Al-Azhar University and spent time in an Egyptian prison camp because of his ties to the Muslim Brotherhood. He has written about the Islamic awakening—his many books have sold in the hundreds of thousands—and emphasized the important role of the *ulama*, the religious teachers of the Muslim community, as its leaders. He has championed the independence of the ulama and argued that Islam requires freedom of thought and discussion.[32]

Al-Qaradawi has proved himself adept at shaping his message to meet the demands of new media. As Anderson noted, he is "wholly orthodox in theology but expressing it in a more modern idiom that attracts a transnational audience among professional middle classes."[33] Modern does not mean moderate. Al-Qaradawi has endorsed suicide bombing attacks on Israeli civilians as a legitimate tactic in the effort to reclaim Muslim territory.[34] He also, however, issued a fatwa that defends democracy not as a form of unbelief but as a system that properly gives people the right to choose their leaders without compulsion and to question and remove them. On another occasion, he denounced Abu Musab al-Zarqawi, leader of al Qaeda in Iraq, as a murderer.[35]

Whatever al-Qaradawi's views on particular issues may be, he unquestionably wields greater influence by virtue of being a media personality. His political clout as "the global mufti" is enhanced by the reach and frequency that satellite television and the Internet provide. Al-Qaradawi and numerous other public figures constitute an expanding religious-political group that makes sophisticated use of new media. Gary Bunt observed, "For an elite, the Internet now forms part of a religious conceptual framework, incorporating symbols, divine utterances, sacred texts, and the power to inspire and motivate individuals in both their personal practice and in wider worldly and sacred goals. . . . It is through a digital interface that an increasing number of people will view their religion and their place in the Muslim world."[36]

The Quran is central to Islam's online presence. This is, in part, a function of *da'wah*, the rallying of believers to the faith or, as some would have it, the exhortation to return to premodern, unblemished Islam. (Those who advocate the second approach apparently see no irony in using the Internet to turn back the clock.) Even Web sites that present news and softer features place primary emphasis on the religion itself. The IslamiCity Web site (www.islamicity.com) streams Radio Al Islam, which offers calls to prayer, recitations of the Quran, tools to aid in searching the Quran's content and memorizing the text, as well as locating mosques and determining local times for prayer.[37]

Unlike the holy books of other religions, the Quran is considered to be the untouched word of God, as revealed to God's messenger, Muhammad, who then recited it. This is the essence of its sacred nature. Its recitation remains central to the practice of Islam, so when it is broadcast or presented online, its words and rhythms find a large and rapt audience. Just as the muezzins' call to prayer brings people to mosques, so too does a media-delivered call or recitation pull together the virtual community.

Quran-related use of the Internet has been under way for about two decades. Jon W. Anderson noted, "Islam was brought online in the 1980s, initially by students from Muslim countries who studied and worked in some of the high-tech institutes where the technology was being developed or extended. . . . They brought interests in Islam on line as pious acts of witness in the new medium of their work." In their early online content, they created "discussion groups that mixed debate about religion with questions about applying the texts to contemporary life and to issues of Muslim life in the diaspora that ranged from where to find places of worship, Muslim bookstores, and halal butchers to news about home, cheap flights, and even matrimonials." This content was expanded "to include digital newsletters, which were often addressed to particular national populations or focused on Muslim populations in particular Western countries." The content was often "creolized discourse," mostly in English, sometimes in French, with transliterated Arabic, Persian, and other languages.[38] Those early efforts have evolved into a more sophisticated Internet presence, as can be seen on many of the easily accessible Islam-related Web sites. A quick Google search will turn up several thousand such sites.

The digital *minbar*, or cyber-pulpit, is of special importance to diasporic Muslims. It should be noted that even in far-flung centers of Muslim immigration such as Paris, London, and New York, imams and mosques quickly establish themselves, and so Muslim residents there do not need to depend solely on a virtual connection for religious sustenance. As a platform for globalized Islam, however, online offerings may have special allure: as a connection to a nostalgia-misted past and a remedy for homesickness.

In reality, economic hardship and political conflict may have made this earlier life far less attractive than it appears in memory. Nevertheless, new media may create such a convenient bridge across distance and time that a Web site or a satellite channel can become cherished as a tie to real or imagined "home." Peter Mandaville noted, "New media are likely to play an increasingly important role among young Muslims born and raised in the West as they search for spaces and languages in which to shape an Islam that is both relevant to their socio-cultural situatedness and free from the hegemony of traditional sources of interpretation and authority." Mandaville also observed, "More than anything else, the Internet and other information technologies provide spaces where Muslims, who often find themselves to be a marginalized or extreme minority group in many Western communities, can go in order to find others 'like them.'"[39]

Al Jazeera's approach to certain news stories illustrates how globalized journalism can affect globalized Islam. Sam Cherribi wrote that Al Jazeera used its coverage of the banning of the *hijab*, a veil, from French schools "to build a global Muslim identity [and] mobilize a shared public opinion." According to Cherribi, Al Jazeera framed the veil story in its reporting from 2002 to 2005 as "not only a problem for girls and women in public schools in France; it is a problem for Muslim women and men around the world." The veil coverage, he wrote, was part of a "civilization message" delivered by Al Jazeera, in this case because "the veil gives the immediate recognition of otherness: non-Muslims do not wear it." Cherribi also argued that Al Jazeera is a religious channel, more Christian Broadcasting Network (CBN) than CNN, with an agenda that focuses on Islam even above pan-Arabism.[40] Others, however, contend that Al Jazeera's content is relatively balanced when it addresses religious topics, reflecting the intricate spiderweb of Islamism and pan-Arabism that is part of the mind-set of many of the people who live in the Arab world and watch the channel.

Beyond the news coverage of specific issues, the importance of new media is found in its providing an arena where the future of Islam will be contested. This takes place on several levels: doctrinal debate between moderates and conservatives about defining the beliefs and practices of "true Islam" and political argument about Islam's stance toward the non-Islamic world. For those who argue that Islam is not a party to a clash of civilizations but is instead undergoing an internal struggle to determine its direction, the huge number of media venues—particularly online—provides the opportunity to watch the various sides present their cases.

For this direction-setting process, the Internet and satellite television transform and transcend traditional hierarchies. Robert Hefner noted, "The classically educated scholars (*ulama*) who long dominated the religious tradition awoke to face a host of new challengers, including secularly educated new Muslim intellectuals, independent preachers, Internet Islamists, and other beneficiaries of new technologies and organizations."[41]

Merlyna Lim wrote that by expanding the number of voices to which a mass audience may listen, the Internet

> tremendously enhances the prospects for an egalitarian type of communications in which every voice is potentially as important as another. For Muslim Internet users, this capability opens space to examine religion with no authority except the texts of the *Qur'an* and *Hadith*. By learning from the Internet, people can feel they have acquired enough Islamic knowledge to guide important life decisions without having recourse to more traditional scholars such as an imam or Islamic teachers in local mosques. At the same time, radical fundamentalist groups can also use the Internet to bypass local authorities—national/sub-national authorities, an imam, local religious leaders, and parents—and directly reach ordinary Muslims in cyberspace.

As an example of this, wrote Lim, "the reductionist tendency and simplicity of narratives of conspiracy and Salafi jihadism fit better with the mass nature of the Internet. It is thus understandable why this kind of message is even more popular in cyberspace than it is in other media."[42]

In such ways the structure and substance of Islam are being reshaped by new media. Another aspect of the Internet's effect on the religion is the changing role of Arabic. Much as the Catholic Church relied for centuries on Latin, regardless of whether people understood it, many Islamic ulama insist that Arabic is the true language of Islam because it was spoken by Muhammad and so even non-Arabic speakers should learn at least enough of the language to be able to recite parts of the Quran in it. In theory, the common language could further Islamic unity. Faisal Devji observed, "Arabic not only moves beyond regional boundaries but also transforms the places in which it is uttered. These places where Arabic is spoken come therefore to represent an Islamic universality that extends to the furthest reaches of the globe."[43]

A single language that everyone within the ummah could speak might make increased cohesion more feasible, but having a common language for everyday discourse is unrealistic. That is not the nature of today's world, and so reliance on Arabic is intrinsically limiting, partly because most Muslims do not speak Arabic. Dale Eickelman and Jon Anderson wrote, "While Arabic remains a universal medium at one level, language differences within the Muslim world significantly constrain the circulation of ideas. Some Indonesian religious intellectuals, often trained in the United States and Canada, interpret developments in the Arab world, but virtually no Arab intellectuals follow debates on Muslim intellectual and political life in Southeast Asia."[44]

With the Internet providing information in many languages, particularly English, dependence on Arabic has been reduced and the audience has expanded. Jocelyne Cesari noted that abandonment of Arabic and other ancestral languages "has led to the growth of 'vernacular' forms of Islam in Europe and America, where sermons, religious literature, and public discussions are increasingly in English, which has now become the second language of Muslims all over the *ummah*."[45]

Traditionalists may lament the disincentive to learn Arabic, but an increased number of languages used to disseminate information could enable more people to feel that they are truly part of the *ummah* and could contribute to the cohesion that new communications technologies may foster. This acceptance of linguistic diversity is particularly important for Web sites and blogs, which within a short time have grown spectacularly in their number and range of outlook.

Whatever the language of online content, the Internet is bringing added religious and political depth to existing or new constituencies. In Indonesia, reported Merlyna Lim, "the Internet has played a key role in creating and sustaining political legitimation, resistance, and identity projects among Islamic fundamentalists. . . . The Internet is becoming a major factor in identity formation—one that can allow users to access global sources of information while interpreting that information in local identity contexts through key nodes and sources."[46]

Sufism, which is criticized by some fundamentalists as non-Islamic while its advocates say it is the true essence of Islam, has seen its tenets debated and its visibility increased through new media. Carl Ernst wrote that Sufi Web sites have been primarily created by one segment of the Sufi population: "members of the cosmopolitan and globalizing classes: either emigrant Sufi leaders establishing new bases in America and Europe, immigrant technocrats who happen to be connected to Sufi lineages, or Euro-American converts to Sufism in one form or another."

Ernst also noted that one Sufi leader in Southeast Asia, when asked if he was interested in setting up a Web site, said, "We are not vendors who hawk our wares in the bazaar. . . . People come to us." But his Malaysian followers have set up an online site on which they sell English-language publications by the leading masters of the order.[47]

The Redrawn Map and Foreign Policy

When the United States and other Western nations formulate policy, they often do not take into account the sophisticated political culture and staying power of virtual states. In developing strategies for dealing with Islamic states and peoples, the reality of the substantive *ummah* has been neglected while disproportionate effort has been devoted to courting "the Arab street" (without bothering to define exactly what "the Arab street" might be) and paying too little attention to Islam beyond the Arab world.

Fifty years ago, it was easy to dismiss the notion of the *ummah* as a cohesive entity because the mechanisms needed to pull it together did not exist. But to do so today is to disregard the enormous capabilities of information and communication technologies. At the very least, policymakers in the non-Islamic world should more carefully consider the potential ramifications of technology-enhanced pan-Islamism.

On another level, a case can be made that instead of a "clash of civilizations," as described by Samuel Huntington, there is a clash *within* Islam between progressive and reactionary elements. If this is so, the ripple effects of such a contest are likely to be far more consequential if they emanate from an *ummah* that is unified to any degree.

Communications technology could be this unifying tool. During the coming decade, Al Jazeera and its satellite television brethren will deliver their messages in more languages to more people, many of them Muslims. This expanded reach will enhance media influence, particularly if these information providers deliver their products with a political slant. More significant, during this time the Internet audience will expand exponentially and online offerings will foster expanded discourse and other connections within the virtual *ummah*.

Policymakers can sit back and watch all this happen or they can participate in the process. The latter course requires a realistic plan. As American public diplomacy efforts since 9/11 have proved, competing head-to-head is often pointless. Al Hurra, the satellite television channel sponsored by the U.S. government, has been an inconsequential competitor for Al Jazeera, Al Arabiya, and other indigenous broadcasters. Self-serving online products fare no better. A smarter course of action would involve less competition and more cooperation. The Islamic-oriented media with the largest audiences—on air and online—are generally open to presenting a range of perspectives, and these media have credibility that will increase the chance that the messages they carry will receive a fair hearing.

Information from *someone* will reach the virtual *ummah*. This intellectual contest should not be left to be dominated by one viewpoint. If the United States and other democracies want to make their case to the Islamic community, their policymakers must develop a more sophisticated appreciation of the influence of new media.

Virtual states are part of geopolitical reality. Their essence is connectivity rather than territoriality. Whether they have the *ummah*'s population of more than a billion or a much smaller constituency, their technology-enhanced existence as virtual entities deserves to be recognized.

5
Global Connections, Global Terrorism

One example of the Internet being used specifically to build a global *ummah* can be found in the online presence of Hizb ut-Tahrir, the Party of Liberation, which is reportedly active in at least forty countries. Its cyber-presence—with a principal Web site available in Arabic, English, Russian, Turkish, Urdu, and German—illustrates how a broader *ummah* might coalesce through use of the Internet.

Hizb ut-Tahrir has been described as a radical Islamic political movement that wants to establish widespread adherence to "pure Islamic doctrine" and creation of an Islamic caliphate in Central Asia that would unite the entire Islamic world community. The group endorses a three-step process to achieve this: educating Muslims about its goal of a shariah-based society; encouraging Muslims to spread these views among others, especially members of government, the military, and other power centers, in their countries; and then, through its faithful adherents, causing secular governments to crumble as loyalties come to lie solely with Islam—not with nationalities, politics, or ethnic identifications. At that point, a supreme Islamic leader, a caliph like those of past centuries, would exercise political and religious authority over all Muslims.[1]

Hizb ut-Tahrir relies heavily on the Internet. Zeyno Baran wrote, "The Internet's global reach is perfect for a group that denies the legitimacy of political borders. Hizb ut-Tahrir's Web sites can be easily accessed by Muslims anywhere, and the Internet is especially effective at facilitating communications with and among people living in repressive societies." Baran added that Hizb ut-Tahrir "has essentially constructed a virtual Islamist community in cyberspace, frequented by members, prospective members, and sympathizers. Hizb ut-Tahrir's Web sites are designed to draw in Web-surfing Muslims who feel alienated from the societies in which they live, providing them with a place to obtain news and analysis, exchange ideas, and feel part of a global Muslim community."[2]

This offer of a virtual "home" is a good illustration of sophisticated use of new media and ties into the organization's appreciation of the processes of supranational connectivity. As reflected in Hizb ut-Tahrir's approach, the *ummah*'s potential for increased cohesion is partly a function of globalization. Establishing a caliphate to rule a global, if abstract, *ummah* is a precept of neofundamentalism, which, said Olivier Roy, "valorizes the uprootedness of uprooted people. By pretending to ignore the cultural context and by providing a code of conduct that functions in a similar manner in any part of the world, it is a perfect tool of globalization. It works along the same lines as globalization—individualization, deculturation, and deterritorialization—and promotes a reconstructed identity based on the homogenization of patterns of conduct."[3]

Hizb ut-Tahrir's Web presence is an instructive illustration of how the virtual *ummah* could take shape. The primary—www.hizb-ut-tahrir.org—and subsidiary sites, such as the one for Britain—www.hizb.org.uk—are user-friendly and otherwise well designed to hold the attention of anyone visiting for a quick look. But most important is that the site gives the organization an easy-to-find, always available virtual presence. This is, in many ways, preferable to a physical headquarters. The virtual location can be observed by anyone, but it is less vulnerable to intrusion by law enforcement agencies or opponents. It can be monitored but not raided or penetrated in the same ways that a conventional base of operations could be, although it can be disrupted by hacking. Its sympathizers can safely make virtual "visits."

Anyone with access to the Internet has access to Hizb ut-Tahrir, and of course the same can be said of any group with a

Web site. But the site's political effects, some of which cannot be known even to its proprietors, and its method of recruitment as a virtual transaction put it in a special category. Through the site, the organization engages in constant proselytizing, trying to convince its visitors that its approach to the future of Islam deserves their support and participation.

The Web site describes membership as an invisible affiliation: "The person in question imposes himself on the Party when he melts into it and when the *dawah* interacts with him and he adopts the thoughts and the concepts of the Party." Then the member presumably aids the party's political missionary work, which involves convincing fellow Muslims of the importance of government being based on Islamic law. After that, the party intends to restore the *ummah* "to her previous might and glory such that she wrests the reins of initiative away from other states and nations, and returns to her rightful place as the first state in the world, as she was in the past, when she governs the world according to the laws of Islam."[4]

Hizb ut-Tahrir's conception of the *ummah* and the party's plan of action reflect its goal of building a new caliphate initially in virtual territory. It relies on cyberspace as a political location in which organizing a virtual state can take place. Except for occasions when the party undertakes localized activity, such as protesting a proposed British anti-terrorism statute, conventional borders are disregarded and traditional sovereignty is also treated as irrelevant. The *ummah* as righteous political entity supersedes such secular constraints, and cyberspace rather than conventionally defined territory is seen as a congenial home for the *ummah*.

Although no acts of violence have been directly attributed to Hizb ut-Tahrir, several governments have labeled it a terrorist organization. As of April 2008, the party was not on the U.S. State Department's list of foreign terrorist groups, but in Russia and some Central Asian countries, Hizb ut-Tahrir activists have been jailed, with a flurry of arrests in Tajikistan and Kyrgyzstan in mid-2006. The party is illegal in Germany, Pakistan, and most Arab countries. In Britain, party leaders have been charged with promoting anti-Semitism. During the fall of 2006, Hizb ut-Tahrir activity accelerated with members' efforts such as placing posters throughout Zanzibar that urged the establishment of a caliphate as a way to halt the corruption of Muslim life there by Western tourists.[5]

By 2007 Hizb ut-Tahrir had become active in the United States, largely by relying on online marketing such as video sharing, social networking, and even sponsoring online hip-hop boutiques. The group seemed to be positioning itself to take advantage of any rift that might develop between the American Muslim community and the U.S. government.[6]

Presumably, security forces throughout the world keep watch on people thought to be Hizb ut-Tahrir members. But little imagination or effort appears to have been devoted to considering how to deal with a putative foe that so intensively relies on the Internet as a political medium.

O ⁀ O

Despite the opportunities afforded by new communications and information technologies, obstacles to peaceful coexistence within the broad spectrum of Islam remain formidable. Muslim-versus-Muslim warfare in Iraq has displayed the deep wounds sectarianism can inflict, and this conflict has an online component, with Sunni and Shia each using Internet forums to urge the destruction of the other. On a less sanguinary level, Muslims' worldviews differ so much that finding common ground for a Sufi mystic and a Hizb ut-Tahrir strategist may be difficult. Fundamentalist and modernist may each feel strongly that the other is following a path toward disaster. Such diversity does not mean that the *ummah* cannot come together, but if it does so it will probably be loosely knit.

It would, however, still be a significant geopolitical presence, and the weave of its fabric could be tightened by external factors, such as actions by perceived common foes—primarily Israel and the United States—as depicted in news reports and from other sources, many of them relying on new media. When images from Gaza and Lebanon in 2006 showed the agony of fellow Muslims, the reports that were most trusted were provided by Arab news organizations that are credible among their particular regional and global audiences. When such reports reach households in Cairo, Karachi, Djakarta, and Paris, Muslims feel the pain of other Muslims and may reflexively seek the embrace of the Islamic community.

Islam has no monopoly on high-tech communication tools. Other religions also use them: Christian Web sites and blogs outnumber all others. Some diasporic communities rely on satellite channels and online forums to sustain identity. But Islam and the members of the global Muslim community are different. At this point in history, Islam in its many manifestations is affecting how much of the world works and is a factor in many of the world's armed conflicts. That is why it makes sense for the United States, among others, to devise a policy toward the *ummah* as well as toward traditional nation-states.

For good or ill, Islam is a special case, and policymakers in the United States and elsewhere in the non-Islamic world should more seriously contemplate how a realized *ummah* might change the world, particularly in the context of the profound effect terrorism has on international affairs.

Al Qaeda as a Virtual State

A virtual state may possess well-defined political characteristics, as in the case of Kurdistan, or may be more nebulous, as with the *ummah*. Whatever its particulars, the virtual state is more than just a presence on the Internet or a technological specter. It is characterized by a uniformity of purpose and a desire for some degree of cohesion. A virtual state can conduct business, such as raising and dispensing money and delivering services to its citizenry. A virtual state might also be capable of waging war. It can have far-flung impact by creating its own network with worldwide reach.

Although it is often labeled as a "network," al Qaeda can be seen as such a state. It is something of a confederation, with affiliates around the world that retain some autonomy while still considering themselves to be parts of the greater whole. Policymakers should look at it as a state rather than as an amorphous organization because treating it as a state might inspire more realistic appraisal of its political and quasi-military capabilities and perhaps bring more coherence to policy decisions. Treating al Qaeda as a state also makes sense if it is an enemy against which a war is to be fought. As a political enterprise requiring public support in a democracy, war requires a foe with an identity that the public can comprehend. War against a network can be difficult to grasp.

The struggle against al Qaeda illustrates this difficulty. The al Qaeda as enemy concept creates problems of definition and policy. Al Qaeda is a principal target of the "war on terror," but waging a "war on terror" makes little sense because "terror" is a concept and an effect rather than a tangible entity that can be targeted as the enemy. Al Qaeda has more substance than "terrorism" per se because it has a self-defined identity and structure, although it remains elusive as a physical opponent. It is not an enemy such as Germany and Japan were when fighting the United States during the Second World War. They were conventional nations and existed as physical territory that could be attacked and eventually occupied.

When the United States invaded Afghanistan in late 2001, U.S. forces were attacking the Taliban that ruled the country, their guest Osama bin Laden, and fighters loyal to al Qaeda. But Afghanistan was not the al Qaeda homeland; there is no such thing, at least not in the traditional, physical sense. Even if Afghanistan were, over the long term, to be successfully occupied and pacified (doubtful in itself), al Qaeda would not necessarily have been conquered. The real al Qaeda homeland is vast and virtual and is given cohesion via cyber-tools and new media rather than by having territory defined by borders.

Al Qaeda has troops, organized in cells rather than divisions. It has a command structure, which—like much of the Internet-centric world—is decidedly nonlinear. For those who fight it, al Qaeda may seem to be a scattered array of psychopaths operating under a common brand name. If that were true, they could be picked off one at a time and eventually the threat would be erased. But as a virtual state, al Qaeda possesses more substance and resilience than might at first be seen, and it continues to evolve. Abdel Bari Atwan wrote that future organizational changes will "further take al Qaeda outside the scope and experience of international security forces. By converting al Qaeda into a set of guiding principles, an ideology, it transcends all national boundaries and makes affiliation or enfranchisement exceptionally easy."[7]

The U.S. 9/11 Commission grappled with such matters, stating in its report,

> National security used to be considered by studying foreign frontiers, weighing opposing groups of states, and measuring industrial might. To be dangerous, an enemy had to muster large armies. Threats emerged slowly, often visibly, as weapons were forged, armies conscripted, and units trained and moved into place. Because large states were so powerful, they also had more to lose. They could be deterred. Now threats can emerge quickly. An organization like al Qaeda, headquartered in a country on the other side of the earth, in a region so poor that electricity or telephones were scarce, could nonetheless scheme to wield weapons of unprecedented destructive power in the largest cities of the United States. . . . Our enemy is twofold: al Qaeda, a stateless network of terrorists that struck us on 9/11; and a radical ideological movement in the Islamic world, inspired in part by al Qaeda, which has spawned terrorist groups and violence across the globe.[8]

A "stateless network" or a networked state? Faisal Devji observed that al Qaeda, like jihadist movements generally, is "non-geographical in nature, using the most disparate territories as temporary bases for its action. This makes it into an impossible enemy for the United States, because it exists beyond America's war-making potential." It is a new global category, wrote Devji, "with the geographical, financial, and technological mobility that defines globalization itself."[9]

Al Qaeda cannot be regarded as an "impossible enemy," but it is a difficult one. If al Qaeda launches another major attack against the United States, Great Britain, or another nation, how would the victim strike back? The supply of inviting "enemy" states is limited: Afghanistan and Iraq have already been checked off the list, Libya wisely removed itself, and diving into Iran or Syria could well prove politically and militarily counterproductive. And suppose it turned out that the attack was planned and directed by al Qaeda operatives living in Paris or Rome or Montreal. Would a military response be feasible, or would the reaction be ratcheted down to the level of a police matter? Such temperate action might be sensible, but would it be macho enough to be politically acceptable within the victim nation, assuming that the attack had caused many casualties?

Variations on such hypothetical questions are beyond counting, and considering how to answer them is a full-time job for antiterrorism strategists. Part of addressing such matters involves understanding what al Qaeda is and is not. It is often treated as an *organization*, which can be misleading because the term conjures up images of a company such as General Motors or a fraternal group such as Rotary International. These organizations rely on clearly defined lines of authority and responsibility, with those at the bottom of the organizational structure—such as salespeople in the field or members of local clubs—linked and ultimately responsible to those at the top. Instructions and other information flow neatly, top to bottom. Such groups generally can be depicted by precise blueprints showing how they are organized.

But as Jason Burke observed, to view al Qaeda "as a coherent and tight-knit organization, with 'tentacles everywhere' and with a defined ideology and personnel that had emerged as early as the late 1980s, is to misunderstand not only its true nature but also the nature of Islamic radicalism then and now."[10] Al Qaeda is not a corporation or a club. It is a political entity with a population—dispersed as it may be—that engages in financial transactions, communications activity, and military operations. With these characteristics and its global reach, al Qaeda should be analyzed as a virtual state.

Michael Scheuer asked,

Do Osama bin Laden, Ayman al-Zawahiri, and the al Qaeda organization and its allies conduct diplomacy in the traditional sense of that activity? Given that al Qaeda and its affiliated factions are not nation-states, have no capital cities, and neither send nor receive representatives who can be accurately termed ambassadors, the answer would have to be 'no.' Yet there is a definite sense in which they conduct a foreign policy that is meant to advance the Islamist movement toward victory. . . . This foreign policy—or political warfare strategy—is to be delivered over the heads of U.S. and Western leaders to voters in non-Muslim countries and is meant to do two things: change the policies of countries allied with the United States by eroding popular support for assisting the United States in fighting the war on terrorism, and, second, slowly strip allies away from the United States and leave it increasingly isolated.[11]

In terms of organizational design, the 9/11 Commission noted that as al Qaeda evolved during the late 1990s it "relied heavily on the ideas and work of enterprising and strong-willed field commanders who enjoyed considerable autonomy."[12] A RAND study reported that before the U.S. invasion of Afghanistan, al Qaeda featured a combination of a hub-and-spoke structure, in which cells of operatives communicated with Osama bin Laden and his lieutenants in Afghanistan, and a wheel structure, where operatives communicated with each other without necessarily going through the leadership.[13]

After the fall of the Taliban and with bin Laden and others in the top echelon on the run, the structure became even more flexible. As Gabriel Weimann noted, "In the loose network structure, group members are organized into cells that have little or no contact with other cells or with a central control or headquarters. Leaders do not issue orders to the cells but rather distribute information via the media, Web sites, and e-mails that can be distributed and accessed anonymously. The advantage of this operational structure is that surveillance, penetration, or capture of operatives does not lead the intelligence agency to other cells or to the central control structure." Al Qaeda and other terrorist groups, added Weimann, "are loosely organized networks that rely less on hierarchical structure and more on horizontal networking. To varying degrees, many modern terrorist groups share the pattern of the loosely knit network: decentralization, segmentation, and delegation of authority."[14]

But al Qaeda might not be so loosely organized. Guidance, if not orders, can be passed down from the top. In mid-2007, as was the case before the 2001 attacks, a *shura*, or leadership council, was meeting regularly and reporting to bin Laden, who would make decisions himself about some matters passed up to him. About two hundred people, many of whom received regular salaries, constituted the core of al Qaeda.[15] A virtual state is more than a network because of its unifying sense of purpose and the related sharing of information—such as how to make an improvised explosive device—through sophisticated use of media. A virtual state does not need a conventional hierarchy. Al Qaeda continues to evolve as a nonhierarchical global enterprise, a new kind of state with operations that transcend conventional structures as well as borders. It has leaders with star power—Osama bin Laden and Ayman al-Zawahiri—but more important it has "citizens" throughout the world, people whose loyalty is to al Qaeda's cause, if not to bin Laden personally. For some, al Qaeda is the state that is fighting many enemies to protect Islam and in doing so is filling a role from which corrupt, co-opted countries such as Saudi Arabia have abdicated. Other al Qaeda citizens see their new state as a temporary manifestation serving as a steppingstone toward the restored caliphate.

Treating al Qaeda as a virtual state rather than as merely a criminal organization may strike some as an undue distinction for terrorists. But however unsavory al Qaeda's people and activities might be, their opponents must recognize that finding one man in a cave will be merely useful, not determinative, in stopping al Qaeda's terrorism. As was proved when Abu Musab al-Zarqawi, the self-proclaimed head of al Qaeda in Iraq, was killed by a U.S. air strike in June 2006, the future of al Qaeda is not tied to any one person. Osama bin Laden's demise will not signal the collapse of al Qaeda, which is much more than simply bin Laden's gang.

Virtual states possess considerable survivability, largely because of their incorporated multidimensional networks. Spanish politician and terrorism expert Gustavo de Aristegui identified four kinds of al Qaeda networks: "First, there is the original network, the one that committed 9/11, which uses its own resources and people it has recruited and trained." Second is the "ad-hoc terrorist network, consisting of franchise organizations that al Qaeda created—often to replace ones that weren't bloody enough—in countries such as the Philippines, Jordan, and Algeria." Third, said Aristegui, is an umbrella network, "a strategic union of like-minded companies" tied to al Qaeda by common purpose and funds provided by bin Laden. In the fourth network are the "imitators, emulators" who agree with al Qaeda's program but have fewer financial connections to bin Laden. Members at this level, said Aristegui, carried out the 2004 Madrid bombings.[16] The third of these levels particularly illustrates that al Qaeda has grown beyond mere network status, becoming more defined and unified.

This is a complex entity, spread out around the world, operating secretly, pursued by law enforcement and probed by infiltrators,[17] all the while needing leadership and funds as it plans its attacks. Global media help sustain this virtual state. Ayman al-Zawahiri said in 2005, "We are in a battle, and more than half of this battle is taking place in the battlefield of the media. . . . We are in a media battle for the hearts and minds of our *ummah*."

Through news reports, satellite television provides al Qaeda citizens and the general public with graphic depictions of al Qaeda's work and occasional glimpses of bin Laden himself. More significant, the Internet provides more detailed and frequent versions of what the news media have covered, all the while furthering operational connectivity and a sense of cohesion. In terms of organization, Michael Scheuer noted, "The Internet today allows militant Muslims from every country to meet, talk, and get to know each other electronically, a familiarization and bonding process that in the 1980s and early 1990s required a trip to Sudan, Yemen, Afghanistan, or Pakistan."[18] To enhance cybersecurity for such connections, the online *Technical Mujahid Magazine* was begun in late 2006 to instruct its readers about electronic data security and other high-tech matters.

The al Qaeda leadership has recognized this and stresses Internet use in directives to its citizens/followers, as is illustrated in this message carried on one of its Web sites:

Due to the advances of modern technology, it is easy to spread news, information, articles, and other information over the Internet. We strongly urge Muslim Internet professionals to spread and disseminate news and information about the Jihad through e-mail lists, discussion groups, and their own Web sites. If you fail to do this, and our site closes down before you have done this, we may hold you to account before Allah on the Day of Judgment. . . . We expect our Web site to be opened and closed continuously. Therefore we urgently recommend any Muslims that are interested in our material to copy all the articles from our site and disseminate them through their own Web sites, discussion boards, and e-mail lists. This is something that any Muslim can participate in easily, including sisters. This way, even if our sites are closed down, the material will live on with the Grace of Allah.[19]

Even when under attack by U.S. forces in late 2001, al Qaeda clung to its high-tech tools. A Pakistani journalist who was on the scene wrote that while retreating from the attack, "every second al Qaeda member was carrying a laptop computer along with his Kalashnikov."[20]

Al Qaeda has adroitly managed its cyber-affairs while building the global al Qaeda nation. Weimann found that al Qaeda's Web presence grew from one site during the late 1990s to more than fifty by 2006. Other jihadist sites number in the thousands. When a site is hacked or pulled down by a service provider, the content soon pops up on a new site. Weimann reports, "A widespread network of Web sites is used to feed directions and information from those at the top of al Qaeda to supporters and sympathizers around the world. Lectures, taped announcements, videos of terrorist attacks, guidebooks, and manuals are disseminated through al Qaeda's Web sites, forums, chat rooms, and online bulletin boards."

An example of these products is *Sawt Al-Jihad* (*Voice of Jihad*), an online magazine that first appeared in February 2004 and touts the accomplishments of mujahedin. The tone of the magazine is illustrated by this excerpt from an October 2004 editorial:

Muslims! Go out to [fight] Jihad for the sake of Allah! Paradise has already flung open its gates and the virgins of paradise are already decked out in anticipation of their grooms—this is Allah's promise. He [Allah] will not grant peace of mind to anyone who has a heart until he has gone out to fight against Allah's enemies, as he was commanded. He who does not act [i.e., fight the Jihad] out of obedience to Allah's command, and out of zeal for the honor of the Muslim women which was defiled at Abu Ghraib and in the other prisons of the leaders of unbelief, and out of fervor, and out of mortification at [the thought of] shirking [battle]—what else could arouse him [to go to battle] other than all of these?[21]

As Weimann noted, *Sawt Al-Jihad* reflects the multiple purposes of such al Qaeda ventures: "Orchestrating attacks against Western targets is important, but the main objective remains that of mobilizing public support and gaining grassroots legitimacy among Muslims."[22] Another aspect of this effort to build a Web-based constituency is an online library of training materials explaining how to mix ricin poison, how to build a bomb using commercial chemicals, how to sneak through Syria and into Iraq, and other such advice. Some of these items are supported by experts who answer questions on message boards and chat rooms.

Another al Qaeda online magazine, *Muaskar Al-Battar* (*Camp of the Sword*), underscored the value of online instruction: "Oh Mujahid brother, in order to join the great training camps you don't have to travel to other lands. Alone in your home or with a group of your brothers, you too can begin to execute the training program."[23]

The Al Neda Web site, which al Qaeda began using in early 2002, has published analyses of the wars in Afghanistan and Iraq, commentary by Islamic clerics about al Qaeda operations, and explanations of how al Qaeda's war aims would benefit the *ummah* by undermining the power of the United States, Israel, and unfaithful Muslim governments. The content of al Qaeda–related sites, wrote Michael Scheuer, "adds up to a tremendous contribution to what bin Laden always has said is his and al

Qaeda's first priority: the instigation to jihad of as many Muslims in as many locales as possible."[24]

Nadya Labi observed that al Qaeda strategists have "recognized that the Internet could become a vast global recruiting ground—in effect a new, borderless Afghanistan."[25] Propaganda video, disseminated primarily through the Internet, has been used to reinforce the commitment of al Qaeda's citizens, intimidate the public, and enlist newcomers. British and American Muslims have been targeted by the recruiting efforts, such as a 2006 video that emphasized rapes and murders committed by U.S. soldiers in Iraq. Released to mark the first anniversary of the 7/7 bombings in London, the video featured bin Laden's deputy, al-Zawahiri; Shehzad Tanweer, one of the London bombers, who died during the attack; and Adam Gadahn, also known as "Azzam the American," who grew up in California.

Tanweer, delivering his final testament in English with a Yorkshire accent, said, "We are 100 percent committed to the cause of Islam. We love death the way you love life. . . . Oh, Muslims of Britain, you, day in and day out on your TV sets, watch and hear about the oppression of the Muslims, from the east to the west. But yet you turn a blind eye, and carry on with your lives as if you never heard anything, or as if it does not concern you. . . . Oh, Muslims of Britain, stand up and be counted. . . . Fight against the disbelievers, for it is an obligation made on you by Allah." To this, Gadahn added, "It's crucial for Muslims to keep in mind that the American, the British, and the other members of the coalition of terror have intentionally targeted Muslim civilians."[26]

Al Qaeda's sophistication in media matters can be seen in the establishment of its own production company, the As-Sahab Foundation, which produces video of bin Laden's statements and infomercials about al Qaeda and jihad. As-Sahab is part of the media department bin Laden established when al Qaeda was created in 1988. The first message to emerge was that al Qaeda was a brave underdog challenging the mighty Soviet Union and soon thereafter other purported enemies of Islam. During the early 1990s, when bin Laden was based in Sudan, the media message called for reform of the impure government of Saudi Arabia. In 1996 bin Laden issued his "Declaration of War on the United

States" and used the al Qaeda media machinery to spread the call for jihad. Ultimately, the As-Sahab product was presented as an alternative to conventional television news.[27]

For some As-Sahab productions, al Qaeda photographers shoot video of bin Laden, al-Zawahiri, or others at their remote hideouts. The raw footage is taken to another location where it can be uploaded to the Internet and sent digitally to As-Sahab's postproduction facilities. As-Sahab can produce a broadcast-quality product, with logos, digitally inserted backdrops, and subtitles, often in English. The usual setting of the videos had been outdoors with weapons visible, but in some of the newer messages that backdrop has been replaced by a book-lined office, giving the videos the look of a conventional political message and making it harder for intelligence analysts to determine where the footage was shot.

Between 2005 and 2006, al Qaeda quadrupled the number of videos it produced. In 2006 As-Sahab released fifty-eight video and audio messages. In 2007, it released more than ninety. Dissemination was available through roughly 4,500 jihadi Web sites.[28]

For distribution, the standard procedure used to be a physical delivery of videotapes to Al Jazeera or other news outlets, which would edit the material before airing it. The newer method is to upload the finished video onto various Web sites and then publish the addresses of these sites on Internet forums. Al Qaeda sympathizers can then copy and distribute the video files, which means the product is disseminated unedited to a large audience. With more and more jihadi Web sites appearing on the Internet, al Qaeda has a growing network of distributors for its propaganda and is less dependent on news organizations. One jihadist who helps distribute the al Qaeda videos told a reporter, "We become like journalists ourselves," working to "get the message out."[29]

In Iraq, the Islamist State of Iraq has its own media company, patterned after As-Sahab. Its products include a 2007 nineteen-minute video titled "Why Do We Wage Jihad?" The As-Sahab look has also been copied by al Qaeda–related operations outside the center of the Middle East, as could be seen in video productions used in 2007 by Al Qaeda Organization in the Islamic Maghreb.[30]

This kind of media work was taken to a new level by al-Zarqawi in Iraq. Al-Zarqawi first displayed his grisly flair for using media when American businessman Nicholas Berg was abducted and beheaded in Iraq in 2004, with al-Zarqawi apparently the executioner. The beheading was videotaped and offered on a Web site, from which it was copied to other sites and downloaded 500,000 times within twenty-four hours.[31] That may say as much about the audience as it does about al-Zarqawi, but the Jordanian-born insurgency leader had a well-honed instinct for promoting his brand of jihad.

The following year, al-Zarqawi began an online magazine, *Zurwat al-Sanam* (*The Tip of the Camel's Hump,* meaning ideal Islamic practice), which featured forty-three pages of text, including stories about fallen jihadists, and photographs of Osama bin Laden and George W. Bush.[32] Several months later, al-Zarqawi's "information wing" released "All Religion Will Be for Allah," a forty-six-minute video with scenes including a brigade of suicide bombers in training. As the *Washington Post* reported, the video was offered on a specially designed Web page with many options for downloading: versions (Windows Media or RealPlayer) for those with high-speed Internet connections, another version for those with dial-up, and one for downloading to play on a cell phone.[33] A wide range of online products can be found. Even cartoons depicting children as suicide bombers are easily accessible on the Web.[34]

While he was pursuing his ambitious media agenda, al-Zarqawi was chastised by al-Zawahiri for "slaughtering" hostages in public view and for targeting Shiites before defeating the Americans in Iraq. Al-Zarqawi's autonomy was not limitless. Implicit in al-Zawahiri's message was a reminder that much of al-Zarqawi's funding came from sources bin Laden controlled. This is one way the virtual terrorist state polices its citizenry.[35]

As part of his media strategy, al-Zarqawi had an online press secretary working for him. During July 2005, al Qaeda in Iraq released an average of nine online statements each day. These releases often claimed responsibility for attacks, especially against American troops. The media operation also corrected erroneous news accounts, as in 2005 when al-Zarqawi's spokesperson issued

GLOBAL CONNECTIONS, GLOBAL TERRORISM 107

a denial that the al-Zarqawi insurgents had been responsible for a suicide car bombing in Hilla, Iraq, that had killed women and children and had led residents to angrily demonstrate against the violence. The spokesperson said, in an online statement, that their group had claimed responsibility for *another* attack, one directed at U.S. soldiers, and had had nothing to do with the Hilla bombing. The statement warned, "No one should aspire to say about us what we have not said."[36]

Although al-Zarqawi is gone, al Qaeda's media operations in Iraq and elsewhere have become more sophisticated and pervasive. Al Zawra television, featuring video of sniper attacks on U.S. soldiers in Iraq, was broadcasting twenty-four hours a day by early 2007. Operated by Sunni insurgents, the channel claimed to represent "all factions of resistance against the Iranian and American occupation."[37] Although the United States tried to drive Al Zawra's programming off the air, it remained available on Arabsat despite the Saudi government being a major stakeholder in the satellite company. Apparently the Saudis' interest in helping fellow Sunnis was deemed more important than its interest in helping the United States.[38]

Al Qaeda's agenda involves much more than mounting isolated terrorist attacks. The broader political plan includes mobilizing public opinion and pulling more subsidiary groups and individuals into the al Qaeda state. Bin Laden has recognized the breadth and potential power of al Qaeda as part of a unified *ummah*. He has said, "We are the children of one nation [*ummah*], which extends from the Middle East to the Philippines, Indonesia, Malaysia, India, Pakistan, and as far away as Mauritania."[39]

Bin Laden understands the importance of delivering images of violence to this large audience as one part of building al Qaeda because, as Faisal Devji noted, "martyrdom creates a global community because it is collectively witnessed in mass media." But Devji also pointed out that al Qaeda's terrorism should be appraised in a broader context. "In the long run," he wrote, "violence is probably Al Qaeda's most superficial and short-lived effect, though it is certainly one of great importance for the moment. Far greater and almost incalculable in its effects is the jihad's democratization of Islam, accomplished by its fragmentation of traditional forms of religious authority and the dispersal of their elements into a potentially endless series of re-combinations—some represented by Al Qaeda itself."[40]

As a matter of semantics, "democratization" as Devji uses it in this instance can be debated, and jihad is just one factor behind the pressures pushing Islam toward change. New media have altered the dynamics of influence. Information hegemony has shriveled; traditional states, media organizations, and political actors cannot set agendas or establish boundaries of discourse in the ways that they once could. In Devji's example, the many Islamic voices delivered by the Internet and satellite television individually and collectively alter the traditional lines of authority within Islam. Clergy have a place in the virtual state, but they do not control it. When Osama bin Laden or other jihadists participate in the goings on of this virtual world, they assume a leadership role and attain influence beyond that tied to the notoriety of committing acts of violence.

Bin Laden may eventually meet an end similar to that of his understudy al-Zarqawi. Throughout the world, headlines will proclaim that his death means the death of al Qaeda, just as many Western news organizations overrated the significance of al-Zarqawi's death. Losing bin Laden will be a serious blow to al Qaeda but certainly not a fatal one.

Al Qaeda has become a virtual state, with a vicious and ambitious agenda and a dedicated citizenry. As such, it is far too substantial to be erased with the removal of one person and too complex to be regarded as anything less than a new kind of state.

Beyond al Qaeda

For terrorist organizations, new media provide increasing numbers of opportunities to reach a global audience. Instead of using clearinghouses to mail videos—a process that law enforcement was able to disrupt—these groups now rely on pirated video-editing software and Web sites on which material may be uploaded for their followers to access. Web sites feature items such as the 118-page "Comprehensive Security Encyclopedia," which was posted in 2007 with detailed instructions about improving Internet and telephone security, purchasing weapons, handling explosives, transferring funds to jihadist groups, and other useful hints.[41]

One of the masters of this craft was Younis Tsouli, a young Moroccan whose nom de cyber-guerre was Irhabi007. Tsouli provided technical skills needed by al Qaeda after it was forced to leave Afghanistan and establish an online headquarters and by al-Zarqawi when he used the Internet as part of his war plan in Iraq. Tsouli was adroit at tasks such as hacking into servers that he then used to distribute large video files. (One of his hacking victims was the computer system of the Arkansas Highway and Transportation Department.) Arrested in London in 2005 and sent to prison by a British court in 2007, Tsouli understood the Internet's effectiveness in reaching potential recruits for al Qaeda's cause. The importance of this was acknowledged in the 2006 U.S. National Intelligence Estimate: "The radicalization process is occurring more quickly, more widely, and more anonymously in the Internet age, raising the likelihood of surprise attacks by unknown groups whose members and supporters may be difficult to pinpoint."[42]

By mid-2007 Islamist Web sites were broadening their agendas. "Media jihad" included entering online forums with large American audiences in order to influence "the views of the weak-minded American" who "is an idiot and does not know where Iraq is." The "weak-minded" were to be targeted with videos showing American troops under fire and with false messages purportedly from American soldiers and their families lamenting their involvement in the Iraq war. The Islamist Web forums also featured information gleaned from Western news reports, such as poll results showing lack of public support for the war, and occasionally information about weapons systems that found its way into news stories.[43]

Beyond the material directly addressing warfare, the Islamist Web sites devote much of their content to ideological and cultural issues that are at the heart of efforts to win the support of young Muslims. Given the assumption that this war will be a long one, cultivating the next generation is seen by the jihadists as crucial to their eventual success. Perhaps the greatest danger related to these messages is the inadequacy of the responses to them.

Even a flawed argument has appeal when it is allowed to stand in an intellectual vacuum. Recognizing that and acting on it in a sophisticated, comprehensive way is the task that must be undertaken by moderate Muslims and non-Muslims who do not believe that prolonged conflict is inevitable. New media will be indispensable in doing this.

6

The Cyber-struggle for Democracy

The quest for democratization during the late twentieth and early twenty-first centuries has produced some stunning moments: the lone man standing in front of a tank at Tiananmen Square; celebrations at the Berlin Wall; hundreds of thousands of demonstrators protesting unfair elections on the streets of Belgrade and Kiev; women going to the polls in Kuwait. Democracy has grown in quieter ways, as well: governments have agreed to become more transparent and more representative; elections have replaced edicts; debate has begun to occur publicly rather than in hidden corners. These triumphs, large and small, produced ripple effects as the world learned about them through words and pictures that swept across the globe. Others who wanted to pursue their own democratic goals were encouraged as they gathered news from television and computer screens and then used various tools— e-mail, Web sites, text messaging—to organize their own efforts.

At the heart of all this is communication of unprecedented speed and pervasiveness that can disseminate information and pull people together. As part of the machinery of democracy, new media help to restructure the balance between those who govern and those who are governed. Jon Alterman observed, "Governments have lost the near monopoly they used to enjoy over certain kinds of information, and as a result they have less ability to direct domestic politics. The traditional tools of government information ministries, censorship, and propaganda are withering, and governments must create new strategies and tools to cope with the new environment."[1]

Shanthi Kalathil and Taylor Boas have predicted that in certain Arab states the Internet "will complement many other, more longstanding potential forces for liberalization: greater contact with the outside world through tourism and travel, more integration with the global economy, and the increasingly modern outlook of a youthful population." They also noted, however, that "the authoritarian state is hardly obsolete in the era of the Internet. In fact, the state plays a crucial role in charting the development of the Internet in authoritarian regimes and in conditioning the ways it is used by societal, economic, and political actors. Through proactive policies such as instituting e-government and wiring key industries, authoritarian regimes can guide the development of the Internet so that it serves state-defined goals and priorities." In Cuba, for example, "authorities have carefully planned out the diffusion of the Internet within their country, controlling the medium's pace of development and the sectors in which Internet access is granted. Cuban authorities seek control over the Internet not through a massive, centralized censorship mechanism but rather by denying Internet access where it could be potentially subversive."[2]

A realistic appraisal of authoritarian management of communication is important because it underscores the need to be cautious when considering the alluring but in some ways unrealistic technology-creates-democracy formula. Building democracy is always a struggle and even governments in relatively free countries may resist the expansion of democratic processes. Obstacles can be devised to limit the effects of almost every technological innovation. Reporters Without Borders issues an annual report about how governments interfere with Internet freedom, and the 2006 report listed twenty-four countries (including the United States) plus the European Union as being at fault. Their alleged offenses ranged from providing too few privacy guarantees for Net users in the United States to banning Web-based e-mail and spying on what Internet café customers are viewing in Burma. Other obstructions cited in the report include laws requiring registration of all online publications, intimidation of bloggers, and—the most common tactic—blocking access to Web content that a government considers politically or culturally objectionable.³

The new technologies—particularly those that are Internet-based—are so irresistible that even many of the governments that restrict online communication are unwilling to shut them down entirely. In these countries, observed Shanthi Kalathil, "although other programs censor and spread propaganda, e-government initiatives that reshape bureaucracy, dispense education and health information, and increase direct communication between officials and the public actually improve the quality of life for citizens and boost transparency. Understanding these distinct effects of technology is crucial for those interested in using the Internet effectively to increase political liberalization and improve governance in closed societies." Further, she noted, "if cash-strapped authoritarian states wish to tap the global economy, they will face growing pressure to permit private investment and market-led development within Internet sectors."⁴

Reporters Without Borders has cited Singapore, for example, for pressuring bloggers who criticize the government, but Singapore also has one of the world's most sophisticated online government programs. The government presents its online portal as "a unified customer-centric gateway to Government information on four different segments:

○ the Government segment which provides updates about Singapore and the government,

○ the eCitizen segment which provides information and services for Singaporean citizens and permanent residents,

○ the Business segment which offers access to business services, and

○ the Non-Resident segment which offers foreign visitors information about visiting, relocating, working or studying in Singapore."

The Singapore sites are so comprehensive that they have become indispensable parts of everyday life. The eCitizen site provides information about finding housing and medical care, adopting a child, reporting a crime, and even getting married: "This section will help you move towards 'I do' and beyond, easily," it promises.[5]

Given such evidence of benefits for citizens, Kalathil argued, "Rather than treating the Internet as an innately liberating tool that, if unleashed in closed societies, will release a tide of opposition sentiment, policy makers should identify and support specific actions and Internet policies that are likely to promote openness in authoritarian countries."[6] This suggestion is worth incorporating in policy planning, although it should not be taken so far as to undercut efforts to use new media to aid true democratic reform.

While governments design sophisticated online environments to enhance their hold on power, people in the streets may still use short message services (SMS) such as cell phone text messaging to deliver information or organize protests. In South Korea in 2002, e-mails and text messages sent to 800,000 voters on Election Day probably affected the outcome of the presidential voting that elected Roh Moo Hyun. In China in 2004, twelve thousand workers used SMS to mobilize for a strike against a manufacturer. Unlike the Internet, which can be monitored, cell phones used in concert overwhelm attempts at surveillance. They allow their users to deliver messages freely and so have particular value as anti-establishment political tools.[7]

The path toward democratization is never straight or smooth, and media can do only so much to make traveling that path easier. Although information and communication technology is not a panacea, it can provide increasingly significant impetus for local, regional, and global reform. The Internet—to consider just one facet of new media—is changing society in ways that might be taken for granted by those who have become dependent on it. Its transformative effect is far greater than that of television when it was coming of age in the 1950s and 1960s, and its many functions and interactive capabilities make judging its impact a more complex task. Add to the Internet the cell phone, satellite television, and other ICT devices, and the political effects of current and prospective societal connectivity can fuel the imaginations of activists for years to come.

China: The Giant Laboratory

As with many statistics about China's modernization, the numbers about communications are staggering. From 2002 into 2006 the number of Internet-connected computers more than doubled, to 46 million. The number of Internet users increased to 137 million by the end of 2006 and reached 210 million by the end of 2007, which put China second to the United States in that category. By late 2007 more than 75 percent of Chinese Internet users had broadband, up from 7 percent in 2002. Search engines were receiving more than 360 million requests each day, computer-to-computer messaging was being used by 87 million people, and the number of blogs went from near zero to anywhere from 15 to 30 million, depending on the estimate, in three years. During the same period, mobile phone accounts doubled, pushing past 400 million, more than in any other country.[8]

A new economic sector developed around those providing service and content to all these high-tech customers. Sina, the most popular Net portal, offered its 95 million registered visitors in 2004 links to Korean companies for online gambling and to Yahoo for auctions. It reported a US$31 million profit on US$114 million in revenues. Sohu, another portal, has garnered large profits by sending Internet content to its customers' cell phones. Among the other offerings from China's growing ranks of online entrepreneurs are Shanda, which emphasizes online gaming and reported having nearly 19 million paying accounts in 2005, and Linktone, which provides, games, cartoons, and horoscopes to cell phone customers.[9]

This technological progress fits in well with China's development as one of the world's great economic and political powers. Countries that lag behind in these areas, such as many in the Middle East, consign themselves to the lower tiers of global influence. Ideally, when so many people have so many ways to communicate and gather information, democracy should gain traction. Governments, however, can try to impede this process, and depending on how sophisticated and determined their efforts are, they can at least temporarily derail technology-based democratization. Among the nations employing antidemocracy tactics, China is sadly noteworthy for the vigor it has displayed in using pervasive controls.

The Chinese government's actions may have been stimulated in part by optimistic predictions from around the world that new media would encourage open dissent and lead to rapid expansion of democracy in China. Those judgments failed to adequately consider China's political reality—most of those in power do not want democracy, except in ways that they define and control.

The government's tactics have produced mixed results. In 2000 President Bill Clinton said that China's efforts to restrict Internet use were "sort of like trying to nail Jell-O to the wall." A 2002 RAND report found, however, that "the Chinese government has successfully stifled the spread of Internet-based dissent primarily by employing old 'Leninist techniques' [that] include strict government regulations, surveillance, arrests, confiscation of equipment, and the use of informants. . . . There also is evidence that the Chinese government is using the Internet for its own political purposes, spreading criticism of dissidents electronically and bombarding dissidents' e-mail addresses with thousands of bogus messages."[10]

Among the targets for censors have been online news discussion groups, which provided forums for well-known experts about social and political issues and encouraged public comments about matters that state-controlled media touched on softly, if at all. Unfettered discussion of news is free speech and a fundamental democratic activity, which means that from the Chinese government's standpoint it is dangerous and needs to be stopped, particularly when it draws a huge following, as many of these sites did. In February 2004 the government enacted rules banning independent reporting that hadn't been approved by the government, discussion of sensitive issues such as economic problems, and Web postings that criticized the Communist Party. Searches for some sites that featured political opinion elicited the message, "This page cannot be found," and attempts to post comments were met with the warning, "This Web site now has a pre-checking system. Your published messages will have to be checked by management personnel before being seen by other viewers."[11]

A further measure aimed at influencing online discussion is the planting of topics by government-directed monitors. At Shanghai Normal University in 2006, five hundred students were working on a project named "Let the Winds of a Civilized Internet Blow," which was part of a larger "socialist morality" campaign. These monitors, without revealing their official role, steered online discussions toward topics and opinions approved by the government.[12]

Chinese officials have been inconsistent in their efforts to control the Internet because they must deal with conflicting priorities. Their first instinct was to block online access to news sources such as the *New York Times* and the BBC. This action was a relatively minor nuisance because Chinese Internet users could often access the same information by going to other sites. But then the government began periodically barring access to search engines, such as Google, which are essential tools for finding online information. This seemed a good way to keep people away from news about the religious group Falun Gong, the Dalai Lama, and other topics that the government did not want the public talking about or even thinking about. In early 2007 President Hu Jintao was reported to have told a Politburo study session, "Whether we can cope with the Internet is a matter that affects the development of socialist culture, the security of information, and the stability of the state." He said that development of Web usage should not be deterred but should be done in ways that would "nurture a healthy online culture."[13]

About three-quarters of China's Internet traffic is carried by ChinaNet, which is owned by the state telephone company, China Telecom, and all Net traffic in China must pass through gateways—banks of government computers—where e-mail and Web searches can be monitored. This makes it easy for the government to control the connections between ChinaNet and the global Web; routers, like railroad switches, can be programmed to reject incoming data from certain sites. Filters catch certain search terms—"dissident," "independent Taiwan," and the like—and direct the searches to government-approved sites. In addition to this computer-driven censorship, Chinese authorities employ more than thirty thousand people to monitor Web sites and search out politically "unacceptable" content.[14]

Given the vastness of the Chinese bureaucracy, these mechanics of obstruction are not difficult to deploy, at least until computer wizards devise detours around the government's obstacles. But the problem the Chinese government soon encountered was the international business community's reaction when corporate representatives trying to work online in China ran into government-imposed obstacles. Many of these men and women consider Internet access to be a matter of entitlement, and they expect that they and their employees will be able to conduct searches and freely use their computers for other online work. This is so essential to doing business that they quickly made the government aware that China's role in the global marketplace would be constricted if such barriers were maintained.

China wants to be a global player, not a walled-off bastion like North Korea, where the government can act without concern about deterring investment or otherwise antagonizing the international business community. So, although Chinese government decision making is not shaped by devotion to democratic ideals, it is somewhat constrained by global economic realities that make impractical the most draconian blockages of Internet access. Fareed Zakaria observed, "China's Communist Party elites—like all modernizing autocrats—believe that they can manage this balancing act, mixing economic liberalization with political control." Their role model, wrote Zakaria, is Singapore's former prime minister Lee Kuan Yew, who "achieved the dream of every strongman: to modernize the economy, even the society of his country, but not the politics."[15] Lee was an exception, able to reach modernity while delaying some aspects of democracy. China has even grander ambitions and will be tested as it tries to resist powerful forces of global change.

According to a report prepared by Harvard's Berkman Center for Internet and Society, China's Internet filtering regime is "the most sophisticated effort of its kind in the world." If you are a Chinese Internet user and post a message with "democracy" or another word or phrase in the subject line that irritates officialdom, you are likely to receive a warning: "This message contains a banned expression. Please delete." As they control the flow of information in this way, Chinese authorities have not had to work on their own. They have enlisted powerful accomplices, some from the United States. Microsoft altered its blog tool, MSN Space, to assist the Chinese government. Yahoo has limited its searches to exclude politically sensitive results. Cisco Systems has sold equipment to China that will block online access to particular Web sites and pages within certain sites.[16]

The non-Chinese companies that are involved in such activity generally say that they try to juggle values and business interests. Yahoo responded to criticism about its work in China by claiming that it seeks to "balance legal requirements against our strong belief that our active involvement in China contributes to the continued modernization of the country." Google has tailored its search capabilities to meet the Chinese government's demands, and one of its executives defended this by saying, "We are all very aware that entering China requires us to balance two specific needs: the needs of our users and the need of operating within a political climate and a set of government regulations, as we do elsewhere in the world." (The precedence of national law is nothing new for international online business. Since 2000 Yahoo and eBay have conformed to laws in Germany and elsewhere that prohibit sale of Nazi memorabilia and other hate-related material.)[17]

A case can be made, however, that some media organizations have foregone balance and have abandoned values in furtherance of their business dealings in China. Star TV, part of Rupert Murdoch's News Corporation, cut the BBC from its north Asian schedule and HarperCollins, also part of News Corporation, dropped a book by Chris Patten, Britain's last governor of Hong Kong and a nemesis of China's communist leadership. This was a noteworthy retreat by Murdoch, who in 1993 proudly declared that satellite television posed an "unambiguous threat to totalitarian regimes everywhere." By 2005 Murdoch was talking and acting differently, collaborating with China's national broadcaster, CCTV, as part of News Corporation's efforts to secure the huge profits that await within China's media markets.[18]

Cooperating with the Chinese government puts technology and media companies on a slippery slope. In 2005 Shi Tao, a

Chinese journalist, was sentenced to ten years in prison for "disseminating state secrets abroad." Shi's "crime" was to e-mail his notes about an editor warning journalists that no coverage would be allowed of any events marking the fifteenth anniversary of the 1989 Tiananmen Square massacre. The prosecution relied partly on information linking Shi's e-mail to his telephone number, details of which were given to the government by a Yahoo subsidiary. Several months after Shi's trial, Yahoo spent a billion dollars for a 40 percent share of Alibaba.com, China's biggest e-commerce company. This was the largest single foreign investment in China's Internet sector and certainly would not have been approved unless the Chinese government was well disposed toward Yahoo.[19]

Whatever rationales the companies involved might offer, this complicity with the Chinese government's obstruction of speech has a bad smell to it. Based on such cases, the notion that new information and communication technologies would speed the march toward democracy seems little more than fantasy. On the basic level of providing more accurate and thorough news to the public—which is another way to aid democratization—further problems have arisen.

The 2002 outbreak of severe acute respiratory syndrome (SARS) saw the Chinese government tie itself in knots as it tried to control information about the virus. Although by the beginning of February 2003 nine hundred people were ill with SARS in Guangzhou (45 percent of them health care workers), regional Communist Party officials continued to ban news coverage about the disease. The public learned about the outbreak through a terse text message sent on February 8 to mobile phones: "There is a fatal flu in Guangzhou." During the next three days, that message was resent 126 million times, and Internet chat rooms and e-mail messages also spread the word. On February 11 the *Guangzhou Daily* received permission from the provincial governor to run a story about SARS and report that 305 people had been infected and five had died.

But this did not mean that news organizations could cover the story fully. When the World Health Organization (WHO) issued its first global warning about the virus on March 15, China's propaganda ministry ordered Chinese news media not to report the story. Nevertheless, word spread among the Chinese public, primarily through text messaging, a medium popular among Chinese because it is relatively uncensored. (During the first quarter of 2003, the Chinese sent 26.5 billion text messages to each other. By 2007, the number of Chinese using instant messaging had reached 170 million.)

When China's health minister, in response to a WHO travel advisory about SARS, said at a news conference, "SARS has been placed under control," an angry surgeon in Beijing sent e-mails to two Chinese television channels saying that he knew of more than one hundred SARS cases and six deaths just in Beijing. Although neither channel followed up on the tip, it was leaked to *Time* magazine, which posted its report on its Web site. Some Chinese readers translated the *Time* story and other Western articles about SARS and e-mailed them throughout China. One Chinese official told the *Washington Post*, "We got our information from the Web and the Web said the government's information was fake. The first thing we all did when we got to the office was log on and read what the government said and then read what the foreign media said. They had created a situation like this: If you don't speak the truth, people will start believing foreigners. So the government had to change."[20]

That change happened, but slowly. China's new president, Hu Jintao, and premier, Wen Jiabao, pressured officials to provide more information. Finally, the two leaders told officials at a Politburo meeting to stop lying about the extent of the SARS epidemic and demanded sweeping public action to fight the spread of the disease. These orders were immediately printed and broadcast by Chinese media. Several days later, the health minister and the mayor of Beijing were fired for their roles in the cover up.

China's leaders may have learned from this case that they would not be able to hold back the tide of information. No longer could they expect to fully control news content by telling a finite number of print and broadcast executives what they could and could not deliver to the public. The combination of text messaging within China and access (even if limited) to international news sources meant that delivery of information could not be stopped. Nevertheless, Chinese officials were far from embracing openness. Just a month after President Hu ordered the media to tell the truth about SARS, authorities arrested more than a hundred people for sending "rumors" in text messages. It apparently did not matter that many of the rumors were true.[21]

Clamping down on new media continued after the SARS crisis. In December 2003 in Heilongjiang province a woman accused a farmer and his wife of having scratched her BMW automobile with their cart. She yelled at the farmer, his wife, and a group of peasants, and then drove her car into them, killing the farmer's wife and injuring twelve other people. When she received a suspended sentence for an "accidental traffic disturbance" from the usually harsh courts, rumors spread that she was politically well connected. The story became a hot topic on Internet news discussion sites and Sina.com reported 200,000 e-mails about the case, 90 percent of which said the sentence was too light. The provincial governor felt compelled to publicly deny that he was related to the driver and other officials promised to reopen the case. But the government also told news organizations to drop the subject and quickly moved to shut down some Internet chat rooms where the case was a hot topic. After an investigation, the initial court judgment was upheld.[22]

Unlike the SARS story, which had global economic ramifications, this case did not have direct consequences for the national government. In the days before the pervasive presence of new media, the government would have acted behind closed doors to deal with the BMW driver one way or the other. The public would have learned nothing or only what the government wanted to tell them. But now those closed doors can be forced open, or at least eavesdroppers can often find ways to listen to whatever is going on behind them.

The government's unease is justifiable in some respects because "online justice" can quickly become "online injustice." Many e-mails attacking the court's handling of the BMW case were based on hearsay, and rumors flowed freely. Most of the Chinese government lacks the flexibility required for responding to public debate of this kind.

In another case, an online literary discussion in December

2005 attracted thousands of postings. The topic was an essay, "In Memory of Miss Liu Hezhen," written in 1926 by the great Chinese author Lu Xun after one of his students was killed during a demonstration in front of Government House in Beijing. In his essay, Lu Xun had written, "The history of mankind's battle forward through bloodshed is like the formation of coal, where a great deal of wood is needed to produce a small amount of coal. But petitions do not serve any purpose, especially peaceful ones. Since blood was shed, however, the affair will naturally make itself more felt."

That a work published almost eighty years earlier should generate so much discussion may at first have seemed odd, but soon it became clear that the long ago event in Beijing was serving as a proxy for a more recent incident. Several days earlier, Chinese police had fired on farmers protesting land seizures in Dongzhou, reportedly killing as many as twenty people. The government ordered mainstream media not to report about the event and told Internet sites to censor any mention of it. Keywords such as "Dongzhou" were banned from search engines.

Despite the government's attempt to stifle discussion about the incident, one bulletin board site received more than thirty thousand messages reflecting anger and grief about the killings. Administrators of the site deleted these messages several days later. An editor of the site posted a note apologizing to those who had posted the messages and promised to tell "the authorities in charge" about the outpouring of protest.

In the face of such obstacles, Internet users have become adept at devising creative ways around restrictions; hence the discussion of Lu Xun's essay. One of the participants said that authorities probably understood what was going on: "It's not a crime to talk about Lu Xun, but it's a form of protest." Eight well-known dissidents posted an open letter condemning the Dongzhou shooting on Bokee, China's largest blogging site. It was deleted just twelve hours after it appeared. The writers then posted just the title, "A Statement Regarding the Murder Case in Dongzhou," and their own names, assuming that people who saw the title without additional content would track down the entire letter elsewhere on the Web. The Bokee administrators, worried that they would appear so compliant with official censorship that they would alienate their customers, let this abbreviated version remain.

The government's monitors directed most of their attention to the largest Web sites, so many of the protests about Dongzhou were posted on smaller sites. They remained accessible there for a while, but then the censors, alerted by the amount of traffic going to those sites, blocked access to them as well.[23]

These cases reflect the government's determination to control news and the comparable determination of many Chinese to find information. Although it has deployed massive numbers of monitors and censors, the government has not been able to plug every leak or counteract every technology-based maneuver that resolute citizens have used as they search for truth. Saying that one side or the other is "winning" would be simplistic and pointless; the tug-of-war will continue indefinitely.

As this struggle proceeds, technology experts on both sides constantly enhance the skills they will pit against each other. SafeWeb, a private, U.S.-based company (which received CIA funding), created proxy server software, Triangle Boy, which by 2001 was making available proxy servers that the Chinese censors could not immediately find. Chinese Internet users received daily e-mails listing the latest addresses of the Triangle Boy servers, through which they could connect to sites banned by Chinese authorities. The software encrypts the data transmitted between an individual's computer and Web sites that the person accesses, in effect deceiving firewalls and other blocking mechanisms.[24]

Recently, the use of proxy sites has become more common. A censored site, such as Voice of America (voanews.com), sets up a proxy site with an address that the Chinese government has not put on its no-access list. Then mass e-mails are sent to alert Chinese Web users about the uncensored addresses. The Chinese users can then connect to these sites and proceed farther into the Web. When Chinese officials identify the new sites—often within a few days—new proxy sites are set up and the process recycles.[25]

While this cat-and-mouse game proceeds and access to many Internet sites remains problematic, a more intense competition is under way as bloggers match wits with regulators. Li Xinde, a blogger who posts investigative reporting about official corruption, said that he relies on "what Chairman Mao called sparrow tactics. You stay small and independent, you move around a lot, and you choose when to strike and when to run." His stories have included reports about a deputy mayor of Jining who was accused of stealing $400,000, an abduction of a young woman by family planning officials, and the mysterious death of a businessman who was involved in a financial dispute with a police official. Li makes a modest living from contributions provided by well-wishers and by reporters who have used his blog as a source of leads for their own work.[26]

In March 2006 the blogs of Beijing-based journalist Wang Xiaofeng and Guangzhou's Yuan Lei were ordered shut down. Their satirical commentaries had attracted large numbers of readers. Wang's site was visited more than 10 million times, and when it was closed a message on the site said, "Because of unavoidable reasons known to all, this blog is now temporarily closed."[27]

This was not much of a victory for the state. Individual blogs might be shut down, but unless authorities begin jailing thousands of bloggers, the offending blogs will just pop up again with new names or otherwise thinly disguised. With thousands of new blogs appearing every day, even the vast Chinese regulatory bureaucracy is overmatched, so the government gives blog-hosting companies lists of banned words and lets them enforce the rules.

The lack of clear instructions sometimes leads these companies to censor more rigorously than even the government would, particularly when the hosts have larger business interests at stake. In December 2005 Microsoft's MSN Spaces, a blogging platform, shut down the blog of journalist Zhao Jing, who used the online name "Michael Anti" and wrote about issues such as the government's firing editors at a progressive Beijing newspaper.[28] Zhao had previously told other bloggers that Microsoft would not risk having its entire blogging service—which hosted 3.3 million blogs in China—shut down and would "sell me out" by deleting his site if pressured by the government. He wrote about his blog, which he had begun in late 2004, "Most blogs were diaries of entertainment, but I wanted to do something different. I wanted to produce a high-quality blog about politics, like a column, with each entry good enough to publish in a newspaper or magazine." He used strong headlines, compelling photos, and ads on Google to attract readers, and he addressed the Iraq War, democracy in Taiwan, and other controversial topics.

Meanwhile, Microsoft was carefully preparing its entry into the Chinese blogging market, entering into a partnership with a state-owned investment firm run by the son of former president Jiang Zemin. Although MSN Spaces prevented bloggers from using certain words, such as "freedom" and "democracy" in their blog titles, the Microsoft software lured many bloggers. After Zhao switched to this service, his readership more than doubled to fifteen thousand every day.

When Zhao's commentary became too pointed, the government complained to Microsoft and told the company to remove his blog because bloggers were barred from writing about "political, economic, military, or diplomatic news." After this occurred, Zhao, who had worked as a researcher for Chinese bureaus of the *Washington Post* and the *New York Times*, kept writing, using an overseas site that the Chinese government tried to block.[29] He was still there for his readers, if they could find him, somewhere in cyberspace.

On several occasions, *New York Times* columnist Nicholas Kristof has tested the Chinese censors. In 2005 he wrote in a Chinese-language chat room, "If Chinese on the other side of the Taiwan Strait can choose their leaders, why can't we choose our leaders?" His comment remained posted for ten minutes, until a monitor saw and removed it. Then Kristof tried a more subtle comment: "Under the Communist Party's great leadership, China has changed tremendously. I wonder if in 20 years the party will introduce competing parties, because that could benefit us greatly." That clearly advocates a multiparty system, but the censors did not remove it; who would want to challenge the notion of "the Communist Party's great leadership"? A year later Kristof started a blog, written in Chinese, on two Chinese host services. On it he posted a series of provocative messages: he denounced the imprisonment of his *New York Times* colleague Zhao Yan, who had been charged with disclosing state secrets (an allegation wrapped in more than usual official obfuscation); he called for

President Hu Jintao to publicly disclose his financial assets; he asked, "Why can't we discuss Falun Gong?"; and he described how he had seen the Chinese army fire on protestors at Tiananmen Square on June 4, 1989. All his postings remained in full, except for asterisks replacing the Chinese characters for "Falun" and "June 4."

The longevity of Kristof's postings does not signal the Chinese government's new commitment to openness. As Kristof observed, "The Internet is just too big and complex for State Security to control, and so the Web is beginning to assume the watchdog role filled by the news media in freer countries." The persistent blogger Li Xinde told Kristof, "They can keep closing sites, but they never catch up. You can't stop the Yellow River from flowing, and you can't block the bloggers."[30]

That does not mean that the Chinese government will stop trying. In January 2006, when Google introduced a Chinese version of its search engine—Google.cn—it agreed to accept guidance from Chinese officials about blocking content the government deems objectionable. Google wants to get a large share of the quickly growing market that will have hundreds of millions of prospective customers. Google executives characterized the censorship agreement as excruciating but offered a justification common among businesses seeking entry into the Chinese market: "We firmly believe, with our culture of innovation, Google can make meaningful and positive contributions to the already impressive pace of development in China."[31]

Perhaps so, but the Google concessions were in line with China's increasingly sophisticated and comprehensive regulatory measures, codified as the Provisions on the Administration of Internet News Information Services, which were promulgated in September 2005. According to the OpenNet Initiative, a collaborative venture of four universities in Britain, Canada, and the United States, the three most significant changes implemented in the 2005 rules were

> adding categories of prohibited news Web site content (inciting illegal assemblies or conducting activities on behalf of illegal civil organizations), banning non-government

opinion and analysis pieces, and greatly increasing requirements for individuals and small groups posting news. The
two new categories of banned material aim to discourage
use of the Internet for political organization and mobilization, which are viewed by the Chinese state as subversive.
Thus, for example, the increasing use of mobile phone messaging to organize protests not only violates these new
regulations, but also falls under several established categories of prohibited content: harming the interests of the
nation, disrupting the solidarity of peoples, and disrupting
national policies, at least. Rather than changing the legality
of using the Internet for 'subversive' organization, these new
regulations fortify state control over expression on the
Internet and serve as a powerful reminder and warning
against using the Internet for purposes the state views as
threatening.[32]

Enforcement of such regulations has been inconsistent as
Chinese authorities, mildly concerned about world opinion (at
least in terms of its impact on China's economy), have tried to
maintain control while nurturing an image of kinder and gentler
authoritarianism. That concern has not deterred occasional clo-
sures of news providers. In January 2006 authorities suspended
publication of Freezing Point, a well-known weekly section of
the state-run *China Youth Daily*. Articles in Freezing Point frequently challenged the party line and publication was halted after
it published a piece criticizing history textbooks used in middle
schools. The government then barred Chinese news media from
reporting the shutdown and ordered that Web sites not carry any
discussion about it. When Freezing Point's editor confirmed the
suspension on his blog, censors deleted the blog page.
    The story continued. More than two dozen liberal party of-
ficials, academics, and writers protested the closure as word of
the government's action swept through cybernews venues. A
month after shutting down Freezing Point, the government allowed it to resume publication, but without its two top editors
and with an article criticizing the author of the earlier piece about
the history textbooks.[33]

This war of attrition will probably continue indefinitely as censors create new measures to try to control the steadily increasing flow of information and providers create still more ways to disseminate that information. Larger issues about China's political future are affected by this contentiousness. Freedom of expression inevitably leads to freedom of political action, which is what the Chinese government really fears.

This bubbles up periodically. For more than a decade, the Internet has been home to growing Chinese cybernationalism. According to Xu Wu, "Chinese cyber nationalists have been utilizing the Internet as a communication center, organizational platform, and execution channel to promote nationalistic causes." Beginning in 2003, this movement has emphasized anti-Japanese activity. In 2003 an online campaign against Japan's bid to become a permanent member of the UN Security Council gathered more than 40 million signatures. In 2005 large anti-Japan protests in major Chinese cities were organized mainly through online and cell phone networks. Routes for protest marches were posted online and forwarded by e-mail and text messages. Video footage of violence occurring during the protests in Shanghai was banned from regular news outlets but could be found on the Internet. The government also became involved in this process when local police in Shanghai sent a mass text message to cell phone users the night before the protest saying, "We ask people to express your patriotic passion through the right channel, following the laws and maintaining order." Whether that was a warning or encouragement was unclear. Finally, the central government ordered Web sites to filter out anti-Japanese content.[34]

When considering prospects for democracy in China, it is important not to rely on sweeping declarations such as "the Chinese government is unfailingly antidemocratic and oppressive" and "the Chinese public is progressive and wants to be more like the democratic West." It may be that the democratic instincts of the Chinese people are overrated by people outside China. Fareed Zakaria observed, "When speaking about dissent in China, it is easy to believe that more democracy would mean more liberty. In fact, in the short term, the opposite is true. The Chinese government on many important issues is more liberal than its people.

. . . On a wide range of issues, from law and order to attitudes regarding Taiwan, Japan, and the United States, the Beijing regime is less populist, nationalist, aggressive, and intolerant than its people."[35]

And so, the new China continues to take shape as thousands of years of tradition mesh with technologies that evolve from day to day. "Free expression" of the breadth that is possible today is unprecedented in Chinese political culture, which is one reason that the country's leadership remains so cautious as it evaluates the effects of new media. Along with economic growth, political change will continue in China, driven partly by these new media. But the government will continue to allow real progress only at a carefully measured pace.

Change, and Lack of Change, Elsewhere

Governments more repressive than China's devote much effort to blocking information flowing into their countries from various directions.

The Democratic Voice of Burma (DVB), a satellite television channel based in Norway, supports Aung San Suu Kyi, the Nobel Peace Prize–winning leader of opposition to the country's military leaders, and carries news about her while she remains under house arrest in Rangoon. For much of its coverage of Burma,[36] the station recruits clandestine reporters to tape footage and smuggle it to a neighboring country, and from there it is sent to the editorial headquarters in Oslo. Burmese students living in Europe began the radio version of DVB in 1992 after Burma's military junta nullified results of an election won by the opposition. For a time, the Burmese government jammed the radio station's transmissions but relented because, says a station editor, "They wanted to get real information, even about their own country. They cannot rely on reports from their subordinates, so they have to listen to our radio to get real information or to measure the feeling of the grassroots people."[37]

Satellite dishes are legal only if licensed, and watching DVB is officially banned. But people still watch it. In addition to surreptitiously receiving the satellite broadcasts, Burmese with Internet access (only about 64,000 out of a population of 47 million) can get news from DVB online (www.dvb.no) and burmanet.org, although the government has been able to obstruct access to such sites. Among the stories carried on burmanet during August 2006 was a report about the military government's decision to block Google's mail and messenger services.

Efforts to control new media are not surprising. As Reporters Without Borders notes, Burma is

> a paradise for censors. Scissors in hand, the agents of the Press Scrutiny and Registration Division check every article, editorial, cartoon, advertisement and illustration ahead of publication. In 2005, they even began going through death notices placed in Burmese newspapers. They strike out all references to the United Nations, accused of wanting to overthrow the government. More seriously, the authorities censor all independent news on the bird flu epidemic. . . . In Burma, a journalist can earn a seven-year prison sentence simply for having an unauthorized fax, video camera, modem or a copy of a banned publication.[38]

Burma ranks with countries such as Cuba, Libya, Turkmenistan, and North Korea as among the world's worst in terms of press freedom. But information from space and cyberspace—via satellite and the Internet—does penetrate the country. Whether it will have measurable impact on Burma's political rigidity is another matter. When a government is firmly in control and harshly limits freedom—including barring access to information—news media may create a few waves, but that is far from being enough to capsize a country's rulers.

Burma's military leaders might be further convinced that their controls are wise if they look at the outcome of the 2002 elections in far more liberal South Korea. With about 70 percent of the population online—and most using broadband—South Koreans turned increasingly to Internet news providers rather than conservative newspapers for campaign coverage. The most popular of the online news organizations was OhmyNews, which near Election Day registered 20 million page views a day. (The country's population is 49 million.)

OhmyNews showed its willingness to challenge the political establishment in its extensive coverage of the incident in 2002 in which two Korean schoolgirls were crushed by a U.S. armored vehicle on patrol. The OhmyNews reporting was credited with pushing the mainstream press to report more thoroughly about the case, which otherwise it would probably have covered lightly. This coverage was followed by large demonstrations against the U.S. military presence in the country.[39]

The beneficiary of all this was Roh Moo Hyun, the reform candidate for president, who won an upset victory in December 2002. OhmyNews accelerated dissatisfaction with the political status quo, and this, coupled with more conventional campaign factors, helped Roh win a narrow victory over a more conservative opponent.

By focusing on stories that usually were not thoroughly covered by other news organizations and by enlisting "citizen journalists," OhmyNews transformed the media environment and gave a boost to those who embraced similarly anti-establishment politics. This cannot happen everywhere; without fundamental media freedom such iconoclastic news coverage would quickly be suppressed. The contrast between South Korea and countries such as Burma is stark.

But even when press freedom is not as solidly established as it is in South Korea, new media may push the political process toward greater openness and integrity. This could be seen in Georgia, where the peaceful "Rose Revolution" brought tentative democracy to a former Soviet republic. On election night in November 2003, Georgia's Rustavi-2 television ran a crawl showing the official voting results, according to which the in-power party, led by President Eduard Shevardnadze, was winning. Beside those numbers ran reports about exit polling and the returns as counted by independent, Western-funded monitors, which showed a clear victory for the opposition. Above the numbers Rustavi carried live images of demonstrators pouring into Tbilisi to denounce the rigged election. Opposition leaders, brandishing roses, eventually made their way into the parliament building and Shevardnadze relinquished power.[40]

This process illustrated the attributes of "soft power."

Complementing the Georgians' media efforts, the United States, European governments, and NGOs aided the reformers with encouragement and money, not coercive muscle. Georgia's president, Mikheil Saakashvili, said in 2005, "The resources to support change are much wider than to send troops. There is the Internet, TV, NGOs. Americans helped us most by channeling support to free Georgian news media. That was more powerful than 5,000 Marines."[41]

One of the essential ingredients for nonviolent revolution is a civil society substantive enough to sustain independent media that can inform the public and mobilize people who want change. Intervention in the form of financial assistance to media organizations can prove to be money well spent. This was the case in 1999 in Serbia, where the United States spent the equivalent of one dollar per Serb (the population is slightly more than nine million), and European sources also supplied generous support. The real work within Serbia was done by people such as Veran Matic, head of resilient B-92 Radio, but the partnership with Western aid providers enhanced the role of independent Serb media in the ouster of Slobodan Milosevic's regime.

In a case with parallels to the Georgian election, the 2004 Orange Revolution in Ukraine was strengthened through the work of Internet-based newspaper *Pravda Ukraine* and cable television station Channel 5.[42] As Adrian Karatnycky reported, Ukraine's Internet news sites did much to show the public just how corrupt the entrenched government was, partly by disseminating audio recordings that showed how high officials had been engaged in rigging the election. By Election Day in November 2004, 6 million of Ukraine's 48 million citizens had access to the Internet. Many members of this online population lived in Kiev and other major cities, where the protests were the most widespread.[43]

Such examples illustrate the roles of new media in political change. The extent of their effect is situational; media impact depends on other factors, such as the public's willingness to act. Nevertheless, such case histories offer encouragement to those who anticipate increased media influence as these vehicles—particularly those on the Internet—become more pervasive.

Governments throughout the world are not being swept away

by surges of reform; realpolitik does not work that way. Those who hold power continue to try to limit the political influence of new media. The Vietnamese government, for example, has been intent on blocking access to sites related to democracy and political dissidents. The OpenNet Initiative reported in 2006, "Vietnam tries to leverage the Internet to provide economic development and benefit, while simultaneously struggling to limit access to content that might destabilize the Communist state. . . . Among other methods, the state monitors the use of cybercafés and employs filtering of Internet content to control the information its citizens can access online."[44] People using the Internet to collect and disseminate information about democratization have been jailed, and the government has steadily tightened its controls.

This adoption of what might be called the Chinese model has been common in authoritarian states, but controls have also been employed in real or putative democracies. After terrorist bombings in Mumbai that killed more than two hundred people in July 2006, India's Department of Telecommunications ordered the shutdown of seventeen blogs that allegedly carried extremist religious and political content. Without the practiced skills of Internet control such as might be found in China and some other countries, the Indian directive resulted in not just the targeted blogs but also popular sites such as Geocities and Typepad being shut down, despite angry protests from their customers.[45]

Meanwhile, India continues to build its online infrastructure, reaching out to its rural population—700 million farmers. Villages begin with perhaps one personal computer and a power source that includes solar panels hooked up to car batteries that function during frequent power losses. With most Internet connections difficult and expensive, the best plan for these villages is for them to be provided with Wimax technology for wireless broadband access.[46]

The India example illustrates the divided approach to new media by relatively progressive governments. They want to expand their high-tech infrastructure so more of their citizens can benefit from enhanced access to information and communication, but they are wary of the political effects the new media bring with them. Over time, it is likely that governments' efforts to control new media content will prove increasingly futile as advances in technology that aid openness will outstrip blocking techniques.

Until this happens, governments will keep trying to censor media, new and old, but will be met with determined attempts to get information to the public, sometimes by old-fashioned methods. In Nepal in 2005, when the government banned news broadcasts on the nation's independent radio stations, one reporter took a loudspeaker to the top of a three-story building and each evening read the news to an audience of about three hundred gathered in the streets below. In a country that still has few computers and Internet cafés, this was a practical as well as symbolic response to the government's restrictions. (Police did not interfere because the sessions were deemed public meetings, which were legal, rather than newscasts, which were not.)[47]

The Chinese and other governments carefully watch Singapore and Malaysia because these two countries have fostered extensive development of information and communication technologies while not seeing an appreciable diminution of centralized political control, which they had established mainly by using licensing to regulate who is allowed to speak. These governments have sought to balance their interests. Singaporean journalist Cherian George noted, "The Internet's perceived economic value dominated the authorities' policy formulation, subordinating the goal of political control that historically shaped media policy. . . . Rather than abandon their economic dreams for the Internet, the two governments decided to tolerate a lesser degree of political control than they were accustomed to and that continued to prevail in their treatment of other media."

But when Internet content—which is not susceptible to traditional licensing controls—became more bothersome, the governments were not willing to embrace openness and free speech. As George observed,

> Traditionally the two regimes have maintained control partly through coercion, but mainly through hegemonic consensus. Their preferred mode is not routine repression of dissident opinion, but an ideological domination that makes compliance with the regime seem like common

sense. Restricting the range of opinions publicly uttered—by prior restraint of media outlets through licensing—is a key part of this strategy. The governments' failure to apply this mode of control to the Internet, and their resulting need to reach for more coercive methods, should be seen as representing strains on their hegemony.[48]

Following the 9/11 attacks on the United States, the Malaysian and Singaporean governments cracked down on their political opponents, citing plotting by Islamic militants. The mainstream—i.e., state-controlled—media paid little attention to the rights of those arrested, but reported George, "The two countries' alternative media, operating mainly through the Internet, kept these issues alive from the moment the news of the arrests broke. Although not oblivious to the terrorist threat, these media incorporated the perspectives of human rights groups and opposition politicians, or wrote their own editorials to argue that liberty and justice should not be abandoned in the struggle to maintain order."

Among the Singaporean new media organizations is ThinkCentre.org. According to George, "ThinkCentre's Web site developed as an adjunct to traditional offline political activities. Its founders were engaged in the printing of political tracts and the organization of public meetings—two ancient forms of democratic participation." They began the Web site to further mobilize public opinion. ThinkCentre.org is at heart a political venture that, wrote George, practices an "activist journalism abhorred by believers in objective and disinterested reporting."[49] Given the characteristics of new media that have such appeal to organizations such as ThinkCentre, traditional boundaries between journalism and political action will frequently be crossed.

On the journalism side, the Singaporean case indicates that online news products, which can be slippery for regulators to grasp, may take advantage of their relative freedom by becoming more aggressive in their acquisition and delivery of news. This is not always the case, but the instances in which it has occurred offer encouragement to those who hope to see new media foster more vibrant and meaningful journalism that is not merely another vehicle for the establishment's conventional wisdom.

Journalism is one thing; propaganda disguised as journalism is something else. Even governments that generally allow incoming news from throughout the world without restrictions have had to consider the impact of Internet and satellite television messages that are clearly designed to generate hatred. In France in 2004, the French public broadcasting regulator granted a license to Hezbollah-affiliated Al Manar television. To receive the license, Al Manar had to agree "not to incite hate, violence, or discrimination on the basis of race, sex, religion, or nationality." Within a week, however, Al Manar broadcast one report claiming that Israel had spread the AIDS virus and other diseases in Arab countries and another calling for war against Jews and the destruction of Israel.

Given the country's licensing rules, French regulators could not ban the satellite channel immediately. They had to wait until a French court ruled that the operators of French satellite Eutelsat could be ordered to drop Al Manar because the channel had violated its licensing pledge and also violated French antihate laws. After the French ruling against the channel, the European Union, in March 2005, banned all EU countries' satellites from carrying Al Manar.[50]

Totally preventing access to Al Manar or any other information provider is nearly impossible without restricting Internet access, which France and other democracies do not want to do, or knocking out the source itself. Al Manar remained available on the Web and continued to broadcast throughout most of the 2006 Israel-Hezbollah war, despite being targeted by Israeli air strikes. With its population including six million Muslims and 600,000 Jews, France is understandably sensitive to the problems that Al Manar could exacerbate. But the reality of this new technology is such that in France the government can be only partially successful in keeping the station from reaching French audiences, and so policymakers must be prepared to deal with the effects of Hezbollah's message being available.

Aside from pressing political issues such as those central to the Al Manar broadcasts, new media are at the heart of new policy fields in countries trying to catch up to the world's most technologically developed states. Russian president Vladimir Putin has endorsed E-Russia, a project that calls for high-speed Internet that will enhance research, increase productivity, and improve governmental accountability. This is a massive program for Russia, which as recently as 2001 found that only 2 percent of its schools had Internet access and which had no domestic producers of information technology hardware. Given the Russian government's traditional wariness about free-flowing information, the implementation of E-Russia is being accompanied by new efforts to monitor electronic communications. Old habits die hard; one Russian IT manager observed that government bureaucrats saw the new technologies as tools to obtain more information *about* citizens rather than to deliver more information *to* citizens.[51]

An even wider digital divide awaits narrowing in parts of Africa. The lack of easily available Internet access in Zimbabwe, for instance, frustrates efforts of exiled journalists to deliver news in the face of government obstruction. Because so few people have Internet access in their homes, those wanting online information must use Internet cafés. The Zimbabwean government, as of mid-2006, had not blocked Internet sites but was considering e-mail censorship and was jamming Studio 7, which broadcasts from Voice of America studios in the United States. On the ground, journalists had to be licensed by the government, and those not supportive of the Mugabe administration were frequently harassed and arrested.[52]

On a more positive note, projects in Burundi and Burkina Faso have used the Internet in AIDS treatment programs for record-keeping and teaching prevention and treatment techniques. A venture in South Africa has taught rural women about drip irrigation as a way to increase the yields of village vegetable gardens. In another South African case, someone was saved from a poisonous snakebite by a neighbor who had learned the essential first aid procedures from the Internet.[53] Anecdotes such as these might or might not indicate a broader substantive impact of new media. Many years will pass before the digital divide is reliably bridged. One goal is to get government ministries, hospitals, and schools onto the Internet by 2012.

Meanwhile speculation will continue about what effects new technologies might have on democratization. Will wide distribution of inexpensive laptops and cell phone–based Internet access foster intellectual enfranchisement that will lead to activism with constructive political effect? Or will those who hold power stay ahead of the game, finding ways to control technology-based discourse and frustrate reform efforts? The road toward democracy will be unpredictable, with twists and turns and plenty of bumps, as well as the occasional smooth stretch. In countries such as Russia and Nigeria, there may be spurts of free expression and debate followed by renewal of government controls.

Economics will also play a big role, as media pioneers try to mesh noble intentions with financial reality. Providing news and other information is fundamentally a business, and it requires revenue. In Iraq after Saddam, hundreds of newspapers were born, but many of them died simply because they did not have the wherewithal to keep going. Al Jazeera is a beacon for those who believe that transnational broadcasting will advance freedom, but not every station will have a wealthy emir ready to absorb its debts. Corporations such as Google and Cisco Systems also will continue to face difficult decisions about how to balance doing good politically and doing well financially. As counterpoint to governments, various NGOs will enter the game, exerting pressure and trying to shape agendas.

In 1960, when television was just becoming a common presence in American households, U.S. politics was transformed. To win a presidential election, a candidate had to "look good on camera" as voters began to rely on new criteria to judge their politicians. Politics evolved to meet the demands and capabilities of new technology.

Candidates in the 2008 U.S. presidential campaign began early to court bloggers and campaign on the Web, recognizing it as a virtual forum where money could be raised and supporters mobilized. Once again, politicians adapted to the changing demands of new media.

Depending on individual nations' political systems, such changes will take place in the global public sphere at an ever faster pace. In many ways, on many levels, today's new media and those yet to come will continue to reshape international and national political systems and individual lives throughout the world. These are widespread aspects of the Al Jazeera effect, and as new information and communication technologies take hold, some of the most important tests of media-related progress will occur in the Middle East.

7

Transforming the Middle East

Media effects are just parts of a large political universe, the constituent elements of which must come into alignment if democratization is to take hold. Media cannot force change; media can only inspire it and assist it. Media power has its limits.

That said, the media's role should also not be underrated. Mohammed Jassim Al Ali, former managing director of Al Jazeera, said, "Democracy is coming to the Middle East because of the communication revolution. You can no longer hide information and must now tell the people the truth. If you don't, the people won't follow you, they won't support you, they won't obey you."[1] With numerous caveats related to the need for structural political change, that premise is sound in the sense that democratic tremors, some strong and some faint, are being felt in parts of the Middle East that have rarely been touched by such movement in the past. The increased availability of information is a significant factor in this.

Various players have assumed important roles in the processes of change. None has been more visible than Al Jazeera.

Al Jazeera as Pacesetter

Wadah Khanfar, Al Jazeera's director general, said in 2005, "Everyone is talking about change, reform, political transformation, and democracy in the Arab world. The realities are changing and so is what is dominating the news. . . . The whole discussion taking place in the region has found itself on our screen." That has impact. According to a report by the U.S. Institute of Peace,

Al Jazeera and other satellite channels "offer a locus for the Arab street to vent, formulate, and discuss public affairs. They bring Arabs closer together, breaking taboos and generally competing with each other and their respective governments for the news agenda."[2]

The news media can help to galvanize activism and construct an intellectual framework that gives coherence to reform efforts. But the climb toward political change will be long and steep. In his book about Al Jazeera, Hugh Miles observed, "Optimists theorize that satellite TV will sweep away traditional Arab obstacles to progress and dissolve seemingly intractable problems and that an 'Islamic Glasnost' will ensue. . . . But to believe that satellite television is automatically going to make Arab societies democratic is to presume that the current state of affairs in the Arab world results from an information deficiency, which is not true. Except in the most authoritarian Arab countries, the news has long been available to the determined via the radio, and that has never brought about much democracy." Miles added that even if Arab satellite television viewers see something on the air that leads them to change their minds about an issue, "there is still no political mechanism in place for them to do anything about it."[3]

Miles made a valid point, and expectations should be realistic when evaluating prospects for reform. Unless fundamental processes of democracy—such as an open electoral process and transparent functioning of government—become well established, the impact of Al Jazeera and other news organizations will be limited. But it should also be kept in mind that audience size is important in itself and the significance of sheer numbers of people having easy, frequent access to diverse sources of information should not be underestimated. When a critical mass of the public finds ways to get more information, political processes are likely to change. Pressures will mount on those who govern, and over time, only the most regressive leaders will wholly ignore the public's wishes.

Al Jazeera was born in 1996, when the emir of Qatar, Hamad bin Khalifa, recruited staff members of short-lived BBC Arabic Television (which was reborn in 2008) and invested US$140 million to start his channel. Within a few years, Al Jazeera established itself as the principal television voice of the Arab viewpoint of major events and its coverage attracted the attention of news organizations elsewhere. In 1998, when the United States and Britain bombed Iraq because Saddam Hussein was blocking the work of weapons inspectors, Al Jazeera was there. In 2000, during the Palestinian intifada, Al Jazeera's graphic coverage attracted a large audience throughout the Arab world. And in 2001, when the United States attacked Afghanistan, the Taliban allowed Al Jazeera to remain after Western journalists were ordered to leave. By 2003 and the beginning of the Iraq War, Al Jazeera's success had encouraged rivals, such as Al Arabiya and Abu Dhabi TV, to emphasize live, comprehensive coverage. For the first time, many Arabs did not have to rely on the BBC, CNN, or other outside news sources when a big story broke. They could instead find news presented from an Arab perspective.

One of Al Jazeera's strengths has been its introduction of energetic and sometimes contentious debate into an Arab news business that was previously known for its drab docility. The high production values of the channel's newscasts and the lively exchanges in its talk shows have expanded the news audience and changed the nature of political discourse within the Arab public sphere. Getting more people to pay attention to and talk about news is an important facet of larger issues related to democratization. Overall, noted Bernard Lewis, television "brings to the peoples of the Middle East a previously unknown spectacle—that of lively and vigorous public disagreement and debate."[4]

The style and substance of Al Jazeera's programming has led its audience to become more engaged with the issues addressed in coverage. This is largely because the channel is trusted more than many of its competitors. Critics of Al Jazeera, particularly in the West, often challenge the channel's objectivity, but such criticism misses the point in terms of understanding the channel's baseline strength. Rather than judging the news product they receive according to standards prescribed by outsiders, most of Al Jazeera's viewers consider *credibility* to be a news provider's most important attribute, and these viewers want news that is gathered independently for Arabs by Arabs and that sees events through *their* eyes. In the new era of proliferating satellite television channels,

state-controlled and Western broadcasters have found that they
are at a significant competitive disadvantage in the Arab world
because they are not as credible as Al Jazeera. Furthermore, the
presentation of news on Al Jazeera reflects a passion that is well
suited for an audience that feels passionately about many of the
issues and events that the channel covers.

The combination of energetic news presentation and a broadened flow of information can affect politics. As Marc Lynch noted,
"News coverage of political protests and struggles has opened up
the realm of possibility across the Arab world, inspiring political
activists and shifting the real balance of power on the ground."
Coverage by Al Jazeera's newscasts and talk shows has altered
public perceptions of politics, letting people see more of what is
going on and implicitly encouraging them to become involved.
The talk shows, wrote Lynch,

> have contributed to the evisceration of the political legiti-
> macy of the Arab status quo. Relentless criticism of all aspects
> of social, economic, and political life has exposed the cruel
> failings of the Arab order for all Arabs to see. The cumula-
> tive effect of program after program in which Arab leaders
> are savaged for their failures, where the Arab street is ridi-
> culed for its impotence, where the Arabs are held up as 'the
> joke of the world,' where sham elections and cults of per-
> sonality are mocked is to generate an urgency for change
> and impatience with traditional excuses.

The talk shows might not cause specific political upheavals,
wrote Lynch, "but they prepared the ground for them by legiti-
mizing dissent and exposing the regimes."[5]

Al Jazeera's coverage of Egypt in 2005 illustrated how the
channel can infringe on a government's control of politics. On
Election Day in September, when President Hosni Mubarak won
the country's first multicandidate election, Egypt's state-run television made no mention of anti-Mubarak protests in Cairo or
calls by opposition parties to boycott what they claimed to be a
rigged process to keep Mubarak in power. Al Jazeera, however,

aired an interview with political commentator Mohammed Hassanein Heikal, a well-known opponent of the president. Not allowed to appear on Egyptian channels, Heikal in his Al Jazeera appearance voiced his skepticism about Mubarak's promises to enact democratic reforms.

In the parliamentary elections two months later, the state-run Egyptian channels did not report the violence that accompanied the voting. Al Jazeera ran footage of voters with bloody faces and thugs waving machetes while police officers stood by. Al Jazeera also carried a news conference at which judges charged that the vote had been rigged and that police had intimidated people who wanted to vote. Mustafa el-Menshawy wrote that Al Jazeera's coverage "stifled official attempts by the state-run stations to deny—or disregard—the electoral violations." Columnist Salama Ahmed Salama said of this, "Al Jazeera has initiated a transformation in Egyptian society. We would not have known about these violations if it wasn't for Al Jazeera."[6]

When Al Jazeera and its competitors report stories such as these, wrote Lynch, "It establishes a common, core Arab narrative which in the past had existed only in a more abstract sense." Al Jazeera's coverage of events in individual Arab countries is usually set within a broader Arab context, making connections that news organizations focused on just single countries often overlook. This regional approach can shape how members of the Al Jazeera audience see their region in relation to the larger world. Lynch noted, "The rise in anti-Americanism in the region since 2002 might well be partially explained not simply by the appearance of graphic, bloody images from Palestine or Iraq, but also by the common narrative linking America as the common denominator for each of these otherwise distinct issues."[7] This coverage also can give the rest of the world a sense of the prevalent attitudes in the Middle East. Youssef Ibrahim noted that Arab satellite media have become "a platform and an effective means to respond to Western media, and hence the Arab citizen now has a channel to the top leadership in the United States."[8]

Governments outside the Arab world would be foolish to ignore what is being said on the Arab channels. The tone and specific content of news and talk programs on the new Arab media provide daily snapshots and, over time, a more substantive portrait of Arab political opinion.

In an even broader context, observed Bernard Lewis, the mass media have made "Middle Eastern Muslims more painfully aware of how badly things have gone wrong. In the past, they were not really conscious of the differences between their world and the rest. They did not realize how far they were falling behind not only the advanced West, but also the advancing East—first Japan, then China, India, South Korea, and Southeast Asia—and practically everywhere else in terms of standard of living, achievement, and, more generally, human and cultural development."[9]

When such media effects come together in a region that is already volatile, their potential impact is significantly heightened. Rather than grapple with the underlying causes of discontent and violence, government officials from Cairo to Washington blame Al Jazeera and other independent news media for their political problems. This finger pointing has been predictably ineffective, but policymakers continue to eschew meaningful analysis of satellite television's role. Rather than seeking ways to work with Al Jazeera, some governments prefer to fight it. Feeble responses—such as setting up a U.S. government–sponsored satellite channel, Al Hurra—have produced feeble results.

Al Jazeera's long-term impact will be judged according to how its coverage fits into the larger context of social and political change. Mohamed Zayani wrote,

> One should be skeptical about the often ambitious transformative claims for new media as well as the claims about its democratizing potential and its ability not just to increase and widen participation among the various social strata in the Arab world, but to transform social and political organization. Real change cannot be expected solely or mainly from the media sector. Democracy cannot emanate just from the media; the political systems and institutions themselves have to change, evolve, and adapt. . . . We should not be under the illusion that satellite TV can dramatically change society or revolutionize its institutions.[10]

Similarly, Marc Lynch wrote, "What one enthusiast called 'the Democratic Republic of Al Jazeera' does not, in fact, exist. Al Jazeera cannot create democracy on its own, nor compel Arab leaders to change their ways. Television talk shows cannot substitute for the hard work of political organizing and institution building."[11]

Looking at this from another angle, Mamoun Fandi noted that the proliferation of satellite television may create a virtual politics, like an event in an arena, that citizens watch rather than participate in. "Governments in the Arab world," wrote Fandi, "are encouraging the trend whereby the media become a substitute for real politics."[12] That outlook might be unduly pessimistic. Competitive elections in Iraq, Palestine, and other Arab countries may be tumultuous, but they are taking place. Elsewhere in the region and the world, people watch the satellite channels, see what is happening, and take heart as they pursue their own political fortunes.

Bits of optimism appear occasionally in the region. The 2004 *Arab Human Development Report* acknowledged that "formidable obstacles stand in the way of a society of freedom and good governance in Arab countries. And this is an undeniable truth. But at the end of this difficult journey, there lies a noble goal, worthy of the hardships endured by those who seek it."[13]

Dynamics of Democratization

Over the long term, the Internet may prove to be even more potent than satellite television as a force for reform, although this will take extra time given the limited Internet access within most of the Middle East. As more widespread Internet use gradually takes hold in the region, the World Wide Web's political vitality is likely to change the way people view their own countries and the rest of the world. Information from news organizations and other sources that were previously out of reach will be tapped and the Internet's interactive nature may foster the intellectual enfranchisement that opens the way to political change.

The Internet is an increasingly significant presence in international politics, but its lasting impact remains uncertain. Shanthi

Kalathil and Taylor C. Boas noted that the Internet "is only a tool, and its specific uses by political, economic, and societal actors must be carefully weighed and considered,"[14] and Charles Kupchan observed that the "international effects of the information revolution, just like those of economic interdependence, depend upon the broader political context in which these technologies are deployed."[15] In other words, advocates of democracy should not view the Internet as a cure-all. It is a potentially valuable tool for reform, but there must be people willing to use the tool to bring about systemic change. As with any political enterprise, the abilities and determination of participants, the resources available, other political occurrences near and far, and sometimes good or bad luck will affect any given democratization effort.

The Internet can generate political pressure because it is itself intrinsically democratic and can foster populist participation. That is not yet fully understood, but it can be seen in the fervor of political discussion that takes place on a scale and with an audacity new to politics in much of the world. People advocating change don't have to take the risks involved with public demonstrations in a police state, and they don't have to rely on slow and small-scale dissemination such as the circulation of *samizdat* in the Soviet Union. Instead there can be a virtual political presence such as sprang up in late 2005 in Syria, where, according to David Ignatius, "Internet cafes are scattered through Damascus, allowing people to constantly share news and gossip. The security forces have been arresting dissidents, but that doesn't stop people from talking."[16] That talking takes place not only over the tables in the cafés but also over the Internet.

Nevertheless, how much effect the Internet will have in the Arab political world remains speculative, particularly because Arab states lag far behind most of the rest of the world in taking advantage of this technology. As of 2003, according to the United Nations, there were only 18 computers per 1,000 people in Arab countries, compared to the global average of 78 per thousand. By late 2007, 21 percent of the Middle East's population had Internet access (often through shared access), a significant acceleration but still lagging behind much of the rest of the world. By comparison, the figure for Internet users in Eurpose was 48 percent and for North America 71 percent.)[17]

Once access is available, easy acquisition and dissemination of unmediated media may be viewed as information democracy, but because this freedom is available to all, regardless of their intentions, it may be abused, as can be seen in the terrorist examples cited in chapter 5. News organizations are sometimes inadvertently complicit in this when their coverage of terrorists' pronouncements reaches a much larger audience than could be achieved through the original Webcast, videotape, or other message. This raises questions about mainstream media's gatekeeper role, and the European Union has urged media organizations to draw up a code of conduct to ensure that they do not become de facto propagandists for terrorists.[18]

Yet another use of the Internet with significant political potential is blogging. Blogs amplify voices that may have previously gone unheard. As such they foster a degree of democratic parity at least in terms of expanding audience access for those who feel they have something worthwhile to say. The blogging firmament is already crowded and becoming more so, with blog search engine Technorati tracking more than 113 million blogs as of spring 2008. Technorati reported that 175,000 blogs were being created every day and that bloggers were updating their blogs with more than 1.6 million posts each day, or about 18 updates per second.[19]

Despite the crowd, bloggers are good at finding each other and reaching audiences. Particularly in countries where governments have tried to suppress political organizing, blogging may prove to be valuable in orchestrating pressure for reform. In 2005 bloggers in Lebanon and elsewhere spurred debate about the perpetrators and aftershocks of Rafik Hariri's assassination—debate that could be joined by anyone with Internet access, regardless of some governments' desire to stifle these discussions.

Another example of political blogging was seen in 2002, when Bahrainis dissatisfied with conventional media coverage of a scandal related to the national pension fund could read less constrained analysis on blogs such as "Bahraini blogsite" or "Mahmood's Den."[20] Many Bahraini villages have their own Web sites and chat rooms where discussions about the ruling Khalifa family are less restrained than they usually would be on street corners. By late 2005 BahrainOnline.org had become a go-to site for anyone interested in political news. Its iconoclastic success was underscored when the irritated government jailed several of the site's Webmasters for a few weeks.[21]

Talk about politics has expanded from the neighborhood coffeehouse to global proportions. The Internet encourages electronic speech and the thinking behind it. This is networking in the sense that like-minded activists can find each other and form partnerships of various kinds. Information—some of it solid, some of it wild—can be disseminated quickly and widely. Some time will have to pass before this phenomenon's long-term political impact can be determined, but if bloggers' talk leads to expanded activism by their readers, this could be yet another way that mass media provide impetus for democratization.

O ⌐ O

While the Internet is being put to increasing use, an even more common communications device is proving particularly helpful in mobilizing activists. Text messaging on cell phones facilitates the organization of demonstrations and circulation of political information. Especially when political parties are restricted, text messages can be sent to unofficial membership lists. In Kuwait, women organizing protests about voting rights in 2005 could summon young women from schools by sending text messages. (In May 2005 Kuwaiti women were granted the right to vote and to be candidates in parliamentary and local council elections.) In Lebanon, in March 2005, text messages (along with e-mails) were used to mobilize anti-Syrian demonstrators.[22]

Fawzi Guleid of the National Democratic Institute in Bahrain observed that text messaging fosters expansion of speech because it "allows people to send messages that they would not say in public." It should also be noted, however, that text messaging lends itself to the spread of rumors and anonymous attacks. Rola Dashti, one of the organizers of the women's rights demonstrations in Kuwait, was the subject of widely circulated text messages that criticized her for her Lebanese and Iranian ancestry and alleged that she had received funds from the American embassy. Her response: "It means I'm making them nervous . . . and I'd better get used to it."[23]

Such examples provide a sense of the potential long-term value of new media tools. They can have a democratizing effect in the basic sense of enabling more people to involve themselves in politics. As always, however, a gap exists between potential and reality.

Much intransigence exists among those who hold political power in the region. As is the case elsewhere in the world, change will come only in small increments and reformers must be prepared to endure many frustrations. Rola Dashti is just one of the new breed of political activists who has found that although she can use new media to advance her career and her cause, she must also learn to protect herself against the political whiplash that can be inflicted by these same media. Whether the political campaign is taking place in Kuwait or in the United States, using new media requires mastering defensive skills to offset the pernicious effects of a new level of attack politics.[24]

A more optimistic evaluation of media influence was offered by Jon Alterman, who argued that "as literacy and bandwidth both expand dramatically, publics are exposed to a broad, often unregulated, spectrum of views that range from secular to religious, from nationalist to global, and from material to spiritual. Under the new paradigm, information is demand-driven rather than supply-driven, and the universe of available views is far broader than ever before." One consequence of more information being more widely communicated, wrote Alterman, is "greater political spontaneity. Whereas Arab politics have often been characterized by orchestrated demonstrations of solidarity, anger, sorrow, or joy, the regime's ability to organize such demonstrations in the future will be greatly diminished."[25]

Current and prospective effects of new media should be appraised in a politically holistic context. While long-term aspirations are pondered, the gritty politics of the Middle East continues to change, sometimes painfully, with mass media in various forms an increasingly important factor. Media tools have been used in political protests in Lebanon, Egypt, Kuwait, and elsewhere. Transnational satellite television is one such tool because it can, to a certain extent, evade controls imposed on news coverage within a country.

The 2005 "Cedar Revolution" in Lebanon demonstrated how this can work on two levels. Regional/international coverage—such as that provided by Al Jazeera and Al Arabiya—could supply information to Lebanese audiences with less concern about the political repercussions that might constrain Lebanese media organizations. By showing the size and energy of the protests, this coverage helped fuel the demonstrations and encouraged even broader pressure on Syria to withdraw. News organizations based outside the country sometimes might be trusted more than those that are presumed to be susceptible to localized political pressures.

The lines between national and transnational are not always sharply drawn; transnational media are not necessarily external media. Lebanese television channels, some of which are available on satellite, also intensively covered the post-assassination story, as did radio stations and print media that reached regional and global audiences through the Internet. In Lebanon, as in any other country, indigenous news content is likely to be affected by the political, sectarian, and financial interests of those who own and run media organizations. News consumers must take this into account when evaluating information they receive and deciding what mix of sources they will rely on.

News flow keeps expanding. In addition to the television coverage, bloggingbeirut.com provided real-time Web video of the Cedar Revolution demonstrations by hundreds of thousands of people in downtown Beirut. This showed again the Internet's value as a mobilization tool; it can supply information that might not be available from conventional providers and it can keep people abreast of what is happening and pull them into the streets.

The reports from Lebanon influenced longer-term political dynamics as the coverage reached viewers throughout the region, letting them see political activity that they might decide to emulate. During the following months, demonstrations elsewhere incorporated the television-friendly tactics that were seen in the Beirut coverage. In Jordan, as had been the case in Lebanon, national flags were prominently displayed in front of the news media's cameras, which helped prevent having the protests dismissed as simply factional discord.[26] Playing to the cameras this way will become more sophisticated as activists gain media experience. (These ripple effects are not unprecedented. Coverage of events in Tiananmen Square in June 1989 reverberated around the world, especially in Eastern Europe, where the revolutionary events in Berlin took place just five months later.)

The events in Lebanon in 2005 also showed how media affect the competition for political credibility. When the demonstrations after Hariri's assassination began in Beirut, Syrian president Bashar al-Assad told Syria's parliament that the number of protestors was being exaggerated—the demonstrators were actually few in number but the crowds looked bigger because the news cameras were zooming in and making small look large. Al-Assad's comments were carried on television and so at the next demonstration marchers carried big signs saying, in English and Arabic, "Zoom out!" and "Zoom out and count!" When the cameras did pull back for a wide shot, the crowd looked even bigger. An estimated million people (of Lebanon's population of 3.7 million) had come to Martyrs' Square, and the world could watch them.[27]

Within Lebanon, there was plenty of television coverage of the political upheaval. Future TV, which Hariri had owned, paid tribute to him and adopted a strong pro-democracy position, as did several other channels. National Broadcasting Network, considered pro-Syria, and Al Manar, which is controlled by Hezbollah, covered these events in a more understated way, using in-studio reporting rather than constantly showing the huge anti-Syria crowds in Beirut. Rallies in support of Syria received more attention from these two stations. As the Lebanese parliament grappled with the crisis, local and international satellite channels covered the body's acrimonious debate and carried the prime minister's on-camera resignation.[28]

The news coverage and other media usage in Lebanon in 2005 did not transform the country's politics. Sectarianism did not vanish and journalists still had to fear car bombs and other violence directed at them. The country's political future remained uncertain. What can be said, however, about Lebanon 2005 is that democracy advanced, even if in small (and reversible) increments. New media tools, such as blogs and text messaging, coupled with more conventional news coverage engaged the public. The online community and the satellite television audience in Lebanon and throughout the Arab world saw what determined people could do.

The triumph was only briefly sweet. The following year saw Lebanon, so often mangled by conflict, battered again by a war between Israel and Hezbollah.

○ ⌨ ○

Egypt presents another example of the absence of a clear "winner" when activists using new media challenge an established order that is widely recognized as needing reform. Osama el-Ghazali Harb, a journalist and member of the Shura Council (the upper house of Egypt's parliament) made the case for change in a 2005 article: "The real cause for alarm is that the official media, be it the press, radio, or television, has shown itself largely incapable of absorbing new developments and continues to address its audience in an outdated language fundamentally at odds with the logic of political development." The strategy of state media, wrote Harb, was

> based on the premise that to ignore any protest—be it demonstration, strike, or sectarian conflict—denies it recognition and helps limit its 'negative' impact. The information revolution has rendered this strategy obsolete. No state can stem the tide of international media. All one does is force citizens to turn to papers, radio, and satellite channels run by foreign media companies for their news and commentary. The official media, in turn, become nothing more than propaganda. When we realize that satellite television reaches all levels of Egyptian society—no matter how devious some have to be to get hold of it—and the formidable media potential of the Internet, the shortsightedness of official media

policy quickly becomes clear.[29]

Harb's frustration was echoed by Naguib Mahfouz, winner of the 1988 Nobel Prize for Literature, who said in 2004, "I am perturbed by the fact that people often come to me and say they saw this or that on a satellite channel and when I ask them what local channels said about the issue I am told that they broadcast nothing at all. This can't go on—Egypt's terrestrial channels should be the first to broadcast news that concerns us. Egyptian viewers reached the age of maturity a long, long time ago, though this is something our media organizations have yet to realize. And because the media shy away from publicizing information it thinks might be unpalatable, news has been replaced by rumor."[30]

This selective editing could be seen when U.S. Secretary of State Condoleezza Rice gave a speech in Cairo in June 2005 urging a faster pace of political reform. On its front page, the government newspaper *Al-Ahram* quoted Rice as saying that President Mubarak had "unlocked the door for change" by allowing a multicandidate presidential election, but the paper omitted her subsequent comment: "But now, the Egyptian government must put its faith in its own people. We are all concerned for the future of Egypt's reforms when peaceful supporters of democracy—men and women—are not free from violence." Egyptian journalist Hisham Kassem said of this episode, "This is an indicator of how much in denial this regime is. This was all over the satellite stations."[31]

On the streets, protests were increasing in frequency and size, using the Internet as an organizing tool and outpacing the established opposition parties. In May 2005, after demonstrators were beaten by men identified as being controlled by Mubarak's National Democratic Party, a network of blogs was set up to spread the word on short notice about upcoming protests and to let democracy proponents have their say and contact others sympathetic to their cause. One blogger wrote that he was posting political comments "so that future generations cannot accuse us of having remained silent when there was a need to speak out."[32]

Blogs were just one part of the new media presence in the protest movement. Alaa Abd el Fattah, who maintained "Egyptian Blogs," a blog clearinghouse, noted, "The interesting story is how all the various Web sites, which include blogs, forums, independent news pages, official pages of political groups, etc., together became very much the opposition platform." The government took notice of the blogs and other Web-based activity and in May 2005 arrested el Fattah and other bloggers who were supporters of Kifaya, a leading opposition group. From around the world, bloggers rallied and created a "Free Alaa" blog to keep his case visible and to try (without much success) to exert pressure on Egyptian authorities.[33]

In 2007 another blogger, Abdelkarim Nabil Suleiman (known online as Karim Amer) was sentenced to four years in prison for "disparaging religions" and "insulting President Mubarak." Writers in *Al-Ahram* and elsewhere promptly criticized the court's action. This was evidence of the existence of some press freedom and illustrates the growing pains common in the region.

Also spending time in jail was Ayman Nour, leader of the Al-Ghad Party, which came in second in Egypt's 2005 presidential election. Critics of the Mubarak regime immediately labeled his imprisonment a political reprisal and called for his release. Nour's supporters received limited coverage in the mainstream Egyptian media, but they mounted a campaign for Nour's freedom on the Web and secured online signatures from members of the European Parliament and the U.S. Congress. On other reformist Web sites, such as elaph.com and middleeasttransparent.com, Nour's case remained visible, an irritant to the Mubarak government.

An irritant but not a powerful enough force to bring about change. Progressive voices continued to be heard in Egypt, although they had little measurable effect. Journalist Salama Salama called for abolishing the Information Ministry and said, "We need a media that mirrors public concerns, encourages freedom of expression, combats ignorance and fanaticism, and promotes democracy and human rights. We are ready for radical change."[34] Perhaps some journalists and political activists were, but the government was not.

Among traditional media, the weekly English-language

magazine *Cairo Times* and newspapers such as *al-Masri al-Youm* (*The Egyptian Today*) and the Nasserist party's *al-Arabi al-Nasseri* are sometimes harshly critical of government officials and policies. Their effect is incremental, perhaps building toward more substantive reform, but for now real power remains with government.

O   ⚘   O

The Mubarak regime is far from being the only obstructionist government in the region. In other countries, such as Iran, media voices must struggle to be heard while the state blocks them or jails those who dare to use new technologies to demand reform.

While in exile during the 1970s, Ayatollah Ruhollah Khomeini kept his support base within Iran nourished by sending audiocassette tapes that were circulated throughout the country. On the tapes he preached against the pro-Western, corrupt secularism of the shah and extolled the glory of an Islamic state, which he promised to build.

As the next generation matured, Khomeini's audiotapes were replaced, first by the fax machine and photocopier, then satellite television, and now Internet-based media. Alternative media are essential in Iran because under provisions of a 1995 press law the government has shut down more than one hundred publications, including forty-one daily newspapers. Mainstream print and broadcast media now studiously avoid provoking the government. When Iranian lawyer Shirin Ebadi won the Nobel Peace Prize in 2003, the state-controlled media ignored the story for several hours and finally ran a fifteen-second announcement that did not mention her human rights work.[35]

Bloggers, however, had posted congratulatory messages within minutes of the Nobel committee's announcement. Iranian blogs are one of the most significant new media phenomena. As of mid-2007, Persiablog reported hosting 780,000 Persian blogs and, according to Technorati, Farsi is one of the top-ten blog languages. One of the pioneers in Weblogistan, as the Farsi blogs collectively are known, is Hossein Derakhshan, an Iranian journalist who moved to Canada after the government shut down the newspaper at which he worked. In 2001 Derakhshan posted online instructions in Farsi about how to set up a blog. Other Iranian journalists who found themselves without a professional home, thanks to the government, gravitated to the Web, and many began blogging. Bijan Safsari, editor and publisher of pro-democracy newspapers closed by the government, wrote on his blog, "At a time when our society is deprived of its rightful free means of communication, and our newspapers are being closed down one by one—with writers and journalists crowding the corners of our jails . . . the only realm that can safeguard and shoulder the responsibility of free speech is the blogosphere." Reporters Without Borders noted, "In a country where the independent press has to fight for its survival on a daily basis, on-line publications and weblogs are the last media to fall into the authorities' clutches."[36]

Eventually, governments begin paying attention to blogs, recognizing that they reach substantial audiences. Then come the arrests. In 2004 a Tehran prosecutor ordered that more than twenty bloggers be locked up. Charges have included "insulting the country's leader, collaborating with the enemy, writing propaganda against the Islamic state, and encouraging people to jeopardize national security."[37] Some of the accused bloggers received extended jail terms, and some left the country. When other bloggers protested the crackdown, they too were arrested. On a visit to Iran, Derakhshan was detained and had to sign a letter apologizing for his blog writings before he was allowed to return to Canada.

Such harassment has not deterred all bloggers. Even political figures have turned to the Net and set up Web sites, including a former vice president, an ayatollah who was once seen as a potential successor to Khomeini, and the son of the former shah (who lives in the United States). Even President Mahmoud Ahmadinejad has his own blog and Web site. (The blog is posted in Farsi, Arabic, English, and French.)

In addition to targeting individual bloggers, Iran has followed the Chinese model of using Internet filters, which are part of a regulatory process that requires Internet service providers to install the filtering mechanism and requires individuals to agree not to access non-Islamic sites. Iranian bloggers are required to register at a Ministry of Culture site or else face their blogs being filtered and blocked. Taking another tack, the government also sponsored a competition for the best blogs addressing the Islamic revolution and the Quran.[38]

With about 70 percent of Iranians under age thirty and an 80 percent literacy rate, interest in blogging is high, as is interest in social and cultural matters rather than standard political fare. In her book *We Are Iran*, the pseudonymous Nasrin Alavi surveyed the Iranian blogosphere and found much of it occupied by young people who chafe under the restrictions of the country's Islamic regime. Masoud Behnoud, a journalist now in exile, contended that journalists have gone underground to plot an "Internet Revolution" while "Internet sites and weblogs by dissident Iranian youths are independently shouldering the entire mission of a public media network and resistance against the conservative clergy." Behnoud also wrote on his blog, "Each day as I open and look at the websites and blogs by young Iranians, I am filled with a new spirit. I say to myself how gratifying it is that our youth now possess an outlet for their beliefs. . . . They value freedom and do not sell out to fanaticism. Their blogs are reflections of the unveiled and candid views of our youth and future generations of Iran."[39]

Alavi also found that Weblogistan is home to an intellectual life that in Iran is sustained primarily in the virtual world. Alavi cited Akbar Ganji, winner of the European Parliament's 2003 Sakharov Prize and referred to by some as the Islamic world's Vaclav Havel, who while in prison wrote a manifesto, "Republicanism," advocating separation of religion and state. Banned by authorities, it was posted on the Internet and debated by bloggers. Derakhshan observed that Iranians must exist on different levels: "Just like they can switch between state television and Western satellite programs by pressing a button, so they switch in their daily lives. This artificiality is imposed on them and they have to deal with it. In effect, most Iranians live two lives, the private and the public. The Weblog community is one space where Iranians can be themselves. It works against hypocrisy. It can only be good for Iran."[40]

One Iranian blogger, identified online as "Hope," wrote, "Let's not forget that terror always starts with language. . . . Censoring words has always led to the censoring of our identity and ultimately to our oppression."[41]

○   ⌖   ○

Outside Iran, concern about keeping at least some level of openness led Pierre Akel to found Middle East Transparent (middleeasttransparent.com), which by mid-2006 was receiving more than fifty thousand hits each day. The site is based in Paris and appears in Arabic, English, and French, providing a forum for liberal Middle Eastern voices to comment on the news. Akel said of his venture and other new media projects, "In the Arab world, much more than in the West, we can genuinely talk of a blog revolution. Arab culture has been decimated during the last 50 years. . . . Some of the best authors pay to have their books published in the order of 3,000 copies for a market of 150 million. This is ridiculous. Even when people write, they face censorship at every level."[42]

The fundamental conflict that exists between free speech and repressive government occurs in many places throughout the world, not just the Middle East, but in this region it is more the rule than the exception. (The freest press and speech in the region are to be found in Israel, but "Being more like Israel" is unlikely to inspire Arab reform.) When change does occur, it is often one step forward and two steps back. Syria provides examples of the difficulty of bringing about change.

Syrian writer Anwar al Qassem commented that Syrian state television seems to operate on the principle of "See not, hear not, speak not." After Rafik Hariri's assassination in Beirut, Syrian state television was not forthcoming about the accusations of official Syrian involvement in the murder and downplayed the massive anti-Syrian demonstrations occurring across the border in Lebanon. That approach had almost no effect on the Syrian public's ability to get information, as many Syrians simply tuned in to Lebanese satellite channels, which treated Syria's Assad regime harshly.

As a tangential counterpoint to this, it is worth noting that another facet of Syrian media, entertainment television, has been very successful. State-run production companies have offered use of their facilities to private directors in return for first broadcast rights. Plans have been started for a Syria Media City near Damascus that would be home to privately owned Syrian satellite television channels and FM radio stations. Change also has taken place in the cosmetics of television. Conscious of the level of competition from the likes of Al Jazeera, Syrian television presenters have been told to shape up, literally. A television anchor's weight cannot exceed the last two numbers of his or her height: a newscaster 160 centimeters (5' 3") tall may not weigh more than 60 kilograms (132 pounds).[43]

Having svelte news anchors will probably have little effect on content, but at least some in the Syrian media establishment recognize that competition exists in the information marketplace. The government has not, however, decided what to do about a long-term Internet policy. Critical Web sites and blogs are sometimes tolerated, sometimes shut down, although Internet content is not as tightly screened in Syria as in some other countries. At Internet cafés in Damascus, customers can access reports about Syria from Human Rights Watch and can find some news stories and blogs critical of the regime. Ayman Abdel Nour has claimed that his site, "All4Syria," has sixteen thousand subscribers. He was a childhood friend of President Bashar al-Assad, so Nour has been treated relatively gently, although his site has periodically been closed, forcing him to distribute his writings by e-mail.

Other bloggers have found even less official tolerance. Some have been jailed after posting pro-democracy messages. Ammar Abdel Hamid decamped to the United States, where he writes "A Heretic's Blog." He observed that the importance of blogs and other new media is not to build a mass movement but "to connect the elites better, to network the elites, to make them able to share more ideas and organize." Eventually, he added, bloggers will "cross the bridge between the elite and the grass roots," a process that has begun with the posting of information about demonstrations, police brutality, and similar issues.

A 2006 entry about Assad explains why Hamid is no longer welcome in Syria: "In his recent declarations, the president, true to his moronic form, has made it quite clear that as the country's isolation increases, it is the people who will suffer, not the country's corrupt officialdom."[44]

○ ⌐& ○

The media situation in each country in the region varies according to long-term politics and short-term exigencies. Post-Saddam Iraq, even with all its violent instability, has made tenuous progress in establishing a relatively free flow of information as a keystone in efforts to construct a semblance of democracy. Radio Dijla was Iraq's first independent, all-talk station, transmitting from a residential neighborhood in Baghdad and reaching ninety miles. It offered a mix of political, religious, sports, public-service, and entertainment shows. By early 2006, said its executive manager, the station was receiving a thousand telephone calls each day, its Web site was getting more than a million hits a month, and adequate funding was being generated through advertising. Its founder, Ahmad al-Rikabi, said of the station's success: "We've quickly become a part of people's lives. It shows the desperate need of ordinary Iraqis to share and communicate their pains and joys. . . . We are already number one in Baghdad."[45] In 2007 armed men believed to be affiliated with al Qaeda in Iraq attacked the station and burned it down.

Another Iraqi station that found early success was Radio Almahaba, which discussed women's issues and was not shy about playing an advocacy role on behalf of those issues. The station encouraged its listeners to make certain that women's interests were well represented in the drafting of Iraq's new constitution. At a rally for women's rights, an Almahaba reporter conducted interviews, then put down her microphone and helped rally participants pass out fliers and petitions.[46]

By some Western standards, such involvement crosses the line between reporting and making the news. But in today's Iraq, involvement by journalists may be a necessary and healthy part of nation building. Standing apart from issues might meet traditional tests of objectivity, but remoteness is unlikely to attract an audience that is so buffeted by the extremes of hope and fear. Although its future, like the future of the country, remains far from certain, the Iraqi media landscape has already changed dramatically since it was controlled by Uday Hussein, Saddam's murderous son.

As in other countries in the region, the Internet has proved to be a valuable means of expanding Iraqi discourse about public affairs. After Saddam's fall, hundreds of Internet cafés opened around the country. Religious and political Web sites attract sizable audiences and spur public and private debate.[47]

That is encouraging, but only in the context of the disaster that is Iraq. Radio, the Internet, and all other media cannot save the country. The early developments in creating a vibrant, broad-based media community are small steps forward on a very long road. Still, without such new media ventures, Iraq's prospects would be even dimmer.

O ⌐⊕ O

Some of the most dynamic media developments in the region have occurred along the Arabian (or Persian) Gulf. Al Jazeera, Al Arabiya, Abu Dhabi Television, and others make their homes there, and several of the governments in the area have recognized that their political and economic situations can benefit from being perceived as progressive centers of new media. That does not mean, however, that these governments have unreservedly embraced freedom for the media organizations they host.

Dubai opened its Media City in 2001, offering tax breaks, no regulation, and other incentives. This open-arms welcome has attracted news, financial, and other television networks, as well as publications. But local media and Internet access are subject to other rules. The Information Ministry has a censorship office that monitors incoming foreign newspapers and magazines and filters Internet content to block sites related to pornography, gambling, and other forbidden topics. Sometimes the filter reaches farther, knocking out references to alcohol and breast cancer. In 2005 it blocked access to the *New York Times* Web site for most of a day, presumably because certain words in the *Times* triggered the filter.[48]

Site-blocking has also occurred in Bahrain, where Web sites carrying critical comments about the government were banned in 2002. The Information Ministry said it would take action against sites that "create tension between people and provoke resentful sectarianism." The government has wide discretion in defining what viewpoints and words cause those problems. No longer able to control debate as effectively as it could when the only media were print and broadcast, the ruling family in Bahrain has found satellite television and the Internet bothersome. Several people who set up political Web sites have been jailed. The royal family remains on edge partly because its members are Sunni while the country is about 70 percent Shia. Bahraini officials know that Shiites within their country watch Al Manar, Hezbollah's Leba- non-based channel, and increasingly tune in to Iraqi or regional television coverage that provides details about violence in Iraq. When television reports that Iraqi Shiites have been killed in ter- rorist attacks, some Bahraini Shiites respond by wearing black. Noting the restiveness of the Shia in Bahrain, the government remains watchful for signs of Iranian influence, which the Internet could help spread.[49]

Wariness about the Internet is also apparent among mem- bers of the Saudi Arabian royal family. The Saudi government's Internet Services Unit states, "All sites that contain content in vio- lation of Islamic tradition or national regulations shall be blocked."[50] Among these blocked sites are Amnesty International's Web pages related to Saudi Arabia, the Encyclopedia Britannica's entry about "Women in American History," *Rolling Stone* maga- zine, and Warner Brothers Records.

Blogging in Saudi Arabia has been late to arrive and slow to grow. By fall 2006, about two thousand Saudi bloggers were at their keyboards, triple the number at the beginning of the year. An Arabic word for blogging, *tadween,* meaning "to chronicle," was not coined until 2006.[51] Even the small number of bloggers alarmed the Saudi establishment, and so the "Official Commu- nity of Saudi Bloggers" was established, ostensibly without government backing but with the clear intent of freezing out bloggers who criticize the status quo. The organizers of this "community" plan to direct advertisers to the blogging sites that do not annoy the government.

On another front, Saudi officials have had to deal with reformist messages delivered by television and radio. The London-based Saudi Human Rights Center has used satellite radio and television to encourage demonstrations in Riyadh. Islah Radio promoted Saudi reform in its broadcasts from shortwave transmitters at an unrevealed location (thought to be in Lithuania) and via satellite to take advantage of the substantial number of households with satellite reception in Saudi Arabia. Since most of the audience prefers even the most basic visual product, rather than radio alone, Islah Television was born, initially presenting just its logo and text information scrolling on the screen with the radio broadcasts as its audio. The station eventually provided programming with more audience appeal, including a call-in show featuring the station's driving force, Saad Al Faqih, who responded to viewers' e-mails, faxes, and phone calls placed through an Internet phone service (which allowed them to avoid government eavesdroppers). Al Faqih consistently criticized the Al Saud princes, at one point calling them "thieves who should be beheaded instead of petty criminals."

The Saudi government apparently fought back, as the shortwave and television signals were jammed and pressure was brought to bear on the European TV transmission providers to drop the station. In December 2004 the station was on the air with a new satellite home that let it be more insulated from economic pressure. As all this was going on, the station had achieved small but noteworthy results in its efforts to encourage demonstrations in support of human rights within Saudi Arabia.[52]

Without judging the merits of the station's content, its struggle for existence illustrates the kind of battle that can be expected as new media organizations jab at governments that are unaccustomed to being challenged. The on-and-off process will continue as each side deals with the other's latest technological and political gambits. As in the Saudi case, Arab broadcasting and print news organizations based outside the region are expanding the amounts of information available to Middle East publics.[53]

Youssef Ibrahim observed, "The din of democracy talk has been amplified by satellite television, the Internet, and cell phones, and that is a new wrinkle for autocratic regimes experienced at quiet repression."[54]

This "democracy talk" may be having some effect. A Jidda-based radio program, Mubasher (Live) FM features callers who complain about corruption, sexual harassment, government officials' lack of accountability, and similar topics that in the past could not be publicly discussed. But King Abdullah himself encouraged the show's host, Salama al-Zaid, to shine a spotlight on the government's failings. To keep the royal blessing, Zaid does not criticize the religious establishment, and he champions the role of the royal family. Even with these examples of restraint, the program is still more "open" than most Saudi media offerings.[55]

○ ⌐ᶀ ○

In some Middle Eastern countries media-related controversies tend to flare up and subside, but in parts of the region tensions are constant and attitudes about the media reflect that. Palestinian writer Ramzy Baroud recalled how his family had always listened to BBC radio news. He observed,

> Palestinians have had a love-hate relationship with the media. Knowing that the name of our refugee camp was uttered on some radio station thousands of miles away was in some way a recognition that our plight mattered, even if little. . . . Even if such reference was made, it hardly deviated from usual mantras that saw the Israeli occupiers as the ultimate source of information, the primary authority on what had indeed happened. This remains the case today. What the Israeli army acknowledges becomes fact, its narrative is the trusted narrative; what it dismisses has simply never happened. At best, it's a murky Palestinian allegation.

Baroud's point about the dominance of the Israeli viewpoint might be debated, although it is no secret that public relations is an important part of Israel's foreign policy, with well-trained press officers in every embassy and even its soldiers instructed on how to act when cameras are near. The Palestinians have been slow to match this effort, although when Hamas decided that it would run candidates in the 2005 legislative elections, it made an announcement in English, and Baroud cited the increasing use of e-mail and blogs to tell Palestinians' version of events.[56]

The recognition by Palestinians and others that they need to have "our side of the story" told is an important reason for the popularity of Al Jazeera and other indigenous news organizations. It also has been a factor in one of the most controversial media organizations in the Middle East: Al Manar.

When it broadcast its first signal in 1991, Al Manar provided Hezbollah and Lebanon's Shiites access to the larger world, giving voice to their claims of being victimized, primarily by Israel. It claims to be "the true reflection of what each and every Muslim and Arab thinks and believes in" and says it "avoids cheap incitement." Its critics disagree. Dennis Ross wrote that Al Manar "socializes hatred and the spirit of enduring conflict. It rejects the very concept of peace between Arabs and Israelis."[57]

The channel is partially owned and controlled by Hezbollah (and therefore, some observers say, by Iran). Like Al Jazeera, it made its mark with its coverage of the 2000 intifada. The channel had reporters on the ground, and it was overtly pro-Palestinian, which was a bias well received by most of its audience. After the intifada, Al Manar's satellite broadcasts reached a growing number of viewers, and the channel continued to develop a "culture of resistance" to Israeli and Western presence in the Muslim world. In 2004 the U.S. government designated Al Manar as a terrorist organization, and two years later it barred American companies from doing business with the company. Nevertheless, Al Manar has continued to expand its audience through its Web site, its live Internet broadcasting, and its CDs and DVDs of its programming. Throughout, Al Manar has glorified Palestinian and Lebanese "martyrs" while attacking the "Zionist entity" of Israel.[58]

When the war between Israel and Hezbollah began in July 2006, Al Manar's headquarters in a Beirut suburb was an early target for Israeli bombing runs. The headquarters was destroyed, but the station was back on the air after just a few minutes, offering a mix of reporting, cheerleading for Hezbollah, and propaganda vilifying Israel and the United States. It was always ready to serve as a forum for Hezbollah leader Hassan Nasrallah's pronouncements about the war.

It is easy to dismiss Al Manar's content as nothing more than hatred and propaganda, but it would be a mistake to underestimate its influence and its potential as a prototype for media operations serving other militias and insurgent groups. Al Manar has been an important factor in making Nasrallah a hero in the eyes of many within the region, and its portrayal of Hezbollah has encouraged Shiites to be more assertive in countries where they are a minority. When Hezbollah was relatively successful against Israel's armed forces in summer 2006, Al Manar's role became more significant, implicitly advancing the interests of Iran and Syria as well as of Hezbollah itself.

Al Manar's recent history illustrates how the media may be used as a weapon. The station aided the Hezbollah war effort and was targeted as a quasi-combatant by Israel. This is part of a larger trend of news organizations and individual journalists being, or at least being perceived as, political actors, which has resulted in political and sometimes military action being directed against them. Al Jazeera has been categorized this way on numerous occasions. It has been criticized for allegedly serving al Qaeda's interests, but such comments are particularly inane when Al Jazeera's content is compared to that of Al Manar. As was seen during the war with Israel, the Hezbollah station's conventional programming was of secondary importance while its broadcasts provoked and recruited.

Enthusiasm about the arrival of new media outlets should be tempered by recognition that when a media organization abuses its influence, much evil can be done. A striking example was the inflammatory broadcasting of Rwanda's Radio Mille Collines, which in 1994 urged the country's Hutus to attack Tutsi *inyenzi* (cockroaches) and fill the country's rivers with Tutsi dead.[59] When contemplating the future role of new media anywhere in the world, such precedent should be remembered. Many positive prospects are on the horizon, but the potential dangers of the misuse of media power should not be ignored.

What Lies Ahead

Even if technological parity were to be approached and Arabs were to move closer to worldwide levels of new media use, optimism about media-inspired reform should be tempered with much caution. As Jon Alterman pointed out, much of the debate that can be seen on Arab satellite television "is still largely about spectacle and not about participation."

Increased participation may appear primarily on the religious, rather than purely the political, side, with impetus coming from the likes of Muslim television preacher Amr Khaled. Alterman wrote, "Through huge revival-style events in Egypt and increasingly via satellite television broadcasts beamed throughout the Middle East, Khaled has created not just a community of viewers, but also a community of participants. His followers do more than write and call in to his programs. His increasingly global audience participates in charity drives, organizes study groups, and seeks to apply his specific lessons to their daily lives."[60]

Favoring European suits and polo shirts rather than a cleric's robes, Khaled relies on Western vernacular, as when he talks about Islam "empowering" women and describes Muhammad as "the first manager." Born in Egypt and now living in England, Khaled has built a huge following by explaining how Islam can thrive in the modern world. Second-generation European Muslims constitute a considerable part of his audience. His programs on Iqraa, a Saudi-owned satellite channel, reach millions of devoted viewers. His Web site (www.amrkhaled.net), which received 26 million hits in 2005, is the third-most popular Arabic site (behind Al Jazeera and an e-mail portal) and is translated into eighteen languages.

Khaled tells women that they must wear the *hijab*, but—unlike fellow television preacher Yusuf al-Qaradawi—he does not often offer opinions on matters such as whether people should join the Palestinian or Iraqi resistance. His principal themes include fostering an Arab and Islamic revival by increasing literacy and community involvement. When addressing European Muslims, he stresses the importance of coexistence—for those living in the UK, he suggests rooting for a British soccer team rather than Pakistan's, and for those in France, he suggests lobbying for the legal right to wear the *hijab* in school, but in the meantime making do with designer hats.[61]

Khaled's example illustrates the multidimensional aspects of new media influence. If a medium is to foster change, it need not be overtly political, but it must be used creatively and with an eye to its relationship with other social and political institutions.

Moderation, however, has its critics. Al-Qaradawi said that Khaled's conciliatory approach during the Danish cartoon controversy was a sign of weakness, and the senior cleric contended that Khaled "does not hold any qualifications to preach. He is a business school graduate who acquired what he knows from reading and who got his start by way of conversations with friends about things that do not really involve any particular thought or judgment." Lindsay Wise observed, "The more Khaled reaches out to the West and America, the more he tries to speak a language that makes everybody happy, the more he risks losing credibility among Arab and Muslim audiences. It is a conundrum familiar to liberal minded politicians and reformers in the Arab world—a rhetoric of dialogue and conciliation can be a hard sell at times of frustration and conflict."[62]

Increased media-based participation has also affected women's issues. Long treated condescendingly, if at all, by many Arab media organizations, these topics are gaining increased traction thanks partly to new media. A good example is the Lebanon-based Heya ("She") satellite television channel, which as of early 2005 was reaching a daily audience estimated at 15 million with a mixture of news, talk, and entertainment programming. About 70 percent of the station's staff members are women, with correspondents reporting from throughout the Arab world. Heya's founder, Nicolas Abu Samah, said the channel's goal "is to empower women. We want to question taboos and provoke controversy." Among the station's offerings is "Al-Makshouf" (The Uncovered), a talk show that addresses topics such as domestic violence and workplace discrimination. A news program, "From

Day to Day," examines news related to women from around the world. Abu Samah noted that the station proceeds carefully to avoid censorship; political leaders and religious authorities are not directly criticized on Heya programs.[63]

In addition to the increased attention to women's issues, coverage of electoral politics is becoming more comprehensive and freewheeling. In covering the 2005 Iraq elections, Middle Eastern television stations displayed their ambition and the strengths of their hardware. Al Arabiya broadcast from eight satellite trucks throughout Iraq and used videophone links and live feeds from neighboring countries. Al Jazeera, despite being banned from broadcasting from within Iraq (an example of the political obstacles that continue to impede information flow), also offered heavy coverage.[64]

◯ ⸙ ◯

Emerging from the rush of events and the shifting global and local political dynamics is a region that is clearly changing—often quietly and with small steps, but still edging forward. If this is considered to be an area where, in Bernard Lewis's words, "things had indeed gone badly wrong,"[65] maybe these changes will help those who live there by reducing tensions and bringing the Arab world closer to the rest of the global community.

The news media—with their audience expanding through new technologies—will be among the most important players in determining how this process turns out. Gadi Wolfsfeld argued, "Journalists have an ethical obligation to encourage reconciliation between hostile populations" by providing as much information as possible about roots of problems and encouraging rational public debate about options for solving those problems.[66]

Democracy can be blocked or undermined by parties within and outside government. As the authors of the *Arab Human Development Report 2004* noted, "In Arab countries today, there seems to be a contradiction between freedom and democracy because many democratic institutions that exist have been stripped of their original purpose to uphold freedom in its comprehensive sense.

... There are some media outlets that are little more than mouth-pieces for government propaganda, promoting freedom of speech only if it does not turn into political activity. Such captive outlets fail to stimulate intelligent and objective debate, enhance knowledge acquisition, and advance human development among the public at large."[67] Unless new media contribute to constructive debate and enhancement of knowledge, prospects for democracy will weaken. For those contributions to be meaningful, all involved in the information process—from the individual blogger to the big media corporation—must retain independence. Government pressure is inevitable, but it must be resisted if the democratic process is to gain a foothold.

Another element of media freedom is economic. Jennifer Windsor and Brian Katulis have noted, "A much-overlooked restriction on press freedom is the media's lack of economic independence and sustainability. Virtually no media organization in the region covers its own operating costs, including many of the prominent regional satellite television channels. Most media outlets are owned and controlled by governments or heavily dependent on subsidies from small groups of private owners or governments."[68]

While day-to-day matters such as building a secure funding base make the Middle Eastern media business precarious, larger problems—such as how to make the case for democracy—also loom over the region. Gilles Kepel has observed that the Abu Ghraib case and similar scandals have so tarnished the image of Western democratic nations that "the word 'democracy,' preceded by the adjective 'Western,' has negative connotations for a large swathe of the educated Muslim middle class—although that class was the potential beneficiary of democratization. The Arabic word *damakrata*, which designates the democratization process, is frequently used pejoratively, signifying a change imposed from without."[69]

When democratization itself is suspect, prospects for any meaningful political reform are jeopardized. The many complex questions related to such issues can rarely be answered precisely. New tools are available, but whether large numbers of people truly want to use them is open to question. New media's role in progressive political change is hard to define with certainty because most of the path toward democratization in the Middle East, as elsewhere, remains uncharted. No one knows precisely where to go next, and those who move in the general direction of reform do so with more faith than certainty.

8
What It All Means

To varying degrees throughout the world, the connectivity of new media is superseding the traditional political connections that have brought identity and structure to global politics. This rewiring of the world's neural system is proceeding at remarkable speed, and its reach keeps extending ever farther. It changes the way states and citizens interact with each other and it gives the individual a chance at a new kind of autonomy, at least on an intellectual level, because of the greater availability of information.

This is the Al Jazeera effect. The Arab satellite channel itself is just the most visible player in a huge universe of new communications and information providers that are changing the relationship between those who govern and those who are governed. It is also assisting those with previously unachievable political agendas. The advent of television a half-century ago pales in comparison with new media's effects on global political life today.

Political actors respond to this in different ways. Some are quick to appreciate the enhancements of power enabled by new media. The use of the Internet by candidates in the 2008 U.S. presidential campaign illustrates this on one level. More common are the scrambling blogs and Web sites used by political activists in many countries who now have a fast and efficient way to disseminate information and mobilize supporters, often in the face of opposition—sometimes fierce—from the political establishment.

Printing a few leaflets on a basement press and distributing them on street corners has been replaced by creating an electronic product that can be seen by millions in moments. Governments felt confident that those handing out material on a street corner could fairly easily be chased away or arrested, and so their impact could be limited. Those using new media tools are far harder to deal with. In China and many other countries, the flood of new media is intrinsically democratic and governments can do only so much to stop it.

That is transformative progress. Satellite television ensures a new era of political diversity, as different kinds of discourse reach mass audiences. The Internet has even greater effect because it is truly a popular medium—accessible, inexpensive, and far-reaching. Almost anyone can use it to proselytize, recruit, mobilize, or whatever. Whether anyone else pays attention is another matter, but this, too, can be seen as a positive characteristic in that the competition for audience should inspire cyber-articulateness and creativity in order to make a message stand out in the crowded virtual marketplace. This is how elements of democracy can be nurtured.

Wider dissemination of information should be a good thing, but caveats exist. "Information" and truth are not necessarily the same, and the Internet has already proved to be a hospitable laboratory for fraud and other deception, ranging from scams aimed at individuals' bank accounts to hate-filled polemics targeting large audiences. The speed and reach of new media are wonderful when there is need to alert people about an approaching hurricane or such, but those same qualities can be poisonous when vicious rumor is presented as the "news" of the moment.

Political leaders and related organizations, scrupulous and unscrupulous alike, are confronted with media and political environments that have converged to an unprecedented extent. Few individuals or groups have as yet mastered this new realm, but some have shown skill at using parts of it to advantage. Some of these are spokesmen for al Qaeda and its ilk, but on the other side are men and women who are trying to use these media to make the world more humane.

Stories That Need to Be Told

Beyond the world of high-powered activists putting communication to use are places invisible to most, where debate about political systems and esoteric issues is unknown. All that matters in these places is basic survival: finding water, medical care, refuge from violence. These are terrible places, where hope is usually nothing more than illusion. New media cannot solve these problems, but they might help.

First, the world needs to be awakened. New media are looked to because traditional journalism has devoted few resources to reporting about events such as the genocidal war in Sudan. According to an analysis of network newscasts by the American Progress Action Fund, during 2004 ABC, CBS, and NBC combined to air just twenty-six minutes of coverage of the conflict in Darfur on their principal nightly newscasts. By comparison, Martha Stewart's legal problems received 130 minutes of airtime. In June 2005 the big three devoted fifteen minutes to the Darfur genocide while airing 1,608 minutes of reports about Michael Jackson's trial. CNN, purportedly a serious news channel, spent forty-seven minutes that month covering events in Darfur and 878 minutes on Jackson.[1] Writing about this in the *New York Times*, Nicholas Kristof noted that the BBC had outperformed the American networks. That was not surprising, but Kristof pointed out that so too had mtvU, the MTV channel aimed at a college student audience.[2]

The content on mtvu.com is an example of what Web-based information sources can provide, and it also underscores its limitations. The site provides basic background material and links to other providers, such as Amnesty International's satellite imagery pages that show what has happened to selected Sudanese villages during the fighting. It also links to a video game, "Darfur Is Dying," in which players "must keep their refugee camp functioning in the face of possible attack by Janjaweed militias." The game involves tasks such as searching for water while avoiding hostile troops.

For those who have slight interest in conventional news offerings, this approach may have value in creating at least threshold awareness of what is taking place in Sudan. But despite such innovative Web products that call attention to the conflict, there is little evidence that policy has been affected. It is good that new media try to spur action, but in this case, as in most others, expecting the situation to be turned upside down is unrealistic.

Underreported as it is, the war in Darfur receives more attention than other stories that rival it in importance. The UN and Doctors Without Borders prepare lists each year of stories that, as the UN puts it, "the world should hear more about." From Haiti to Congo to Sri Lanka, the list underscores the gaps in most news coverage and perhaps stimulates passing interest in underreported stories of horror and misery. Humanitarian organizations use their Web sites to shine a light on these cases, but no matter how articulately anguished these reports might be, there is no evidence that they do much more than stir a few consciences and elicit some financial help. That's all to the good, but in practical terms even the substantial amount of information that these Web sites can provide has only a tiny fraction of the impact a two-minute story on ABC would have.

At least for now. Changing habits of information gathering may enhance the significance of online alarms about international crises. As more people rely more heavily on the Internet rather than traditional news formats, the structure of influence will also change. This will take a while, as reliance on the long-dominant players continues to diminish (evidenced by declines in newspaper circulation and broadcast news audience) and as some among the almost infinite number of Web sites develop sizable and faithful constituencies. Clearinghouse sites, such as YouTube and Technorati, can lead visitors to lesser known sites, as can new and traditional information providers that already have large audiences. This symbiosis of old and new media will continue indefinitely.

Amid the technology-related expansion of "newsworthiness" are some journalistic verities. Some stories must be covered and must be forced into the public's field of vision. Longtime *Nightline* executive producer Leroy Sievers wrote about covering Rwanda during the 1994 genocide: "Was it a story that needed telling? Absolutely. Did the world listen? I don't know. I fear that people just turned the channel, that the images were too painful." Sievers wrote that years later Elie Wiesel spoke to the *Nightline* staff. "He said that the role of the journalist is to speak for those who have no voice. That was it. That's what we were trying to do. That's what we had to do. There, and after Rwanda—because there was a dividing line, before Rwanda and after Rwanda—anywhere in the world where man was doing the worst that he was capable of."[3]

Despite the heroic efforts and good intentions of a few journalists and news organizations, the coverage of the Rwanda genocide was too little, too late, as was the military and political response by the international community. By the time big news organizations, such as *Nightline*'s ABC, got to Rwanda, the worst was done. A decade later, in Darfur, media in various forms are only inconsistently on the scene, and the public is more likely to hear about the crisis in Darfur from a movie star on a talk show than from a major news organization.

By mid-2007 youtube.com had a large roster of Darfur-related videos available, some of which had been viewed a few thousand times, some more than 100,000 times. Did this result in public anger and activism that influenced policymakers? Apparently not. The agony of the genocide continued. At some point, perhaps a critical mass of awareness can be attained and a political tipping point can be reached.

If that happens, the quantity of information that new media provide will be a contributing factor, although not a determinative one. Some encouragement can be found in the ways that responses to non-conflict-related humanitarian emergencies have changed because of information and communication technologies. Aid donors use new technologies to locate disaster victims and keep track of supplies that have been sent. An essential part of relief operations is the communications center, which allows aid workers to communicate with their organizations and governments, check security updates, and study satellite maps of the areas in which they are working.

To make this possible, among the first respondents on the ground may be volunteers from Télécoms sans Frontières, who keep communication flowing even under horrendous circumstances.

Clearinghouse sites such as the UN's ReliefWeb provide constantly updated information about crises around the world. On any given day, the list might include reports about a cyclone in Pakistan, locust infestation in Yemen, landslides in Nepal, and many more. NetHope, a nonprofit consortium of international NGOs, helps relief groups with organization and finances. For their part, the people who are endangered by disasters have found mobile phones to be invaluable in contacting neighbors and the world during times of peril. Access is increasing; in sub-Saharan Africa, according to the World Bank, the number of mobile phone subscribers increased sevenfold between 2000 and 2006.[4]

In disaster relief as in politics, new technologies do not in themselves solve problems. But they can change the process, making things work better. If you are a victim of a tsunami or a war, that means something.

Satellite News Channels and More

Al Jazeera receives plenty of attention, not just from its audience of 35 million but also from observers intrigued by the station's influence. Without again getting into the debate about satellite channels' objectivity or lack thereof, it is important to consider their overall effect on the populations they serve. Ability to get lively and relatively independent content is a new and energizing phenomenon in areas such as the Arab Middle East, and it has profoundly changed politics there.

People who live in Western democracies take for granted the open exchange of political ideas and rarely ponder what their lives would be like without this. New media are allowing people who have never enjoyed this kind of freedom to revel in it. They learn more and they expect more, and although strong governments—such as those in Egypt and Saudi Arabia—show no inclination to embrace democracy, the pot is boiling and the lid has popped off.

Forces are at work that may be slowed down from time to time, but they will not—and cannot—be brought to a full halt. Eventually people will see a transformation of the structure of sociopolitical life, driven in part by the openness that is a by-product of the work of the hundreds of regional satellite channels and in part by other new communication technologies.

As one of the oldest forms of new media (these age terms are all relative), television has seen ups and downs in the attempts by its champions to prove that it is, in Edward R. Murrow's words, more than "merely wires and lights in a box." The liberating influence of many of the newest television channels gives heart to those who believe television remains, in essence, a worthwhile medium.

Beyond television, new media constitute an even more revolutionary force. "Citizen media," which at one level can be defined as a populist, participatory kind of journalism, allow individuals to play the role filled by traditional information providers such as the major news organizations. Blogs—written and video—create a community that can be energized by swift delivery of impressionistic interpretations of events. How much blog content is true conversation and how much is just self-indulgent ranting is open to debate, but unquestionably the blogosphere is at least a supplemental influence on the news agenda. Individuals peruse online information that they have not seen elsewhere, and the impact of these messages can be magnified when more conventional news media take information from blogs and disseminate it even more widely.

Plenty of noise is emerging from all this activity. Is it symphony or cacophony? It is probably more of the latter at the moment, but that is changing as certain blogs become regular stopping places for information consumers, much as the New York Times and the BBC have been for so long. As in other forms of media, dominant voices will emerge with a rowdy chorus in the background. Clearly, user-generated content is finding a place in the discourse of the global community. More broadly, if information is the fuel for engines of democracy, those engines should be able to run faster and in more places.

Sheer volume means something. Anyone who uses search engines to scan the blogosphere generally and blogs with political content in particular will find the numbers overwhelming. This means that it is impossible to look at everything, but it also means that some material will inevitably find its way to an audience, no matter how draconian the efforts to stop it. Governments that seized documents or jammed radio signals in the past now try to close the portals through which the Internet flows. But even if they succeed for a while, the technology and its users will eventually prevail.

In addition to activists, the quiet information consumer will also rely more on unmediated media. The Internet encourages independent exploration, and people will follow their curiosity along the strands of the Web. This will have ramifications in journalism and politics. Less dependence on traditional media will have economic impact on the already shaky news business. Why rely on a news organization that you already suspect of bias when you can get "news" on your own?

As for politics, why trust a politician whom you believe to be manipulative when you can check countless sources on your own to verify claims and investigate issues? For years, trust in the information provided by the news media and politicians has declined, but there were no alternatives. Now a new level of independence is possible, and millions of people who were passive recipients of information will seek new providers and then themselves will become secondary disseminators of various kinds of news products.

These changes in the information flow will affect the continuation of globalization. For those who fear that a globalized society will be characterized by uniformity as global standards take hold, this media revolution should provide reassurance about the staying power of diversity. Rather than finding bland conformity, information consumers will face the daunting task of deciding which among an unprecedented number of voices deserve attention. This is somewhat similar to the time when people in big cities had dozens of newspapers to choose from each day. Now, if they choose to do so, people living anywhere with Internet access can read dozens of newspapers from dozens of countries, watch hundreds of streaming television channels, and peruse an almost infinite number of additional Web sites, online newsletters, written and video blogs, podcasts, and so on.

Intellectual diversity is an elemental part of the Al Jazeera effect. Uniformity will be far less of a problem than finding time to plunge into all the information that is available.

The Dangers of Media Weaponization

Among the many forms of media used to deliver information, news organizations grounded in traditional journalistic standards and practices retain considerable value. Whether it is the *New York Times, Die Welt, El País, Asahi Shimbun,* the BBC, or one of the newer players among the Arab satellite news channels, the journalistic enterprise—in its many, varied forms—can balance the power of governments if it earns and maintains the public's trust.

Influencing public opinion is not a new role for the media, but recently some governments have responded to this with great aggressiveness, and some media organizations have exacerbated matters by becoming protagonists rather than observers.

The 2006 war between Israel and Hezbollah demonstrated how the news media can be used as weapons. Hezbollah used Al Manar television to inflame public sentiment and generally recruit support for Hezbollah's cause, and so Israel deemed Al Manar to be not a legitimate news organization, but rather a military target that should be attacked. Its headquarters and transmission towers were bombed. Israeli aircraft also attacked transmission facilities of other Lebanese television channels and a convoy of journalists traveling through southern Lebanon.

Neither the political involvement by news organizations nor the targeting of journalists as quasi-combatants is new. In recent years, the United States has attacked Al Jazeera's bureaus in Kabul and Baghdad. American journalists have been kidnapped in Iraq and elsewhere. Lebanese journalists critical of Syria have been murdered. On a broader scale, since 1991 more than six hundred journalists throughout the world have been killed because of their work, often on the orders of government or military officials. (Of these, more than a hundred have been killed in Iraq since the March 2003 invasion.) Other forms of repression of journalists are widespread.

News organizations such as Al Jazeera are widely perceived to be political actors. Their global reach and their influence on public opinion have increasingly led to governments responding with diplomatic protests and, in some cases, military measures.

Weaponization of the media is particularly insidious because it affects all journalists' ability to gather news. Some NGOs are paying close attention to this, even as governments clearly complicit in the targeting of journalists disingenuously proclaim their belief in the importance of independent news media. Making matters worse, terrorist groups in Iraq have attacked journalists as a standard tactic and have been especially vicious when going after Iraqis who worked for Western news organizations. Unless this trend toward increased weaponization of the news media is reversed, the public will soon see a significant shrinkage of reporting from combat zones. Even the newest media technologies cannot compensate for this de facto denial of access.

The Rise of Virtual Communities

One facet of the Al Jazeera effect can be seen in the strengthening of communities of interest that rely on new media to enhance, and in some instances create, cohesion. New media can link people who share cultural, religious, or political characteristics with unprecedented thoroughness. When more people throughout the world gain access to these media, communities that were once just imagined will become more tangible as they expand their populations and their "citizens" assert common interests.

The effect this will have on global politics is hard to predict. Some groups may choose to keep their virtual communities relatively closed, using their media tools for intracommunity purposes. Others may try to use the weight of their numbers to play a more active role on the world stage. Still others may create virtual states with violent intentions. Those who address the dangers of terrorism should consider the virtual state concept in this context because creating such a community can vastly expand the power of terrorist organizations. Communication is an essential element of any organization's unity and effectiveness, and ample documentation illustrates how al Qaeda—to cite just one example—has successfully used new media to proselytize, recruit, instruct, and command.

The virtual community is more than a network. Given the

hard-edged purposefulness of many terrorist organizations, their cyber-communities may be more definitively formed than networks that are more loosely constructed. Furthermore, if a "war" on terrorism is to be conducted, and if it is—as is likely—to entail many years of conflict, then defining the enemy is important. Underestimating its organizational strengths and staying power and dismissing such groups as deranged fanatics operating out of remote caves is a gross strategic error. There is much more to al Qaeda and its brethren than that. Public support for that struggle can be weakened if the nature of the threat is understated, whether for political reasons or out of ignorance. Fighting a war against a state—even a virtual state—requires that the enemy be taken seriously and defined in terms that establish the political as well as military context for a long struggle. A case can be made that al Qaeda should be treated as this kind of state.

Virtual states/communities have spawned their own warrior class. Irhabi007, the name used by the young Moroccan Younis Tsouli, lamented in e-mails to colleagues that he was not engaged in traditional combat in Iraq, but from his home in Britain he became one of the best-known architects of cyber-jihad. As Webmaster for Iraq's al Qaeda leader, Abu Musab al-Zarqawi, and as an instructor of others who use the Internet to disseminate recruiting materials and training manuals about weapons and tactics, Irhabi007 was—until his arrest in 2005—a pioneer in building al Qaeda's electronic infrastructure. With thousands of Web sites in use and a stream of video products designed for its sizable audience, al Qaeda continues to expand its global presence. Although the physical territory it holds is minimal, it occupies as much cyber-territory as it needs.

Governments hostile to al Qaeda should recognize that the limited real estate along the Pakistan-Afghanistan border where some al Qaeda fighters are encamped is meaningless as a measure of al Qaeda's territory. Al Qaeda is, in truth, a criminally violent state that relies on media technologies to constitute its global "homeland." Bin Laden and his lieutenants understand that cyberspace is at least as good a terrain for war as are the mountains of Waziristan. This dark side of the Al Jazeera effect will influence global politics for the foreseeable future.

Beyond Terrorism: Considering the Islamic World

Change affects every part of the globe, but it is important to keep in mind how unsettled the Arab part of the Islamic world continues to be. Undercurrents of dissatisfaction run strongly and have been analyzed not just by Western observers such as Bernard Lewis but also by Arabs such as the Syrian-born poet Ali Ahmad Sa'id, known as Adonis. In 2006 Sa'id said, "If I look at the Arabs, with all their resources and great capacities, and I compare what they have achieved over the past century with what others have achieved in that period, I would have to say that we Arabs are in a phase of extinction, in the sense that we have no creative presence in the world."[5]

This outlook contributes to what Dominique Moisi called a global "clash of emotions" in which "the Western world displays a culture of fear, the Arab and Muslim worlds are trapped in a culture of humiliation, and much of Asia displays a culture of hope."[6]

The word "clash" seems inescapable. At the very least, Samuel Huntington established a semantic structure for those who examine the state of today's world, and debate about his clash concept continues endlessly. Some critics rally to the position articulated by Edward Said when he declared Huntington's theory to be "preposterous" because "cultures are hybrid and heterogenous." Said argued, "Western civilization [is] an ideological fiction, implying a sort of detached superiority for a handful of values and ideas."[7] The same kind of heterogeneity characterizes the Islamic population.

Despite ample ranks of critics, the clash concept remains widely used to frame examinations of Islam's relationship with the non-Islamic world. When 28,000 people in twenty-seven countries were polled from November 2006 through January 2007, they were asked about the inevitability of a violent confrontation between Muslim and Western cultures. Most rejected the notion, but in countries such as Nigeria and Germany, close to 40 percent expected such a conflict to occur, and in the world's most populous Muslim country, Indonesia, 51 percent—about 100 million people—said they anticipated a violent confrontation.[8] That outlook finds its proponents among the likes of Abu Bakar

Bashir, a leader of Indonesia's Jemaah Islamiya, which is an al Qaeda ally. Bashir claimed in 2005 that the Quran says it is destiny for Muslims to fight Christians and Jews, and Westerners must be destroyed unless they accept Islam.[9] He is not alone among both visible and underground promoters of this view.

The tension that accompanies such attitudes takes a toll on political psyches. As Nicholas Kristof observed in late 2006, "There's a fatigue in the West with an Arab world that sometimes seems to put its creative juices mostly into building better bombs. Even open-minded people in the West sometimes feel a sense of resignation that maybe the bigots are right: maybe Islam just is intrinsically backward, misogynistic and violent." Kristof went on, however, to point out that such sweeping judgments are flawed. With a line of argument similar to Edward Said's contention about the West, Kristof noted, as have many others, that Islam is not monolithic—the Arab and non-Arab parts of the Muslim world differ considerably in the ways they integrate religious and political beliefs. He wrote, "There is a historic dichotomy between desert Islam—the austere fundamentalism of countries like Saudi Arabia—and riverine or coastal Islam, more outward-looking, flexible and tolerant. Desert Muslims grab the headlines, but my bet is that in the struggle for the soul of Islam, maritime Muslims have the edge."[10]

Maybe so. It's an interesting, if hard-to-prove point, just as Huntington's hypothesis is easier to speculate about than to prove or disprove. Critics of the idea of homogeneity in this context, such as Said and Kristof, can argue that diversity trumps commonality, but they must contend with the flow of mass media product that blurs differences. The fatigue that Kristof cited is attributable not just to real events but also to the mélange of fact and fiction that information consumers must deal with. One byproduct of the Al Jazeera effect is information overload. Nuance does not fare well in the torrent of rumor-filled blogs, stereotype-dominated entertainment, and oversimplified news offerings.

While uncertainty about what to do with the array of new media increases among the general public, there are those within terrorist organizations who know precisely how they want to use various media. As antiterrorism expert David Kilcullen observed,

"If bin Laden didn't have access to global media, satellite communications, and the Internet, he'd just be a cranky guy in a cave."

Kilcullen also noted that radical Islamist movements devise tactics as part of carefully conceived information strategy. He cited ambushes of American convoys in Iraq as one of these tactics: "They're not doing that because they want to reduce the number of humvees we have in Iraq by one. They're doing it because they want spectacular media footage of a burning humvee." These images are put to use, said Kilcullen, not just as YouTube fare, but on jihadist Web sites where visitors can view the video and then click their way to making donations. (These sites are the products of the likes of Irhabi007.)

George Packer wrote, "The Afghan or Iraqi or Lebanese insurgent, unlike his Vietnamese or Salvadoran predecessor, can plug into a global media network that will instantly amplify his message." That network offers material carefully designed to expand jihadi ranks. Jarret Brachman noted, "The quality of jihadi strategic literature continues to improve, as do the technological sophistication and quantity of propaganda being posted on line."[11]

Enhancing these fringe media messages are images delivered by mainstream sources. Al Jazeera and Al Arabiya have used images of Guantanamo prisoners in promos for the channels, which reinforce the perception of the United States as an oppressor of Muslims.[12] That relatively independent news channels in the Middle East exist and can do this is an example of how the media environment has changed. The percentage of information sources controlled by government or government-friendly media outlets continues to shrink. That fosters freer and sometimes more contentious discourse and alters the information-opinion balance. Governments that once could dictate much "news" content now find themselves scrambling to devise new tactics that go beyond damage control. In early 2008 Arab governments led by Saudi Arabia and Egypt adopted a charter that asserts state control over satellite broadcasting. Within two months, Al Hiwar, a London-based channel that was critical of Egypt's government, was denied access to Nilesat, which is partly owned by Egypt.

The Search for New Strategies

Affecting public opinion in this new environment requires more than traditional propaganda, which is vulnerable when blogs and other new media can quickly provide venues for challenging governments' self-serving messages. The U.S. government has been particularly slow to recognize this, and as a result its public diplomacy efforts have had limited effect.

A change in approach is needed. For instance, jihadist Web sites should be countered by anti-jihadist—but not overtly pro-American—sites. After all, most of the people dying in jihadist terror attacks are not the ostensible American targets but rather are Muslim civilians. The 2005 attacks by an al Qaeda affiliate on hotels in Amman, Jordan, that killed sixty people—almost all of them Arabs—provoked a strong anti–al Qaeda backlash among Arabs.

Publicizing and denouncing such indiscriminate attacks can turn public opinion away from jihadists, which certainly serves the interests of the United States and established regimes in most Muslim countries. But such efforts have to be undertaken in ways that reflect understanding of deeper social attitudes. New media will be most important in reaching younger audiences, who are those most often targeted for recruitment by jihadist organizations. This is another example of media as battleground.

Further, the broad-based dissatisfaction with governments of many Muslim countries must be considered when planning media strategies. Those who appear aligned with the political establishment will never have much credibility unless significant liberalization occurs in countries such as Egypt. Policymakers should be better prepared to take advantage of the Al Jazeera effect's ability to enhance democratization efforts.

As noted earlier, the U.S. government, concerned that Arab satellite channels stoke anti-American sentiment, spent large sums to launch its own Arabic-language television channel, Al Hurra, and Radio Sawa, which was supposed to win friends through music-dominated programming with a sprinkling of news. These efforts have found more critics than allies. Robert Reilly, a former director of the Voice of America, wrote that Sawa's approach "transformed the 'war of ideas' into the battle of the bands." He added, "We do not teach civics to American teenagers by asking them to listen to pop music, so why should we expect Arabs and Persians to learn about America or democracy this way? The condescension implicit in this nearly all-music format is not lost on the audience that we should wish to influence the most—those who think."[13]

Veteran diplomat William Rugh was also critical of Sawa and Al Hurra, writing that Sawa, which had in effect replaced the Voice of America Arabic service, ignored the interests of the Arab policymakers and professionals who had listened to VOA. He added that Al Hurra is not competitive with the likes of Al Jazeera because to Arab viewers "it looks much more like the old-style Arab TV channels that were totally controlled by authoritarian Arab governments and that served primarily as propaganda arms of those governments." As an example of Al Hurra's flawed approach, Rugh cited its coverage of the Abu Ghraib scandal, which, wrote Rugh, "essentially featured commentators friendly to the U.S. government, while Al Jazeera broadcast the Senate hearings that featured Richard Clarke and other critics of the administration, and the latter was much more effective public diplomacy."[14]

Radio and television soak up much of America's public diplomacy budget, but other efforts have been undertaken. Belatedly, U.S. officials stepped up their participation in online conversations and debates. Cultural and educational exchanges, which declined dramatically after 9/11, were revived by the Bush administration's top public diplomacy official, Undersecretary of State Karen Hughes. American diplomats were encouraged, said Hughes, to reach out to the public, not just the government, in the countries where they were serving. Emphasizing U.S. support for health care and education programs displaced some of the more controversial topics.[15] Gradually, the American efforts became more sensible although the overall program has yet to match the magnitude of its task.

Even the most polished public diplomacy messages can easily become lost in the ever more crowded communications universe. That is part of the new media reality that confronts all its users, ranging from international satellite channels to terrorist

Web sites to individuals' blogs. Over time, this universe will attain a kind of order as information consumers gravitate with some regularity to offerings they consider most interesting, truthful, and useful. Everyone will still be able to have her or his own say on blogs, Web sites, and the like, even if their audiences are minuscule. Freedom and self-imposed orderliness should be able to coexist.

○ ⁗ ○

Will the Al Jazeera effect help to advance democracy and, in doing so, reduce the likelihood of a clash of civilizations? The definitive answer to that is, perhaps. Those who look forward to such a clash, be they terrorists or unscrupulous political leaders, may be able to use new media to reach and incite larger audiences than ever before, but they will also face more competing voices than ever before. At some point, hopefulness becomes naïveté, but after surveying the Al Jazeera effect one might believe that in this competition benign common sense will prevail over an agenda that will ensure only great misery.

This phenomenon is not limited to areas of political tension and conflict. Throughout the world, as the power of countries such as China, India, and Brazil continues to grow, their politics and their people's welfare will undoubtedly be influenced by new media's pervasiveness and influence. For now, at least, I remain optimistic about the good that the Al Jazeera effect might do.

As noted at the beginning of this book, "the media" are no longer just the media. They are players in themselves as well as mechanisms, and on many levels they are altering world affairs. Many factors besides communication will shape the next stage of global politics, but understanding and respecting the Al Jazeera effect will help anyone who is concerned about the future to better comprehend the change that swirls about us.

Notes

Chapter 1: Beyond the Clash of Civilizations

1. George Packer, "When Here Sees There," *New York Times*, April 21, 2002.
2. Thomas L. Friedman, *Longitudes and Attitudes: The World in the Age of Terrorism* (New York: Anchor Books, 2003), 390.
3. National Commission on Terrorist Attacks Upon the United States, *The 9/11 Commission Report: Final Report of the National Commission on Terrorist Attacks Upon the United States* (New York: Norton, 2004), 340.
4. Middle East Media Research Institute, *Now Online: Swear Loyalty to al Qaeda Leaders*, Special Dispatch Series, no. 1027, November 18, 2005,www.memri.org/bin/articles.cgi?Page=archives&Area=sd&ID=SP102705.
5. Nicholas Watt and Leo Cendrowicz, "Brussels Calls for Media Code to Avoid Aiding Terrorists," *Guardian*, September 21, 2005.
6. Anthony Shadid and Kevin Sullivan, "Anatomy of the Cartoon Protest Movement," *Washington Post*, February 16, 2006.
7. David Ignatius, "From 'Connectedness' to Conflict," *Washington Post*, February 22, 2006.
8. Bernard Lewis, *What Went Wrong? Western Impact and Middle Eastern Response* (New York: Oxford University Press, 2002), 3.
9. Friedman, *Longitudes and Attitudes*, 165.
10. Yasmine el-Rashidi, "D'oh! Arabized Simpsons Aren't Getting Many Laughs," *Wall Street Journal*, October 14, 2005.
11. Thomas L. Friedman, *The Lexus and the Olive Tree* (New York: Farrar, Straus, Giroux, 1999), 7; Friedman, *Longitudes and Attitudes*, 3-4.
12. Jean Chalaby, "From Internationalization to Transnationalization," *Global Media and Communication* 1, no. 1 (2005), 30.
13. Jon B. Alterman, "The Information Revolution and the Middle East," in *The Future Security Environment in the Middle East: Con-*

flict, Stability, and Political Change, eds. Nora Bensahel and Daniel L. Byman (Santa Monica, CA: RAND, 2003), 243.

14. Marc Lynch, *Voices of the New Arab Public: Iraq, Al-Jazeera, and Middle East Politics Today* (New York: Columbia University Press, 2006), 2.

15. Gilles Kepel, *The War for Muslim Minds: Islam and the West* (Cambridge, MA: Harvard University Press, 2004), 7–8.

16. John R. Bradley, *Saudi Arabia Exposed: Inside a Kingdom in Crisis* (New York: Palgrave Macmillan, 2005), 91.

17. Yossi Alpher, "Strategic Interest: Downloading Democracy (with Some U.S. Help)," *Daily Star*, October 4, 2005; "Palestinian-Israeli Crossfire," Bitterlemons.org, www.bitterlemons.org/about/about.html.

18. Pew Research Center, *Islamic Extremism: Common Concern for Muslim and Western Publics*, Pew Global Attitudes Project, July 14, 2005, http://pewglobal.org/reports/display.php?ReportID=248.

19. Jim Yardley, "A Spectator's Role for China's Muslims," *New York Times*, February 19, 2006.

20. Olivier Roy, *Globalized Islam: The Search for a New Ummah* (New York: Columbia University Press, 2004), 25, 123.

21. Diana Mukkaled, "The World Is Closely Watching," *Asharq Alawsat*, August 30, 2005.

22. Habib Battah, "Watching American TV in Beirut," aljazeera.net, July 14, 2006.

23. Roy, *Globalized Islam*, 102.

24. Pew Research Center, *The Great Divide: How Westerners and Muslims View Each Other*, Pew Global Attitudes Project, June 22, 2006, http://pewglobal.org/reports/display.php?ReportID=253.

25. Kepel, *War for Muslim Minds*, 20.

26. Lynch, *Voices of the New Arab Public*, 194.

27. Faiza Saleh Ambah, "Arab World Riveted by Coverage of the 'Sixth War,'" *Washington Post*, August 14, 2006.

28. Doreen Carvajal, "Big Fish Dive into Arab News Stream," *International Herald Tribune*, June 19, 2006.

29. Middle East Media Research Institute, *"Ya Mohammed" Website Hosted in U.S.: A Part of Internet Jihad*, Special Dispatch, no. 1131, March 31, 2006, www.memri.org/bin/articles.cgi?Page=archive &Area=sd&ID=SP113106; Meris Lutz, "A Cyber-platform for Arab Culture," *Daily Star*, April 6, 2006.

30. Mark Allen, *Arabs* (London: Continuum, 2006), 42.

Chapter 2: Channels and More Channels

1. Fahmy Howeidy, "Setting the News Agenda in the Arab World," in *The Al Jazeera Decade* (Doha: Al Jazeera Channel, 2006), 129.

2. Arab Advisors Group, "48 Percent of Households in Cairo Use the

Internet and 46 Percent Have Satellite TV," news release, January 24, 2005.

3.   Samuel Abt, "For Al Jazeera, Balanced Coverage Frequently Leaves No Side Happy," *New York Times*, February 16, 2004.

4.   Laura M. James, "Whose Voice? Nasser, the Arabs, and 'Sawt al-Arab' Radio," *Transnational Broadcasting Studies Journal*, no. 16 (Spring 2006), www.tbsjournal.com/James.html.

5.   Lynch, *Voices of the New Arab Public*, 36.

6.   Faisal Al Kasim, "*The Opposite Direction*: A Program Which Changed the Face of Arab Television," in *The Al Jazeera Phenomenon: Critical Perspectives on New Arab Media*, ed. Mohamed Zayani (Boulder, CO: Paradigm, 2005), 103.

7.   Friedman, *Latitudes and Attitudes*, 135, 155.

8.   Naomi Sakr, *Satellite Realms: Transnational Television, Globalization, and the Middle East* (London: I. B. Tauris, 2001), 13.

9.   U.S. Institute of Peace, *Arab Media: Tools of the Governments; Tools for the People?* Virtual Diplomacy Series, no. 18, July 2005, 5.

10. Stanley Foundation, *Open Media and Transitioning Societies in the Arab Middle East: Implications for U.S. Security Policy*, report in association with the Institute for Near East and Gulf Military Analysis (Muscatine, IA: Stanley Foundation, 2006), 13.

11. "About MBC Group," MBC, www.mbc.net.

12. Samantha M. Shapiro, "The War Inside the Arab Newsroom," *New York Times Magazine*, January 2, 2005.

13. Ibid.

14. Anthony Shadid, "A Newsman Breaks the Mold in Arab World," *Washington Post*, May 1, 2006; Shapiro, "War Inside the Arab Newsroom."

15. John Kifner, "Massacre Draws Self-Criticism in Muslim Press, *New York Times*, September 9, 2004.

16. Shapiro, "War Inside the Arab Newsroom."

17. Shadid, "Newsman Breaks the Mold in the Arab World."

18. Stanley Foundation, *Open Media and Transitioning Societies*, 15.

19. LBC Group, www.lbcgroup.tv/LBC/En.

20. Raed el Rafei, "Lebanese TV Has a Politically Split Personality," *Los Angeles Times*, December 8, 2006.

21. Sebastian Rotella, "French Ban on Arab TV Station Raises Questions," *Los Angeles Times*, January 10, 2005.

22. Vivian Salama, "Hamas TV: Palestinian Media in Transition," *Transnational Broadcasting Studies Journal*, no. 16 (Spring 2006), www.tbsjournal.com/Salama.html.

23. Craig S. Smith, "Warm and Fuzzy TV, Brought to You by Hamas," *New York Times*, January 18, 2006.

24. Middle East Media Research Institute, *Hamas Al-Aqsa TV: A Mickey*

Mouse Character Teaches Children About the Islamic Rule of the World And to "Annihilate the Jews," Special Dispatch Series, no. 1577, May 9, 2007; *On Hamas Al-Aqsa TV, Nahoul the Bee Replaces Farfour the Mickey-Mouse Character, Vows to Continue Farfour's Path of Martyrdom, Jihad,* Special Dispatch Series, no. 1657, July 15, 2007; and *Hamas Bee Nahoul Abuses Cats, Lions at Gaza Zoo, Calls for Liberation of Al-Aqsa Mosque,* Special Dispatch Series, no. 1683, August 17, 2007. All available at www.memri.org/sd.html.

25.   Javid Hassan and Naif Al-Shehri, "Al Resalah Launched," *Arab News,* March 7, 2006.

26.   Al-Resalah Satellite TV Channel, www.alresalah.net; Middle East Media Research Institute, *Islamic Cleric on Saudi Prince Al-Waleed Bin Talal's New TV Channel,* Special Dispatch Series, no. 1118, March 18, 2006, www.memri.org/bin/articles.cgi?Page=archives& Area=sd&ID=SP111806.

27.   Paul Cochrane, "Is Al-Hurra Doomed?" worldpress.org, June 11, 2004, www.worldpress.org/Mideast/1872.cfm.

28.   Neil MacFarquhar, "Washington's Arabic TV Effort Gets Mixed Reviews," *New York Times,* February 20, 2004.

29.   Cochrane, "Is Al-Hurra Doomed?"

30.   Javid Hassan, "Top Judge Blasts Al-Hurra TV's Ideological War," *Arab News,* March 9, 2004.

31.   Barbara Slavin, "VOA Changes Prompt Staffer Protests," *USA Today,* July 12, 2004.

32.   Arab Advisors Group, "Al-Jazeera Viewers," news release, September 5, 2004.

33.   Dana Zureikat Daoud, "Al-Hurra: An Insider's View," *Adham Center News,* Fall 2004, www.adhamonline.com/News/News.htm.

34.   Shibley Telhami testimony, in Senate Foreign Relations Committee, *The Broadcasting Board of Governors: Finding the Right Media for the Message in the Middle East: Hearing before the Committee on Foreign Relations,* 108th Cong., 2nd sess., April 29, 2004, http://foreign.senate.gov/testimony/2004/TelhamiTestimony040429.pdf.

35.   Anne Marie Baylouny, "Alhurra, the Free One: Assessing U.S. Satellite Television in the Middle East," *Strategic Insights* 4, no. 11 (November 2005), www.ccc.nps.navy.mil/si/2005/Nov/baylounyNov05.asp. See also, Philip Seib, "The Ethics of Public Diplomacy," in *Ethics in Public Relations: Responsible Advocacy,* eds. Kathy Fitzpatrick and Carolyn Bronstein (Thousand Oaks, CA: Sage, 2006), 155–170.

36.   "BBC World Service 2010: Arabic Television," BBC World Service.com, October 25, 2005; Matthew Magee, "BBC Trims European Output to Take on Al Jazeera," *Sunday Herald* (Glasgow), October 23, 2005.

37.   "Bush House of Arabia," *Economist,* October 29, 2005, 57; Heba

el-Qudsy, "Q and A with BBC Arabic's Salah Najm," *Asharq Alawsat*, October 7, 2006.

38. Juan Forero, "And Now, the News in Latin America's View," *New York Times*, May 16, 2005; "Telesur: A Counter-hegemonic Project to Compete with CNN and Univision," *La Jornada* (Mexico), February 27, 2005.

39. Humberto Marquez, "Telesur, a Latin American TV Network, Is on the Air," Global Information Network, May 25, 2005; Reed Johnson, "World News from a New Point of View," *Los Angeles Times*, June 19, 2005.

40. Theresa Bradley, "Telesur Buys Caracas TV Channel, Expanding Chavez Media Reach," Bloomberg.com, December 14, 2006; Marquez, "Telesur."

41. "Telesur: A Counter-hegemonic Project."

42. Aram Aharonian, "Todo lo que usted quiere saber de Telesur (Everything You Want to Know About Telesur)," www.rebelion.org, July 13, 2005, translated by BBC Monitoring Media, July 20, 2005.

43. Forero, "And Now the News in Latin America's View"; Marquez, "Telesur"; Bradley, "Telesur Buys Caracas TV Channel."

44. Doreen Carvajal, "All-News Television Spreading Its Wings," *International Herald Tribune*, January 8, 2006.

45. About France 24, www.france24.com/en/about-france-24.

46. "Everybody Wants One Now," *Economist*, November 30, 2006; John Ward Anderson, "All News All the Time, and Now in French," *Washington Post*, December 7, 2006.

47. Caroline Wyatt, "World News to Get a French Flavor," BBC News, December 6, 2006.

48. Anderson, "All News All the Time."

49. "Russia's TV Broadcasting Not Limited by Language," Novosti, June 27, 2005.

50. "Journalism Mixes With Spin on Russia Today: Critics," Canadian Broadcasting Corporation, March 10, 2006; Kim Murphy, "Russia Will Air Its View of the World," *Los Angeles Times*, June 8, 2005.

51. Murphy, "Russia Will Air Its View of the World."

52. Carvajal, "All-News Television Spreading Its Wings."

53. "News of the World," *Economist*, November 1, 2006.

54. Carvajal, "All News Television Spreading Its Wings."

55. "Background: DW-TV Focus on News and Information," Deutsche Welle, www.dw-world.de/dw/article/0,2144,823127,00.html.

56. "About CNN-IBN," IBN Live, www.ibnlive.com/aboutus.html.

57. Jessica Bennett, "G. Scott Paterson: The CEO Is Aiming JumpTV at Immigrants Who Want to Watch Ethnic Programming," *Newsweek International*, January 1, 2007; Steve Gorman, "Webcast Network JumpTV to Launch Iraqi Service," Reuters, January 24, 2006.

58. Bridges TV, www.bridgestv.com.

59. Siraj Wahab, "Muslims Need to Be Media Savvy," *Arab News*, September 14, 2006.

60. Kingdom Holding Company, www.kingdom.com.sa.

Chapter 3: The Internet Surge

1. Elham Ghashghai and Rosalind Lewis, *Issues Affecting Internet Use in Afghanistan and Developing Countries in the Middle East*, RAND Issue Paper, 2002, 3.

2. James Steinberg, "Information Technology and Development: Beyond 'Either/Or,'" *Brookings Review*, Spring 2003, 46.

3. Steinberg, "Information Technology and Development"; "Behind the Digital Divide," *Economist*, March 12, 2005, 22.

4. "Behind the Digital Divide," 22, 25.

5. Ibid., 25; Ghashghai and Lewis, *Issues Affecting Internet Use*, 3.

6. Catherine Yang, "Wireless Heads for the Hills," *Business Week*, November 28, 2005, 13; Ghashghai and Lewis, *Issues Affecting Internet Use*, 3; "Intel Reveals Wimax Wireless Chip," BBC News, April 18, 2005, http://news.bbc.co.uk/2/hi/technology/4455727.stm.

7. Jeffrey R. Young, "MIT Researchers Unveil a $100 Laptop Designed to Benefit Children Worldwide," *Chronicle of Higher Education*, November 25, 2005, A 41; One Laptop per Child, www.laptop.org.

8. Sharon LaFraniere, "Crowds of Pupils but Little Else in African Schools," *New York Times*, December 30, 2006.

9. Young, "MIT Researchers Unveil," A 42.

10. Ghashghai and Lewis, *Issues Affecting Internet Use*, 4.

11. Victoria Shannon, "What Laptop per Child?" *International Herald Tribune*, November 19–20, 2005.

12. Kevin Sullivan, "Internet Extends Reach of Bangladeshi Villagers," *Washington Post*, November 22, 2006.

13. Jonathan Curiel, "Arab Media Present Varied Viewpoints on Prisoner Abuse," *San Francisco Chronicle*, May 9, 2004.

14. Hendrik Hertzberg, "Big News Week," *The New Yorker*, May 30, 2005; Evan Thomas, "How a Fire Broke Out," *Newsweek*, May 23, 2005, 32.

15. Michael Getler, "Yet Another Wake-Up Call," *Washington Post*, May 22, 2005.

16. Hertzberg, "Big News Week."

17. "Yesterday's Papers," *Economist*, April 23, 2005, 59.

18. "War Beyond the Box," Center for Social Media, www.centerforsocialmedia.org/warbeyondbox.

19. Olesya Dmitracova, "Russians Do in Blogs What Few Can Do in Media: Argue," washingtonpost.com, December 18, 2006, www.washingtonpost.com/wp-dyn/content/article/2006/12/18/AR2006121800087.html.

20. Garry Kasparov, "Putin's Critics: A Web Strategy," *Business Week*,

June 4, 2007, 112; The Other Russia, theotherrussia.org; Russian Live Journal, community.livejournal.com/daily_russian.

21. David Mattin, "We Are Changing the Nature of News," *Guardian*, August 15, 2005.

22. Mattin, "We Are Changing"; iTalkNews, www.italknews.com.

23. "The Whole World Is Reading," journalism.org, December 13, 2006, http://journalism.org/node/3276; *Global Voices*, www.global voicesonline.org.

24. "We Had 50 Images Within an Hour," *Guardian*, July 11, 2005.

25. "Execution Footage a Dilemma for TV News," Television Week, January 8, 2007.

26. Michael Coren, "Internet Aids Tsunami Recovery," CNN.com, January 5, 2005, www.cnn.com/2005/TECH/01/05/tech.tsunami/index.html; Stephanie Strom, "Storm and Crisis: Donations," *New York Times*, September 13, 2005.

27. Live 8, www.live8live.com; "Over 26 Million Text Messages Sent Backing Live 8," *New York Times*, July 4, 2005.

28. Thomas Crampton, "French Police Fear That Blogs Have Helped Incite Rioting," *New York Times*, November 10, 2005; Molly Moore and Daniel Williams, "France's Youth Battles Also Waged on the Web," *Washington Post*, November 10, 2005, "French Youths Turn to Web, Cell Phones to Plan Riots," *New York Times*, November 9, 2005.

29. Emily Wax, "African Rebels Take Their Battles Online," *Washington Post*, January 14, 2006.

30. Robert W. Hefner, "Civic Pluralism Denied? The New Media and Jihadi Violence in Indonesia," in *New Media in the Muslim World: The Emerging Public Sphere*, eds. Dale F. Eickelman and Jon W. Anderson, 2nd ed. (Bloomington: Indiana University Press, 2003), 161, 171.

31. Faisal Devji, *Landscapes of the Jihad: Militancy, Morality, Modernity* (Ithaca, NY: Cornell University Press, 2005), 96.

32. Friedman, *Longitudes and Attitudes*, 169.

33. "Dial M for Mujahideen," *Economist*, May 20, 2006, 45.

34. Habib Battah, "SMS: The Next TV Revolution," *Transnational Broadcasting Studies Journal*, no. 16 (Spring 2006), www.tbsjournal.com/Battah.html.

35. Moises Naim, "The YouTube Effect," *Foreign Policy*, January–February 2007, 103–104.

Chapter 4: The Rise of the Virtual State

1. Benedict Anderson, *Imagined Communities: Reflections on the Origin and Spread of Nationalism* (London: Verso, 1991), 6, 7.

2. Merlyna Lim, *Islamic Radicalism and Anti-Americanism in Indonesia: The Role of the Internet* (Washington, DC: East-West Center,

2005), viii.

3. Andrew Cockburn, "Iraq's Resilient Minority," *Smithsonian*, December 2005, 44.

4. Christopher Catherwood, *Winston's Folly: Imperialism and the Creation of Modern Iraq* (London: Constable, 2004), 113, 180.

5. Christiane Bird, *A Thousand Sighs, a Thousand Revolts: Journeys in Kurdistan* (New York: Random House, 2005), 143.

6. Cockburn, "Iraq's Resilient Minority," 54.

7. William Merrifield, "MED-TV: Kurdish Satellite Television and the Changing Relationship Between the State and the Media," *Transnational Broadcasting Studies Journal*, no. 14 (Spring 2005), www.tbsjournal.com/Archives/Spring05/merrifield.html.

8. Sakr, *Satellite Realms*, 62; M. Hakan Yavuz, "Media Identities for Alevis and Kurds in Turkey," in *New Media in the Muslim World*, 193.

9. Merrifield, "MED-TV."

10. "Medya TV CEO Denies Links with PKK," www.clandestineradio.com, February 25, 2004, www.clandestineradio.com/crw/news.php?id= &stn=684&news=345.

11. Yigal Schleifer, "Denmark Again? Now It's Under Fire for Hosting Kurdish TV Station," *Christian Science Monitor*, April 21, 2006.

12. "About KWR," KurdistanWeb.org, http://kurdistanweb.org/kw/about-kw.html.

13. Kurdish Media, www.kurdmedia.com/.

14. Roy, *Globalized Islam*, ix, 18, 146.

15. Anthony Shadid, *Legacy of the Prophet: Despots, Democrats, and the New Politics of Islam* (Boulder, CO: Westview Press, 2002), 252, 253, 266.

16. Devji, *Landscapes of the Jihad*, 22, 72, 74.

17. Friedman, *Longitudes and Attitudes*, 137.

18. Lawrence Pintak, *Reflections in a Bloodshot Lens: America, Islam and the War of Ideas* (London: Pluto Press, 2006), 244, 241.

19. Devji, *Landscapes of the Jihad*, 28.

20. Quintan Wiktorowicz, "The Salafi Movement: Violence and Fragmentation of Community," in *Muslim Networks from Hajj to Hip Hop*, eds. miriam cooke and Bruce B. Lawrence (Chapel Hill: University of North Carolina Press, 2005), 220.

21. Sakr, *Satellite Realms*, 34.

22. Anthony Bubalo and Greg Fealy, *Between the Global and the Local: Islamism, the Middle East, and Indonesia*, Brookings Institution, U.S. Policy Toward the Islamic World, Analysis Paper, no. 9, October 2005.

23. Karim Raslan, "The Islam Gap," *New York Times*, February 15, 2006.

24. Eickelman and Anderson, *New Media in the Muslim World*, 1.

25. Pew Research Center, *Islamic Extremism: Common Concern for Mus-*

lim and Western Publics, Global Attitudes Project, July 14, 2005, http://pewglobal.org/reports/display.php?ReportID=248.

26. Reza Aslan, *No God but God: The Origins, Evolution, and Future of Islam* (New York: Random House, 2006), 237.

27. David Martin Jones and M. L. R. Smith, "Greetings From the Cybercaliphate: Some Notes on Homeland Insecurity," *International Affairs* 81, no. 5 (October 2005): 941.

28. Roy, *Globalized Islam*, 19.

29. IslamOnline.net–About Us, www.islamonline.net/english/aboutus.

30. Roy, *Globalized Islam*, 112.

31. Jon W. Anderson, "The Internet and Islam's New Interpreters," in *New Media in the Muslim World*, 45, 48.

32. Jakob Skovgaard-Petersen, "The Global Mufti," in *Globalization and the Muslim World: Culture, Religion, and Modernity*, eds. Birgit Schaebler and Leif Stenberg (Syracuse, NY: Syracuse University Press, 2004), 155–156.

33. Jon W. Anderson, "New Media, New Publics: Reconfiguring the Public Sphere of Islam," *Social Research* 70, no. 3 (Fall 2003): 898.

34. Kepel, *War for Muslim Minds*, 19.

35. Shadid, *Legacy of the Prophet*, 68; Marc Lynch, "Al Qaeda's Media Strategies," *National Interest*, March 1, 2006, www.nationalinterest.org/Article.aspx?id=11524.

36. Gary R. Bunt, *Islam in the Digital Age: e-Jihad, Online Fatwas, and Cyber Islamic Environments* (London: Pluto Press, 2003), 211.

37. IslamiCity—Islam & the Global Muslim eCommunity, www.islamicity.com.

38. Jon W. Anderson, "Wiring Up: The Internet Difference for Muslim Networks," in *Muslim Networks from Hajj to Hip Hop*, 255–256.

39. Peter Mandaville, "Communication and Diasporic Islam: A Virtual *Ummah*?" in *The Media of Diaspora*, ed. Karim H. Karim (London: Routledge, 2003), 135, 146.

40. Sam Cherribi, "From Baghdad to Paris: Al Jazeera and the Veil," *Harvard International Journal of Press/Politics* 11, no. 2 (Spring 2006): 122, 124, 128.

41. Hefner, "Civic Pluralism Denied?" 160.

42. Lim, *Islamic Radicalism and Anti-Americanism in Indonesia*, 44, 46.

43. Devji, *Landscapes of the Jihad*, 66.

44. Eickelman and Anderson, *New Media in the Muslim World*, 8.

45. Jocelyne Cesari, "Islam in the West: Modernity and Globalization Revisited," in *Globalization and the Muslim World*, 86.

46. Lim, *Islamic Radicalism and Anti-Americanism in Indonesia*, viii.

47. Carl W. Ernst, "Ideological and Technological Transformations of Contemporary Sufism," in *Muslim Networks from Hajj to Hip Hop*, 203.

Chapter 5: Global Connections, Global Terrorism

1.   "Hizb ut-Tahrir al-Islami (Islamic Party of Liberation),"
     GlobalSecurity. org, www.globalsecurity.org/military/world/para/
     hizb-ut-tahrir.htm.

2.   Zeyno Baran, "Fighting the War of Ideas," *Foreign Affairs*, November–December 2005, 72–73.

3.   Roy, *Globalized Islam*, 238, 270.

4.   Hizb ut Tahrir, www.hizb-ut-tahrir.org.

5.   James Brandon, "Hizb ut-Tahrir's Growing Appeal in the Arab World," *Jamestown Foundation Terrorism Monitor* 4, no. 24 (December 14, 2006).

6.   Madeleine Gruen, "Hizb ut-Tahrir's Activities in the United States," *Jamestown Foundation Terrorism Monitor* 5, no. 16 (August 16, 2007).

7.   Abdel Bari Atwan, *The Secret History of al Qaeda* (Berkeley: University of California Press, 2006), 222.

8.   National Commission on Terrorist Attacks, *9/11 Commission Report*, 362–363.

9.   Devji, *Landscapes of the Jihad*, 137.

10. Jason Burke, *Al Qaeda: Casting a Shadow of Terror* (London: I. B. Tauris, 2003), 12.

11. Michael Scheuer, "Al Qaeda Doctrine for International Political Warfare," *Jamestown Foundation Terrorism Focus* 3, no. 42 (October 31, 2006).

12. National Commission on Terrorist Attacks, *9/11 Commission Report*, 145.

13. Michele Zanini and Sean J. A. Edwards, "The Networking of Terror in the Information Age," in *Networks and Netwars: The Future of Terror, Crime, and Militancy*, eds. John Arquila and David Ronfeldt (Santa Monica, CA: RAND, 2001), 34.

14. Gabriel Weimann, *Terror on the Internet: The New Arena, the New Challenges* (Washington, DC: U.S. Institute of Peace Press, 2006), 115–116.

15. Craig Whitlock, "The New al Qaeda Central," *Washington Post*, September 9, 2007.

16. Lawrence Wright, "The Terror Web," *The New Yorker*, August 2, 2004, 44.

17. See Ron Suskind, *The One Percent Doctrine* (New York: Simon & Schuster, 2006).

18. Michael Scheuer, *Imperial Hubris: Why the West Is Losing the War on Terror* (Washington, DC: Brassey's, Inc., 2004), 81.

19. Weimann, *Terror on the Internet*, 66.

20. Atwan, *Secret History of al Qaeda*, 122.

21. Weimann, *Terror on the Internet*, 65, 67; Robert Spencer, "Al Qaeda Internet Magazine *Sawt al-Jihad* Calls to Intensify Fighting During

Ramadan," *Jihad Watch*, October 23, 2004, www.jihadwatch.org/archives/003647.php.

22. Weimann, *Terror on the Internet*, 44.

23. Steve Coll and Susan B. Glasser, "Terrorists Move Operations to Cyberspace," *Washington Post*, August 7, 2005.

24. Scheuer, *Imperial Hubris*, 79, 81.

25. Nadya Labi, "Jihad 2.0," *Atlantic Monthly*, July–August 2006, 103.

26. Middle East Research Media Institute, *American al Qaeda Operative Adam Gadahn, al Qaeda Deputy al-Zawahiri, and London Bomber Shehzad Tanweer in New al Sahab/al Qaeda Film Marking the First Anniversary of the 7/7 London Bombings*, Special Dispatch Series, no. 1201, July 11, 2006, www.memri.org/bin/articles.cgi?Page=archives&Area=sd&ID=SP120106; Jessica Stern, "Al Qaeda, American Style," *New York Times*, July 15, 2006.

27. Michael Scheuer, "Al Qaeda's Media Doctrine: Evolution from Cheerleader to Opinion-Shaper," *Jamestown Foundation Terrorism Focus* 4, no. 15, May 22, 2007.

28. Dan Murphy and Jill Carroll, "Al Qaeda Ramps Up Its Propaganda," *Christian Science Monitor*, July 16, 2007; Bruce Riedel, "Al Qaeda Strikes Back," *Foreign Affairs* 86, no. 3 (May–June 2007): 30.

29. "As-Sahab: Al Qaeda's Nebulous Media Branch," *Stratfor Daily Terrorism Brief*, September 8, 2006, www.stratfor.com; Hassan M. Fattah, "Al Qaeda Increasingly Reliant on Media," *New York Times*, September 30, 2006.

30. Middle East Media Research Institute, *Islamist Websites Monitor No. 85*, Special Dispatch Series, no. 1543, April 13, 2007, www.memri.org/bin articles.cgi?Page=archives&Area=sd&ID=SP15410; Andrew Black, "Al Qaeda in the Islamic Maghreb's Burgeoning Media Apparatus," *Jamestown Foundation Terrorism Focus* 14, no. 14 (May 15, 2007).

31. Labi, "Jihad 2.0," 102.

32. Robert F. Worth, "Jihadists Take Stand on Web, and Some Say It's Defensive," *New York Times*, March 13, 2005.

33. Susan B. Glasser and Steve Coll, "The Web as Weapon," *Washington Post*, August 9, 2005.

34. Various examples available at the MEMRI TV Web site, www.memritv.org.

35. Paul Jenkins, "Redefining Terror," *World Today*, August–September 2006, 8.

36. Worth, "Jihadists Take Stand on Web."

37. Marc Santora and Damien Cave, "Banned Station Beams Voice of Iraq Insurgency," *New York Times*, January 21, 2007.

38. Paul Richter, "U.S., Saudis at Odds Over TV Station," *Los Angeles Times*, May 31, 2007.

39. Kepel, *War for Muslim Minds*, 114.
40. Devji, *Landscapes of the Jihad*, 99, 162.
41. Evan F. Kohlmann, "The Real Online Terrorist Threat," *Foreign Affairs* 85, no. 5 (September–October 2006), 117; Middle East Media Research Institute, *Islamist Websites Monitor # 82–85*, Special Dispatch Series, no. 1543, April 13, 2007, www.memri.org/bin/articles.cgi?Page=archives&Area=sd&ID=SP154307.
42. "A World Wide Web of Terror," *The Economist*, July 14, 2007, 28–29.
43. Middle East Media Research Institute, *Islamist Website Instructs Mujahideen in Using Popular U.S. Web Forums to Foster Anti-War Sentiment Among Americans*, Special Dispatch Series, no. 1508, March 20, 2007, www.memri.org/bin/articles.cgi?Page=archives&Area=sd&ID=SP150807; and *How Islamist Internet Forums Are Used to Inform Mujahideen of News From Western Media*, Special Dispatch Series, no. 1615, June 8, 2007, www.memri.org/bin/articles.cgi?Page=archives&Area=sd&ID=SP161507.

Chapter 6: The Cyber-struggle for Democracy

1. Alterman, "Information Revolution and the Middle East," 245.
2. Shanthi Kalathil and Taylor C. Boas, *Open Networks, Closed Regimes: The Impact of the Internet on Authoritarian Rule* (Washington, DC: Carnegie Endowment for International Peace, 2003), 128, 136, 44.
3. Reporters Without Borders, *2006 Internet Annual Report*, www.rsf.org/IMG/pdf/report.pdf.
4. Shanthi Kalathil, "Dot Com for Dictators," *Foreign Policy*, March–April 2003, 44.
5. Singapore i-Government, www.igov.gov.sg/programmes/eGap_II; eCitizen: Your Gateway to All Government Services, www.ecitizen.gov.sg.
6. Kalathil, "Dot Com for Dictators," 48.
7. Cathy Hong, "New Political Tool: Text Messaging," *Christian Science Monitor*, June 30, 2005.
8. "The Party, the People, and the Power of Cyber-talk," *The Economist*, April 29, 2006, 28; Edward Cody, "Despite a Ban, Chinese Youth Navigate to Internet Cafes," *Washington Post*, February 9, 2007; China Internet Network Information Center, www.cnnic.net.cn.
9. Bruce Einhorn, "The Net's Second Superpower," *Business Week*, March 15, 2005, 54–55.
10. "The Party, the People," 27; RAND, "RAND Report Says Internet Unlikely to Spark Major Political Change in China in Near Future," news release, August 26, 2002, www.rand.org/news/press.02/dissent.html.
11. Mark Magnier, "China Clamps Down on Web News Discussion," *Los Angeles Times*, February 26, 2004.

12. Howard W. French, "As Chinese Students Go Online, Little Sister Is Watching," *New York Times*, May 9, 2006.

13. Cody, "Despite a Ban."

14. Peter S. Goodman and Mike Musgrove, "China Blocks Web Search Engines," *Washington Post*, September 12, 2002; Bruce Einhorn and Ben Elgin, "The Great Firewall of China," *Business Week*, January 23, 2006, 34.

15. Fareed Zakaria, *The Future of Freedom: Illiberal Democracy at Home and Abroad* (New York: Norton, 2003), 85.

16. Anne Applebaum, "Let a Thousand Filters Bloom," *Washington Post*, July 20, 2005.

17. Kathy Chen and Geoffrey A. Fowler, "Microsoft Defends Censoring a Dissident's Blog in China," *Wall Street Journal*, January 6, 2006.

18. "The End of the Affair," *The Economist*, September 24, 2005, 80.

19. Tina Rosenberg, "Building the Great Firewall of China, With Foreign Help," *New York Times*, September 18, 2005.

20. John Pomfret, "Outbreak Gave China's Hu an Opening," *Washington Post*, May 13, 2003.

21. Ibid.

22. Magnier, "China Clamps Down on Web News Discussion"; Tim Luard, "China Clamps Down on Online Justice," BBC News Online, January 19, 2004, http://news.bbc.co.uk/2/hi/asia-pacific/3409995.stm.

23. Philip P. Pan, "Chinese Evade Censors to Discuss Police Assault," *Washington Post*, December 17, 2005; Howard W. French, "Beijing Casts Net of Silence Over Protest," *New York Times*, December 14, 2005; "In Memory of Miss Liu Hezhen," www.marxists.org/archive/lu-xun/1926/04/01.

24. Michael Singer, "Triangle Boy Unleashed," internetnews.com, March 8, 2001.

25. Ethan Gutmann, "Who Lost China's Internet?" *Weekly Standard*, February 25, 2002; Ben Elgin, "Outrunning China's Web Cops," *Business Week*, February 20, 2006, 38.

26. Chris Buckley, "Internet Muckraker Challenges China's Censors," *Washington Post*, February 17, 2006; Nicholas D. Kristof, "Death by a Thousand Blogs," *New York Times*, May 24, 2005.

27. "China Shuts Two Popular Blogs in Latest Crackdown," Reuters, March 8, 2006.

28. Einhorn and Elgin, "Great Firewall of China"; Chen and Fowler, "Microsoft Defends Censoring a Dissident's Blog in China."

29. Philip P. Pan, "Bloggers Who Pursue Change Confront Fear and Mistrust," *Washington Post*, February 21, 2006.

30. Kristof, "Death by a Thousand Blogs"; Nicholas D. Kristof, "In China, It's ＊＊＊＊＊＊＊ vs. Netizens," *New York Times*, June 20, 2006.

31. "Google to Censor Results on New Chinese Search Site," *Washington Post*, January 25, 2006.

32. OpenNet Initiative, *China Tightens Controls on Internet News Content Through Additional Regulations*, Bulletin 012, July 5, 2006, www.opennetinitiative.net/bulletins/012.

33. Philip P. Pan, "Leading Publication Shut Down in China," *Washington Post*, January 25, 2006; Jim Yardley, "Chinese Journal Closed by Censors Is to Reopen," *New York Times*, February 16, 2006; Minxin Pei, "Media Control Gets More Tricky," *Straits Times*, February 27, 2006.

34. Xu Wu, "A Chronicle of Chinese Cyber Nationalism" (paper presented at the International Studies Association annual convention, March 23, 2006), 1, 5; Jim Yardley, "A Hundred Cell Phones Bloom, and Chinese Take to the Streets," *New York Times*, April 25, 2005.

35. Zakaria, *Future of Freedom*, 85.

36. "Myanmar" is the name invented by the junta calling itself State Law and Order Restoration Council when it forcibly seized power in 1989. Some news organizations, governments, and political leaders, including the president of the United States, continue to refer to the country by its historic name, Burma, so I have used Burma here.

37. Lars Bevanger, "Burmese TV Broadcasts from Norway," BBC News Online, August 22, 2005, http://news.bbc.co.uk/2/hi/asia-pacific/4173748.stm.

38. Reporters Without Borders, *Burma Annual Report—2006*, www.rsf.org/article.php3?id_article=17346.

39. Howard W. French, "Online Newspaper Shakes Up Korean Politics," *New York Times*, March 6, 2003.

40. David Anable, "The Role of Georgia's Media—and Western Aid—in the Rose Revolution," *Harvard International Journal of Press/Politics* 11, no. 3 (Summer 2006): 7.

41. David Ignatius, "Reality Check for the Neo-Wilsonians," *Washington Post*, January 26, 2005.

42. Anable, "Role of Georgia's Media," 10.

43. Adrian Karatnycky, "Ukraine's Orange Revolution," *Foreign Affairs* 84, no. 2 (March–April 2005): 43.

44. OpenNet Initiative, "Internet Filtering in Vietnam in 2005–2006: A Country Study," www.opennet.net/studies/vietnam.

45. Randeep Ramesh, "Bloggers' Fury as India Blocks Sites," *Guardian*, July 19, 2006.

46. Spencer Kelly, "Getting Connected in Rural India," BBC Click Online, October 21, 2005, http://news.bbc.co.uk/2/hi/programmes/click_online/4364168.stm.

47. Gopal Sharma, "Banned From the Air, Nepal News Radio Hits Streets," Reuters, June 21, 2005.

48. Kalathil and Boas, *Open Networks, Closed Regimes*, 73; Cherian George, *Contentious Journalism and the Internet: Towards Democratic Discourse in Malaysia and Singapore* (Singapore: Singapore University Press, 2006), 56, 76.

49. George, *Contentious Journalism and the Internet*, 2, 121.

50. Elaine Sciolino, "A New French Headache: When Is Hate on TV Illegal?" *New York Times*, December 9, 2004; Doreen Carvajal, "French Court Orders a Ban on Hezbollah-Run TV Channel," *New York Times*, December 14, 2004; "Europeans Ban Hezbollah-Run TV Channel," *New York Times*, March 18, 2005.

51. Jeremy R. Azrael and D. J. Peterson, *Russia and the Information Revolution*, RAND Issue Paper (Santa Monica, CA: RAND, 2002).

52. Mark Glaser, "Journalist Paints Bleak Picture for Media in Zimbabwe," *Media Shift*, PBS, September 6, 2006, www.pbs.org/mediashift/2006/09/digging_deeperjournalist_paint.

53. "Narrowing the Digital Divide," *Wired News*, November 12, 2005; "Can Technology Ease Africa's Woes?" Reuters, November 15, 2005.

Chapter 7: Transforming the Middle East

1. Mohamed Zayani, "Introduction—Al Jazeera and the Vicissitudes of the New Arab Mediascape," in *The Al Jazeera Phenomenon: Critical Perspectives on New Arab Media*, ed. Mohamed Zayani (Boulder, CO: Paradigm Publishers, 2005), 33.

2. Robin Wright, "Al Jazeera Puts Focus on Reform," *Washington Post*, May 8, 2005.

3. Hugh Miles, *Al-Jazeera: The Inside Story of the Arab News Channel That Is Challenging the West* (New York: Grove: 2005), 327, 328.

4. Bernard Lewis, "Freedom and Justice in the Modern Middle East," *Foreign Affairs* 84, no. 3 (May–June 2005): 46.

5. Marc Lynch, "Assessing the Democratizing Power of Satellite TV," *Transnational Broadcasting Studies Journal*, no. 14 (Spring 2005), www.tbsjournal.com/Archives/Spring05/lynch.html.

6. Mustafa el-Menshawy, "Little Matchbox, Lots of Spark," *Al-Ahram Weekly*, December 29, 2005.

7. Lynch, "Assessing the Democratizing Power of Satellite TV."

8. Mohamed Darwish, "Once Again Divided," *Al-Ahram Weekly*, October 16, 2003.

9. Lewis, "Freedom and Justice in the Modern Middle East," 47.

10. Zayani, "Introduction," 35.

11. Marc Lynch, "Watching Al Jazeera," *Wilson Quarterly*, Summer 2005, 44.

12. Miles, *Al-Jazeera*, 328.

13. UN Development Program, *Arab Human Development Report 2004: Towards Freedom in the Arab World* (New York: UN Publications, 2005), 22.

14. Kalathil and Boas, *Open Networks, Closed Regimes,* 150.

15. Charles A. Kupchan, *The End of the American Era: U.S. Foreign Policy and the Geopolitics of the Twenty-first Century* (New York: Knopf, 2002), 106.

16. David Ignatius, "Careful With Syria," *Washington Post,* November 18, 2005.

17. UN Development Program, *Arab Human Development Report 2003: Building a Knowledge Society* (New York: UN Publications, 2003), 63; Internet Usage World Stats: Internet and Population Statistics, www.internetworldstats.com.

18. Nicholas Watt and Leo Cendrowicz, "Brussels Calls for Media Code to Avoid Aiding Terrorists," *Guardian,* September 21, 2005.

19. Technorati: About Us, http://technorati.com/about.

20. Madeleine K. Albright and Vin Weber, *In Support of Arab Democracy: Why and How: Report of an Independent Task Force* (New York: Council on Foreign Relations, 2005), 30.

21. Neil MacFarquhar, "In Tiny Arab State, Web Takes on Ruling Elite," *New York Times,* January 15, 2006.

22. Hong, "New Political Tool: Text Messaging."

23. Steven Coll, "In the Gulf, Dissidence Goes Digital," *Washington Post,* March 29, 2005.

24. Zayani, "Introduction," 35.

25. Alterman, "Information Revolution and the Middle East," 243.

26. Lynch, "Assessing the Democratizing Power of Satellite TV."

27. Ramez Maluf, "Arab Media in a Shrinking World," *Stanley Foundation Courier,* no. 48 (Summer 2005), 14.

28. Magda Abu-Fadil, "Live from Martyrs' Square: Lebanon's 'Reality TV' Turns Coverage of Peaceful Protests Into Media Battle," *Transnational Broadcasting Studies Journal,* no. 14 (Spring 2005), www.tbsjournal.com/Archives/Spring05/abufadil.html.

29. Osama el-Ghazali Harb, "Fear of Freedom," *Al-Ahram Weekly,* April 14, 2005.

30. Naguib Mahfouz, "The Media's Long Road," *Al-Ahram Weekly,* December 23, 2004.

31. Tom Perry, "Egyptian State Media Ignore U.S. Calls for Reform," *Reuters,* June 22, 2005.

32. Dina Ezzat, "Now Showing," *Al-Ahram Weekly,* June 9, 2005; Daniel Williams, "Appalled at Beating of Protestors, Egypt's Opposition Leaps to Action," *Washington Post,* July 6, 2005; "Egypt Bloggers Spearhead Anti-Mubarak Dissent," Agence France Presse, August 29, 2005.

33. Mark Glaser, "Blogs, Wiki, Google Bomb Used to Free Egyptian Activist," *Media Shift,* PBS, May 23, 2006, www.pbs.org/mediashift/2006/05/digging_deeperblogs_wiki_googl_1.html.

34. Salama A. Salama, "Media Reform!" *Al-Ahram Weekly,* July 1, 2004.

35. Nasrin Alavi, *We Are Iran: The Persian Blogs* (Brooklyn, NY: Soft Skull Press, 2005), 219, 280.

36. Saeed Kamali Dehghan, "Iran's Big Brother for Bloggers," *Guardian*, June 7, 2007; Alavi, *We Are Iran*, 1, 2, 4; Nahid Siamdoust, "Iranian Blogger Returns From Exile for Vote," *Los Angeles Times*, June 23, 2005; "Iran Cracks Down on Bloggers," Associated Press, March 28, 2006.

37. "Iran Cracks Down on Bloggers," Associated Press, March 28, 2006.

38. Siamdoust, "Iranian Blogger Returns"; "Iran Cracks Down on Bloggers"; Amol Sharma, "Muckraking Mullahs," *Foreign Policy*, May–June 2002, 99; Dehghan, "Iran's Big Brother for Bloggers."

39. Alavi, *We Are Iran*, 248–49, 319.

40. Ibid., 102; Siamdoust, "Iranian Blogger Returns."

41. Alavi, *We Are Iran*, 345.

42. Middle East Media Research Institute, *Interview With Editor in Chief of the Reformist Web Site Metransparent.com*, Special Dispatch Series, no. 1193, June 28, 2006, www.memri.org/bin/articles.cgi?Page=archives&Area=sd&ID=SP119306.

43. Marwan Kraidy, "Syria: Media Reform and Its Limitations," *Arab Reform Bulletin* 4, no. 4 (May 2006): 3–4.

44. "Syria's Internet Serves as Platform for Dissent," *Daily Star*, March 15, 2006; Gal Beckerman, "The New Arab Conversation," *Columbia Journalism Review*, January–February 2007, 19.

45. James Palmer, "Baghdad Radio Lets Foes Talk Things Out," *Washington Times*, January 18, 2006; "Talk Radio Comes to Baghdad," BBC News, June 19, 2004, news.bbc.co.uk/2/hi/middle_east/3821307.stm.

46. Yochi J. Dreazen, "Women Find a Voice at Iraq Radio Station," *Wall Street Journal*, July 29, 2005.

47. Anne Alexander, "Iraqi Web Sites," *Global Media and Communication* 1, no. 2 (August 2005): 226.

48. Hassan M. Fattah, "Dubai Opens Door Wide to News Media, but Journalists Note a Catch," *New York Times*, September 11, 2005.

49. Adnan Malik, "Bahrainis Ask for Information Minister's Resignation Over Internet Censorship," Associated Press, May 4, 2002; MacFarquhar, "In Tiny Arab State, Web Takes on Ruling Elite."

50. "Local Content Filtering Policy," Internet Services Unit, www.isu.net.sa/saudi-internet/contenet-filtring/filtring-policy.htm.

51. Faiza Saleh Ambah, "New Clicks in the Arab World," *Washington Post*, November 12, 2006.

52. Andrew Hammond, "Outspoken Saudi Bloggers Wary of 'Official' Group," Reuters, May 3, 2006; David Crawford, "Battle for Ears and Minds: As Technology Gives New Voice to Dissent, a Saudi Vies to Be Heard," *Wall Street Journal*, February 4, 2004; Bradley, *Saudi Arabia Exposed*, 193–195.

53. UN, "Mass Media, Press Freedom and Publishing in the Arab World: Arab Intellectuals Speak Out," news release, October 20, 2003.

54. Youssef M. Ibrahim, "Will the Mideast Bloom?" *Washington Post*, March 13, 2005.

55. Hassan M. Fattah, "Challenging Saudi Arabia's Powerful, One Caller at a Time," *New York Times*, May 5, 2007.

56. Ramzy Baroud, "Citizen Journalism," *Al-Ahram Weekly*, July 20, 2006; "The Battle for Public Relations," *The Economist*, March 26, 2005, 48.

57. Al Manar, www.almanar.com.lb; Avi Jorisch, *Beacon of Hatred: Inside Hizballah's Al-Manar Television* (Washington, DC: Washington Institute for Near East Policy, 2004), ix.

58. Jay Solomon and Mariam Fam, "Air Battle: Lebanese News Network Draws Fire as Arm of Militant Group," *Wall Street Journal*, July 28, 2006.

59. Philip Seib, *The Global Journalist: News and Conscience in a World of Conflict* (Lanham, MD: Rowman and Littlefield, 2002), 68.

60. Jon Alterman, "The Key Is Moving Beyond Spectacle," *Daily Star*, December 27, 2004.

61. Samantha M. Shapiro, "Ministering to the Upwardly Mobile Muslim," *New York Times Magazine*, April 30, 2006.

62. Lindsay Wise, "Amr Khaled vs. Yusuf Al Qaradawi: The Danish Cartoon Controversy and the Clash of Two Islamic TV Titans," *Transnational Broadcasting Studies Journal*, no. 16 (Spring 2006), www.tbsjournal.com/Wise.htm.

63. Will Rasmussen, "Heya Satellite Channel Tackles Women's Core and Controversial Issues in Middle East," *Daily Star*, February 25, 2005.

64. Hassan Fattah, "Voting, Not Violence, Is the Big Story on Arab TV," *New York Times*, January 30, 2005.

65. Lewis, *What Went Wrong?* 151.

66. Gadi Wolfsfeld, *Media and the Path to Peace* (Cambridge: Cambridge University Press, 2004), 102, 2, 5.

67. UN Development Program, *Arab Human Development Report 2004*, 65.

68. Jennifer L. Windsor and Brian Katulis, "Three Keys to the Cowed Arab Media," *Daily Star*, May 17, 2005.

69. Kepel, *War for Muslim Minds*, 293.

Chapter 8: What It All Means

1. "Overview of Research and Methodology," BeAWitness.org, www.beawitness.org/methodology.

2. Nicholas Kristof, "All Ears for Tom Cruise, All Eyes on Brad Pitt," *New York Times*, July 26, 2005.

3. Leroy Sievers, "There Is Evil," *Los Angeles Times,* June 12, 2005.

4. "Flood, Famine, and Mobile Phones," *The Economist,* July 28, 2007, 61–62; ReliefWeb, www.reliefweb.int; NetHope: Wiring the Global Village, www.nethope.org.

5. Middle East Media Research Institute, *Renowned Syrian Poet "Adonis": "We, in Arab Society, Do Not Understand the Meaning of Freedom,"* Special Dispatch Series, no. 1393, December 14, 2006, http://memri.org/bin/articles.cgi?Page=archives&Area=sd&ID=SP139306.

6. Dominique Moisi, "The Clash of Emotions," *Foreign Affairs* 86, no. 1 (January–February 2007): 8.

7. Edward W. Said, *Orientalism* (New York: Vintage, 2003), 347.

8. "If You Want My Opinion," *The Economist,* March 10, 2007, 58.

9. Scott Atran, "In Indonesia, Democracy Isn't Enough," *New York Times,* October 5, 2005.

10. Nicholas Kristof, "The Muslim Stereotype," *New York Times,* December 10, 2006.

11. George Packer, "Knowing the Enemy: Can Social Scientists Redefine the 'War on Terror'?" *The New Yorker,* December 18, 2006, 60, 64; "The Future of the Jihadi Movement: A Five-Year Forecast," *Chronicle of Higher Education,* October 20, 2006.

12. Somini Sengupta and Salman Masood, "Guantanamo Comes to Define U.S. to Muslims," *New York Times,* May 21, 2005.

13. Robert R. Reilly, "Britney vs. the Terrorists," *Washington Post,* February 9, 2007.

14. William A. Rugh, "Broadcasting and American Public Diplomacy," *Transnational Broadcasting Studies Journal* 14 (Spring 2005), www.tbsjournal.com/Archives/Spring05/rugh.html.

15. William McKenzie, "Karen Hughes Q and A: Public Diplomacy in Real Time," *Dallas Morning News,* December 12, 2006.

Selected Bibliography

Books

Alavi, Nasrin. *We Are Iran: The Persian Blogs.* Brooklyn, NY: Soft Skull Press, 2005.

Albright, Madeleine K., and Vin Weber. *In Support of Arab Democracy: Why and How: Report of an Independent Task Force.* New York: Council on Foreign Relations, 2005.

Anderson, Benedict. *Imagined Communities: Reflections on the Origin and Spread of Nationalism.* London: Verso, 1991.

Atwan, Abdel Bari. *The Secret History of al Qaeda.* Berkeley: University of California Press, 2006.

Bensahel, Nora, and Daniel L. Byman, eds. *The Future Security Environment in the Middle East: Conflict, Stability, and Political Change.* Santa Monica, CA: RAND, 2003.

Bird, Christiane. *A Thousand Sighs, a Thousand Revolts: Journeys in Kurdistan.* New York: Random House, 2005.

Bradley, John R. *Saudi Arabia Exposed: Inside a Kingdom in Crisis.* New York: Palgrave Macmillan, 2005.

Bunt, Gary R. *Islam in the Digital Age: e-Jihad, Online Fatwas, and Cyber Islamic Environments.* London: Pluto Press, 2003.

———. *Virtually Islamic: Computer-Mediated Communication and Cyber Islamic Environments.* Cardiff: University of Wales Press, 2000.

Catherwood, Christopher. *Winston's Folly: Imperialism and the Creation of Modern Iraq.* London: Constable, 2004.

Cooke, Miriam, and Bruce B. Lawrence. *Muslim Networks From*

Hajj to Hip Hop. Chapel Hill: University of North Carolina Press, 2005.

Devji, Faisal. *Landscapes of the Jihad: Militancy, Morality, Modernity.* Ithaca, NY: Cornell University Press, 2005.

Eickelman, Dale F., and Jon W. Anderson, eds. *New Media in the Muslim World: The Emerging Public Sphere.* 2nd ed. Bloomington: Indiana University Press, 2003.

Friedman, Thomas L. *Longitudes and Attitudes: The World in the Age of Terrorism.* New York: Anchor Books, 2003.

George, Cherian. *Contentious Journalism and the Internet: Towards Democratic Discourse in Malaysia and Singapore.* Singapore: Singapore University Press, 2006.

Handbook for Bloggers and Cyber-dissidents. Paris: Reporters Without Borders, 2005.

Kalathil, Shanthi, and Taylor C. Boas. *Open Networks, Closed Regimes: The Impact of the Internet on Authoritarian Rule.* Washington, DC: Carnegie Endowment for International Peace, 2003.

Kepel, Gilles. *The War for Muslim Minds: Islam and the West.* Cambridge, MA: Harvard University Press, 2004.

Lewis, Bernard. *What Went Wrong: Western Impact and Middle Eastern Response.* New York: Oxford University Press, 2002.

Lim, Merlyna. *Islamic Radicalism and Anti-Americanism in Indonesia: The Role of the Internet.* Washington, DC: East-West Center, 2005.

Lynch, Marc. *Voices of the New Arab Public: Iraq, Al-Jazeera, and Middle East Politics Today.* New York: Columbia University Press, 2006.

Miles, Hugh. *Al-Jazeera: The Inside Story of the Arab News Channel That Is Challenging the West.* New York: Grove, 2005.

National Commission on Terrorist Attacks Upon the United States. *The 9/11 Commission Report: Final Report of the National Commission on Terrorist Attacks Upon the United States.* New York: Norton, 2004.

Pintak, Lawrence. *Reflections in a Bloodshot Lens: America, Islam and the War of Ideas.* London: Pluto Press, 2006.

Roy, Olivier. *Globalized Islam: The Search for a New Ummah.* New

York: Columbia University Press, 2004.

Sakr, Naomi. *Satellite Realms: Transnational Television, Globalization, and the Middle East.* London: I. B. Tauris, 2001.

Schaebler, Birgit, and Leif Stenberg, eds. *Globalization and the Muslim World: Culture, Religion, and Modernity.* Syracuse, NY: Syracuse University Press, 2004.

Seib, Philip. *The Global Journalist: News and Conscience in a World of Conflict.* Lanham, MD: Rowman and Littlefield, 2002.

Shadid, Anthony. *Legacy of the Prophet: Despots, Democrats, and the New Politics of Islam.* Boulder, CO: Westview Press, 2002.

Weimann, Gabriel. *Terror on the Internet: The New Arena, the New Challenges.* Washington, DC: U.S. Institute of Peace Press, 2006.

Wright, Lawrence. *The Looming Tower: Al-Qaeda and the Road to 9/11.* New York: Knopf, 2006.

Zayani, Mohamed, ed. *The Al Jazeera Phenomenon: Critical Perspectives on New Arab Media.* Boulder, CO: Paradigm Publishers, 2005.

Articles, Chapters, and Reports

Al Kasim, Faisal. *"The Opposite Direction*: A Program Which Changed the Face of Arab Television." In *The Al Jazeera Phenomenon: Critical Perspectives on New Arab Media,* edited by Mohamed Zayani. Boulder, CO: Paradigm, 2005.

Alterman, Jon B., "The Information Revolution and the Middle East." In *The Future Security Environment in the Middle East: Conflict, Stability, and Political Change,* edited by Nora Bensahel and Daniel L. Byman. Santa Monica, CA: RAND, 2003.

Anable, David. "The Role of Georgia's Media—and Western Aid—in the Rose Revolution." *Harvard International Journal of Press/Politics* 11, no. 3 (Summer 2006): 7–43.

Anderson, Jon W., "The Internet and Islam's New Interpreters." In *New Media in the Muslim World: The Emerging Public Sphere,* edited by Dale F. Eickelman and Jon W. Anderson. 2nd ed.

Bloomington: Indiana University Press, 2003.

―――. "New Media, New Publics: Reconfiguring the Public Sphere of Islam," *Social Research* 70, no. 3 (Fall 2003): 887–906.

―――. "Wiring Up: The Internet Difference for Muslim Networks." In *Muslim Networks From Hajj to Hip Hop*, edited by miriam cooke and Bruce B. Lawrence. Chapel Hill: University of North Carolina Press, 2005.

Azrael, Jeremy R., and D. J. Peterson. *Russia and the Information Revolution*. RAND Issue Paper. Santa Monica, CA: RAND, 2002.

Baran, Zeyno. "Fighting the War of Ideas." *Foreign Affairs,* November–December 2005, 68–78.

Brinkerhoff, Jennifer M. "Digital Diasporas and Conflict Prevention: The Case of Somalinet.com." *Review of International Studies* 32, no. 1 (January 2006): 25–47.

Bubalo, Anthony, and Greg Fealy, *Between the Global and the Local: Islamism, the Middle East, and Indonesia*, Brookings Institution, U.S. Policy Toward the Islamic World, Analysis Paper, no. 9, October 2005.

Bunt, Gary. "Defining Islamic Interconnectivity." In *Muslim Networks From Hajj to Hip Hop*, edited by miriam cooke and Bruce B. Lawrence. Chapel Hill: University of North Carolina Press, 2005.

Cherribi, Sam. "From Baghdad to Paris: Al Jazeera and the Veil." *Harvard International Journal of Press/Politics* 11, no. 2 (Spring 2006): 121–138.

Cockburn, Andrew. "Iraq's Resilient Minority," *Smithsonian,* December 2005, 43–55.

Eickelman, Dale F., and Jon W. Anderson. "Redefining Muslim Publics." In *New Media in the Muslim World: The Emerging Public Sphere*, edited by Dale F. Eickelman and Jon W. Anderson. 2nd ed. Bloomington: Indiana University Press, 2003.

Ernst, Carl W. "Ideological and Technological Transformations of Contemporary Sufism." In *Muslim Networks From Hajj to Hip Hop*, edited by miriam cooke and Bruce B. Lawrence. Chapel Hill: University of North Carolina Press, 2005.

Hefner, Robert W. "Civic Pluralism Denied? The New Media and

Jihadi Violence in Indonesia." In *New Media in the Muslim World: The Emerging Public Sphere,* edited by Dale F. Eickelman and Jon W. Anderson. 2nd ed. Bloomington: Indiana University Press, 2003.

Jones, David Martin, and M. L. R. Smith. "Greetings From the Cybercaliphate: Some Notes on Homeland Insecurity." *International Affairs* 81, no. 5 (October 2005): 925–950.

Kalathil, Shanthi. "Dot Com for Dictators." *Foreign Policy,* March–April 2003, 43–49.

Labi, Nadya. "Jihad 2.0." *Atlantic Monthly,* July–August 2006, 102–108.

Mandaville, Peter G. "Communication and Diasporic Islam: A Virtual *Ummah*?" In *The Media of Diaspora,* edited by Karim H. Karim, 135–147 London: Routledge, 2003.

———. "Reimagining the *Ummah*? Information Technology and the Changing Boundaries of Political Islam." In *Islam Encountering Globalization,* edited by Ali Mohammadi, 66–90. London: RoutledgeCurzon, 2002.

Merrifield, William. "MED-TV: Kurdish Satellite Television and the Changing Relationship Between the State and the Media." *Transnational Broadcasting Studies Journal,* no. 14 (Spring 2005), www.tbsjournal.com/Archives/Spring05/merrifield.html.

Packer, George. "Knowing the Enemy: Can Social Scientists Redefine the 'War on Terror'?" *The New Yorker,* December 18, 2006, 60–69.

Shadid, Anthony, and Kevin Sullivan. "Anatomy of the Cartoon Protest Movement." *Washington Post,* February 16, 2006.

Shapiro, Samantha M. "Ministering to the Upwardly Mobile Muslim." *New York Times Magazine,* April 30, 2006.

Stanley Foundation. *Open Media and Transitioning Societies in the Arab Middle East: Implications for U.S. Security Policy.* Report in association with the Institute for Near East and Gulf Military Analysis. Muscatine, IA: Stanley Foundation, 2006.

Wiktorowicz, Quintan. "The Salafi Movement: Violence and Fragmentation of Community." In *Muslim Networks From Hajj to Hip Hop,* edited by miriam cooke and Bruce B. Lawrence. Chapel Hill: University of North Carolina Press, 2005.

Wright, Lawrence. "The Terror Web." *The New Yorker*, August 2, 2004, 40–53.

Yavuz, M. Hakan. "Media Identities for Alevis and Kurds in Turkey." In *New Media in the Muslim World: The Emerging Public Sphere*, edited by Dale F. Eickelman and Jon W. Anderson. 2nd ed. Bloomington: Indiana University Press, 2003.

INDEX

Abu Dhabi TV, 22, 143, 163
Abu Ghraib, 172, 190
Abu Samah, Nicolas, 170–71
advertising, 22, 40
Afghanistan, 5, 61, 76, 96, 143
Aharonian, Aram, 33–35
Ahmadinejad, Mahmoud, 158
Akel, Pierre, 160
Al-Ahram, 155–56
Al Ali, Mohammed Jassim, 141
Al Aqsa TV, 27
al-Arabi al-Nasseri, 157
Al Arabiya, 10, 16, 22–25, 30, 32,
    143, 163, 171, 188
al-Assad, Bashar, 153, 161–62
Alavi, Nasrin, 159
Al-Banna, Hassan, 80
Al Faqih, Saad, 165
Al-Ghad Party, 156
al-Hakawati, 17
Al Hiwar, 188
Al Hurra, 29–32, 89, 146, 189–90
Alibaba.com, 120
al-Ibrahim, Walid, 23
Al Jazeera, 19–25, 36, 81–82, 85–
    86, 141–47, 163, 167–68,
    171, 180, 183, 188; audi-
    ence, 20, 25, 30; coverage of
    Israel by, 10; creation of,
    142–43; credibility of, xi,
    15, 143–44; influence of, ix,

14–16, 42, 161, 183–84; as
    paradigm, x, 139; religious
    content, 24, 83, 85–86; talk
    shows, ix, 142–44
Al Jazeera English, 42–43, 81–82
Al Kasim, Faisal, 21
Al-Khudairi, Ibrahim, 30
Allen, Mark, 17
Al-Maeena, Khaled, 51
Almahaba Radio, 162
Al Manar, 26–27, 137, 153, 164,
    167–68, 183
al-Masri al-Youm, 157
Al Neda, 103
Alpher, Yossi, 10–11
al Qaeda, 2–3, 76, 95–110, 185–
    86, 189
al-Qaradawi, Yusuf, 24, 83, 169–
    70
al Qassem, Anwar, 160
al-Rashed, Abdul Rahman, 23–24
Al Resalah, 28–29
al-Rikabi, Ahmad, 162
Al-Suwaidan, Tarek, 29
Alterman, Jon, 9, 111, 151, 169
Al-Wafd, 52
al-Zaid, Salama, 166
al-Zarqawi, Abu Musab, 83, 100,
    106–108, 185
al-Zawahiri, Ayman, 75, 98, 100–
    101, 104–106

ABOUT THE AUTHOR

Philip Seib is professor of journalism and public diplomacy at the University of Southern California. He is the author and editor of many books, including *Headline Diplomacy: How News Coverage Affects Foreign Policy; The Global Journalist: News and Conscience in a World of Conflict; Beyond the Front Lines: How the News Media Cover a World Shaped by War; Media and Conflict in the 21st Century; Broadcasts from the Blitz: How Edward R. Murrow Helped Lead America into War;* and *New Media and the New Middle East.* He is co-editor of the journal *Media, War, and Conflict.* He lives in Pasadena, California.